Economics of Planning Public Works

Also Published in

Reprints of Economic Classics

BY JOHN M. CLARK

STRATEGIC FACTORS IN BUSINESS CYCLES [1934]

ECONOMICS
of
PLANNING PUBLIC WORKS

BY

John Maurice Clark

Professor of Economics, Columbia University

[1935]

REPRINTS OF ECONOMIC CLASSICS

Augustus M. Kelley, Bookseller
New York 1965

*Originally published for the National Planning Board of the
Federal Emergency Administration of Public Works*

Library of Congress Catalogue Card Number
65 - 19647

PRINTED IN THE UNITED STATES OF AMERICA
by SENTRY PRESS, NEW YORK, N. Y. 10019

PREFACE

This volume presents a part of the research work carried on by a staff serving under the National Planning Board (later incorporated in the National Resources Board). The National Planning Board was set up under the Public Works Administration but distinct from the work of carrying out the current Public Works program, and consisted of Mr. Frederick A. Delano, chairman, and Profs. Wesley C. Mitchell and Charles E. Merriam. Under this Board a number of distinct but related researches were carried out. A study of the general problem of economic and social planning was made by Dr. Lewis L. Lorwin of the Brookings Institution and Prof. A. F. Hinrichs of Brown University. In the field of Public Works, recent experience was surveyed by Dr. Arthur D. Gayer of Barnard College, physical aspects by a panel of planning engineers under Mr. Russell V. Black, administrative aspects by Mr. Frederick Powell who succeeded Dr. Leonard White after the latter was called to other duties, and economic aspects by the present author, with the assistance of Dr. J. Wilner Sundelson on the financial angles of the problem.

This sketch of the organization of the research may serve to explain what is left out of this volume, as well as what is included. Detailed history and statistics of the recent experience in this country will be found in Dr. Gayer's study, to be published by the National Bureau of Economic Research; and only such basic facts are included here as are necessary to an understanding of the problem. The physical possibilities of Public Works in this country are dealt with in Mr. Black's study. Administrative problems are dealt with only incidentally. What remains affords a sufficient range of problems, centering in the one which is most vital for the country today: How may Public Works be so handled as to contribute as much as they are capable of contributing to industrial stability?

Acknowledgments are due to the Board and to its executive officer, Mr. Charles W. Eliot 2d, who has afforded every facility for the study and furnished much valuable material. Mr. C. R. Chambers of the Division of Economics and Statistics of the Public Works Administration has cooperated whole-heartedly, and placed his records at the author's disposal. On financial conditions in State and local governments Mr. Lent D. Upson of the Bureau of the Census and Mr. Wylie Kilpatrick of the Public Works Administration have furnished both data and suggestive discussion. The chapter on the cumulative effects of Public Works expenditures has been read by Prof. J. W. Angell and Alvin H. Hansen; and their criticisms have resulted in materially improving the treatment; though needless to say they are not responsible for the views expressed or the conclusions reached. As for those who have contributed by conference and conversation, the author can only express a general debt of gratitude to them for the help they have rendered.

The conclusions reached in this study will naturally not find universal agreement. The author holds that it is possible for Public Works expenditures, rightly handled, to furnish a real stimulus to business in a depression; and some will object to that view in any form. He also concludes that there are limits to the possibility of lifting ourselves in this way, that this method alone cannot haul us out of a serious depression, and that some ways of attempting it may very easily result instead in imbedding us more firmly in the slough. And some will reject such counsels of caution and moderation.

Unfortunately, these major conclusions are not susceptible of such hard-and-fast proof as a scientist properly likes to demand. They are scientific probabilities—largely deductions from assumptions carefully selected on the basis of available evidence as to the important controlling conditions. The controlling conditions are many, some of them capriciously variable, reaching into the human imponderables. Some of these probabilities approach certainty; others are much more doubtful. It takes courage to act on such probabilities, and caution to act without running unnecessary risks. And it is this combination of courage and caution which, with good will as a foundation, is the prime necessity if we are to come safely through the inspiring and disquieting enterprise of social experimentation to which the country is now committed.

This study of economic aspects was made within rather severe time limitations, during the spring and summer of 1934, and pressure of other duties has prevented the author from making any general revision taking account of later developments. If such revision had been made, warnings against expecting too much might have been made stronger; but nothing seems to have happened to alter the general character of the conclusions reached as to the kind of action which needs to be taken.

JOHN MAURICE CLARK.

TABLE OF CONTENTS

Page

I. THE BACKGROUND OF THE AMERICAN PROBLEM. 1
   A. Introduction.
   B. Work Relief or Relief Work.
   C. Public Works as an Antidote to Depressions.
   D. The Development of City and Regional Planning.

II. HARMONIES AND CONFLICTS BETWEEN THE PURPOSES 8
    IN VIEW.

III. RELIEF WORK: ADVANTAGES AND DISADVANTAGES AS 22
     COMPARED WITH DOLES OR INSURANCE.
   A. General Characteristics of Relief Work.
   B. Unemployment Insurance or Reserves.
   C. Outright Relief.
   D. Conclusion.

IV. VARIETIES OF ECONOMIC DISLOCATIONS. 31
   A. Importance of the Question.
   B. General Character of Business Movements.
   C. The Shorter Type of Business Cycle.
   D. The Different Phases of a Cycle.
   E. Possible Longer Cycles.
   F. Noncyclical Disturbing Factors.
   G. Progressive Changes, and their Possible Disturbing Effects.
   H. Present Prospects.

V. TYPES OF PUBLIC WORKS PROJECTS. 54
   A. General Grading According to Value of Urgency.
   B. Particular Characteristics Bearing on Choice of Projects.
   C. Conclusions.

VI. VARIETIES OF TIMING POLICY. 61
   A. The Contraction Side of Timing.
   B. The Expansion Side of Timing.
   C. Expansion without Contraction: A Progressive Increase in
      Public Spending.

VII. LIMITATIONS ON ALTERING NATURAL TIMING OF 71
     PUBLIC WORKS.
   A. General Limitations.
   B. Political and Administrative Difficulties.

VIII. PREPARATORY MEASURES. 75

IX. CUMULATIVE EFFECTS OF PUBLIC EXPENDITURES. 80
   A. Indirect Primary Employment and Production.
   B. Secondary Effects: the Problem.
   C. Secondary Effects: the Successive-Spendings Approach.
   D. Secondary Effects: the Approach via Volume and Velocity of
      Circulating Medium.
   E. Differences and Attempted Reconciliation.
   F. Recent Experience in the United States.

X. NULLIFYING INFLUENCES.   105
  A. Contraction of Expenditures in the General Budget while Public
       Works are Expanding.
  B. Methods of Raising Funds which May Counteract the Effect of
       Spending them so far as Concerns Stimulus to Business or the
       Sustaining of Purchasing Power.
  C. Public Expenditures which Will Ultimately Reduce the Field for
       Private Investment.
  D. Reactions in the Field of International Trade and Exchange.
  E. Conclusion.

XI. PROBLEMS AND METHODS OF FINANCING.   113
  A. General Need of Fiscal Overhauling.
  B. The General Financial Stringency.
  C. The Stabilization of Public Spending Power.
  D. Borrowing and Repayment.
  E. Kinds of Taxes To Be Used.
  F. The Relation of Federal, State, and Local Finance.
  G. Limits on a Public Works Program Imposed by Financial Con-   127
       siderations.

XII. PROBLEMS OF LABOR POLICY.
  A. Selection of Workers.
  B. The Avoidance of the Use of Machinery.
  C. Wages and Hours.
  D. Employment Exchanges.

XIII. THE CONSTRUCTION INDUSTRIES IN RELATION TO A   131
       PUBLIC WORKS PROGRAM.

XIV. SPECIAL PROBLEMS IN PARTICULAR FIELDS.   133
  A. Public Utilities as Adjuncts to a Public Works Program.
  B. Transportation Coordination.
  C. Watershed Authorities.
  D. Land Utilization.
  E. The Problem of Low-Cost Housing.
  F. Efforts at Self-Help or Self-Sufficing Production.

XV. THE PLACE OF PUBLIC WORKS PLANNING IN A GEN-   144
       ERAL POLICY.
  A. An Organic Network of Problems.
  B. Interrelationships of the Public Works Problem.
  C. Conclusions Bearing on Basic Governmental Organization.

XVI. CONCLUSIONS BEARING ON A PUBLIC WORKS PROGRAM.   155
  A. Essential Elements in a Consistent Policy.
  B. Optional Features of a Public Works Program.
  C. A Minimum Program.
  D. A Sample Program of a More Adequate Sort.
  E. Program of Permanent Expansion of Public Works to Absorb
       Oversavings.
  F. Conclusion.

APPENDIX.   169
  Fiscal Aspects of Planned Public Works.

I. THE BACKGROUND OF THE AMERICAN PROBLEM

A. Introduction

For the purposes of this study there is no need to enter into elaborate definitions of what is meant by "planning" as applied to economic life in general. The field of public works is one in which planning in the narrower and more literal sense of the term is appropriate, possible and even necessary, because the authority that does the planning is the authority under which the works are carried out; namely, the government. Whoever has a piece of work to be carried out under his direction must naturally plan the work, if it is to be well done. He must decide on the details, or delegate that responsibility to others and decide himself on the main features only; and in any case he must decide how much he is to decide and how much he is to delegate. Not even in the field of public works does planning mean that one mind or one committee must determine every detail. It becomes a question not so much of exercising authority of a kind that determines everything, but rather of coordinating the work of a large number of bodies, each of which has its plans, its ambitions, its standards of judgment; and each of which has a certain realm in which its word is final and other realms in which its activities have to be fitted in with what other bodies may be doing.

Those who are talking about planning for economic society as a whole naturally face a problem in which central authority has a still narrower field, and the various bodies, organizations, and interests whose activities have to be fitted together, have a still greater measure of independence. For that reason it would probably express more clearly what is in the minds of persons who contemplate general economic "planning," without a thoroughgoing socialistic system, to use the word "coordination" in place of the word "planning."

Another phase of the attempt to make the economic machine work as a planning mind might want it to work, without putting it under completely socialistic control, is expressed by Walter Lippmann in the term, "a compensated economy." This means that those things which business does within its sphere of liberty, which result in evils or disasters, but over which government is not ready to take direct control, may be made up for by things which government does and which have an opposite effect. The chief example is probably the spending of more money on public works at a time when business is spending too little, and less money on public works at a time when business is spending too much. Thus the literal planning of public works, necessarily carried out by the Government, may be asked to play a part in bringing about a coordinated general economy, and in that scheme one of its principal functions (though not the only one) is to act as a compensator.

So far as State and local works are concerned, there is no one central authority over them, and as a result whatever effects they may have on the economic system of the Nation as a whole are more or less left to chance, to the extent that there may be good or bad

1

effects resulting outside the territory or jurisdiction of the local unit whose activities bring the effect about. Local streets and local fire protection may be wholly a local matter. Local education may be so construed without any obvious evil arising, so long as no localities fall too far behind a proper standard. But when that happens, it appears that the quality of education is a general interest, even a national one, and should not be left wholly at the mercy of local opinions or local poverty.

If a road is built for the sake of employing local workers, that again, is a local matter, on its face. But if that kind of provision comes to be generally needed, we shall have the roots from which may grow systems corresponding to the system of parish settlements and other obstacles to a proper mobility of labor throughout the Nation, against which the early classical economists struggled. One local community would be unwilling to invite wanderers from other communities by offering relief work not limited to actual residents. And if one of the considerations in the building of the road is not merely the employment of the workers on the spot, but the employment of workers to make materials and render all the contributory services which are rendered elsewhere, then we have a clear case where one locality is bearing burdens largely for the benefit of other localities all over the country.

These local governmental units as they stand do not comprise within their boundaries all the interest which are materially concerned in the things they do. Therefore these interests need to be coordinated in some way and for much the same reasons as the conflicting interests of private business. One of the large tasks of the Federal Government in this matter is to bring about just such coordination between the policies of State and local agencies. Its planning must be directed, not toward determining for the localities just what works should be constructed, but rather toward bringing about conditions under which the general volume and output of construction (in which the Federal Government is legitimately interested) shall be such as fit in with a program in the interest of the Nation as a whole.

As for the definition of public works, there seems to be no reason for departing materially from the customary idea of what this includes. It consists of durable goods, primarily fixed structures, produced by government. It does not include, ordinarily, the rendering of intangible services, although here the dividing line between tangible and intangible becomes shadowy in spots, as many such lines do. Under pressure of the current crisis, there has been a strong compulsion to extend the conception of public works as far as possible into the field of intangible services, mainly for the simple reason that, in the field of public works, there was money to be had and employment to be afforded, while in other fields there was pressure to reduce expenses in order to balance budgets. And this difference in fiscal policy did not coincide with any difference in the community's need either for different kinds of works or services, or for the added employment they would afford. Given those conditions, it might be entirely justifiable to attempt any enlargement of the conception of public works which could possibly have any chance of acceptance. But it would seem better in the long run to adopt a defensible and consistent fiscal policy toward all forms of government employment, whether concerned with durable goods or perishable services.

The general background of the American situation consists in the main of three parts. One is work relief, in which there has been a long and baffling experience. One is the idea of using public works as a remedy for business fluctuations. In this we have not had a long experience, and such experiments as are now being tried have not gone far enough to show whether their results will be baffling or not. Prominent public expression of the idea dates back less than 40 years, and any attempt to practice it on a large scale dates back only to the depression of 1929–34. Those parts of the idea which are concerned with the planning of such efforts in advance have never been effectively tried on any considerable scale. The third element in the background of public works planning is drawn from the growth of city and regional plans and planning. In its modern form this has not had a long history, neither is it a mere theory, but a movement well under way— young but thoroughly established and destined to grow.

These three elements make up the background for public works planning—a background which is far from unified and involves some definite conflicts. To understand the problem and to interpret the attitudes of persons approaching it from the standpoints of different parts of this multiple background, one must understand something about each of the parts.

B. Work Relief or Relief Work

Both of these terms are used, and both are probably appropriate, with differences of emphasis. The early English workhouse was clearly work relief, while the more successful operations in the American Civil Works Administration of 1933–34 seem to deserve the name of "relief work." The background of work relief which is most pertinent for our purposes includes the whole history of the English poor laws.[1] The poor laws have gone through a number of different stages, and in construing what is said about them one must be on one's guard against the tendency of the chronicler to exaggerate the differences between such stages for the sake of a more clean-cut and simplified picture of each successive period. The individuals who carried out the system did not change as much as the system did; and neither did the needs and difficulties of the human material they had to deal with. And they tended to modify the system in application, softening its worst rigors when these were most extreme.

The medieval church had encouraged rather indiscriminate alms-giving, and although this tendency was reduced by the Reformation, in Elizabethan England there was still a fairly liberal poor law, and parishes kept stocks of materials on which the poor could be set to work. Possibly as a result of too great liberality there was, around 1700, a "plague of sturdy vagabonds."

The spread of Puritan morals, with their emphasis on the individual's duty to succeed in the world, led to the passing of severe laws, which were, however, not uniformly enforced, whether through the negligence, the inefficiency, or the humanity of local officers.

Under the impact of the Napoleonic Wars, conditions were again liberalized. Possibly it was in part because the great upheavals of the time upset the individualistic basis of the Puritan attitude in much the same way as a great fire or earthquake does, being a community and not an individual calamity, before which the helplessness

[1] Cf. Sydney and Beatrice Webb, English Poor Law History.

of individuals is recognized, and relief loses its stigma. Almost certainly it had something to do with the fear of revolution, which was very real in England at that time. In either case, the result was the same—relief was more freely given.

There was then no unified system of relief, but a mixture of methods involving a certain amount of outdoor relief in cash, a certain amount of subsidized private employment, and certain attempts at making the conditions such as to deter applicants. The general character of the period is described as one of undue and indiscriminate liberality.

In 1834 there came another reversal of policy involving two basic principles. The first was the principle of "less eligibility", or the rule that relief must be made more undesirable than the conditions of self-dependence. The second was the principle of the workhouse test and the rule that there should be no outdoor relief, with some insignificant exceptions. Under this system the poor were set to work at picking oakum or breaking stone and the product of a workyard cost from five to ten times what it could be bought for. Conditions in the workhouse were made deliberately unpleasant, and the result was not merely a deterrent, but virtually a penalizing of the pauper. The workhouses were semipenal institutions.

This system was really directed at the chronic unemployable who had reached a stage of utter destitution. For unemployment resulting from an industrial depression, which falls upon reasonably competent and willing workers, these methods of treatment were utterly unsuited. If the unemployment had not yet wrecked the worker, such a system of relief would have done so. Cities with a genuine unemployment problem had to get special permission for the giving of outdoor relief.[2] During the same period there were also intermittent experiments with outside relief works. These were, on the whole, less useless than the workhouse labors, although even that conclusion may be doubtful.[3] Other resources for the relief of poverty included trade-union insurance and private charity.

The relief works were commonly managed by special local funds to meet special needs, and their defects are summed up by the Webbs who conclude that they were not prompt enough in getting under way, that the amounts raised were not proportional to the need, and that there were less effective safeguards against fraud than in ordinary poor relief.[4] Relief works on this basis of special local funds were intended for the "elite of the unemployed", the sober and industrious, with preference for men with families. They paid a mere pittance, and the work was spread out by limiting it to a few days a week or a few hours a day.

The kinds of work found were various. Sometimes regular city work would be done by workers on the special-relief fund, with the fund making good the extra cost to the city of the work done in this way. Much of the work was of secondary importance, which ordinarily would not have been considered worth doing, although some of it was of a sort which would be classed as normal economic production, such as potato growing, and some of it represented an anticipation of regular public works, such as roads and sewers. There was

[2] Davison, The Unemployed, p. 10.
[3] Ibid., pp. 13–14.
[4] Sidney and Beatrice Webb, English Poor Law History, part II, pp. 640–643.

tree planting, foreshore and swamp reclamation, cleaning of town water courses, grooming of parks, etc.

Through the nineteenth century, spasmodic resorts to this method of relief continued. Some of the most useful forms of work appear to have been devised after the Unemployed Workmen's Act of 1905 brought about a considerable enlargement of work relief. This special effort was brought to an end by improved conditions of trade in 1909. Thus there was a long period marked by no basic change in the official theory of the workhouse system except by increasing use of outside relief work, and also by increasing freedom in the use of outdoor cash relief. Naturally, the whole spirit of the system was gradually changing with the growth of industrial unemployment as distinct from individual pauperism and with the general change in the social attitude toward the problem.

In the meantime France had tried a rather spectacular and much misrepresented experiment, following the Revolution of 1848. Louis Blanc had been responsible for the issuance of a proclamation of "the right to work", by which the provisional government was committed to doing something, though apparently it was not ready to give the principle its whole-hearted support. The result was a perfunctory performance destined to failure from the start. Davison estimates that probably not over 6,000 were ever employed, and these largely at quite futile "work"; but 120,000 received a dole of 1 franc 50 centimes a day, which was sufficient to lure 12,000 into Paris from the provinces and to attract 20,000 away from existing employment. The end of such an experiment was inevitable; the riots and bloodshed which attended it were hardly to be wondered at, once these thousands had been collected in Paris on such impossible terms. Neither the failure nor the bloodshed accompanying it has anything to do with the principle of intelligent work relief. In the meantime, Louis Blanc himself had been establishing some actual cooperative workshops, mostly outside Paris, 20 of which were still in existence 10 years later.[5]

This French experience points out one of the more elementary things to be avoided in a system of relief work, namely, employment at tasks which are obviously so much waste motion. More particularly, it points to the danger of paying people more for doing nothing than they can earn at their regular work. These would seem to be dangers which men of sincerity, intelligence, and foresight should be able to avoid without the need of lurid lessons from history.

In Ireland, for some 50 years following the potato famine, relief was necessary at intervals. Those who attempted relief work here encountered the difficulty that they could find no work to relieve the unemployed or destitute which the majority of the people would not gladly do. This illustrates the general difficulty of relief work in a situation where the conditions of the private economy are so bad that a humane relief administrator can hardly avoid making the conditions of relief more attractive if he is to meet simple human necessities. Even in an economic system which is far less poor than Ireland was then there may be a great many situations in private industry where earnings are so extremely low as to raise the same difficulty for the relief worker. Even outside the so-called "sweated trades", and in trades where wage rates are not inordinately low,

⁵ Davison. op. cit., pp. 26-27.

short time may disastrously reduce earnings during a severe depression without the possibility of the workers escaping into other occupations affording fuller time and better earnings.

At the time of the American Civil War, the cotton industry in Lancashire was ruined by the cutting off of the supply of cotton. Here there was a demand for work on the part of the unemployed themselves, not merely as a moral exercise to certify their worthiness to receive relief, but because a self-respecting worker wanted to produce something of real utility and to get wages as payment. In short, there appeared here the counterpart of the desire for "real work at real wages" which was so strong in the United States in the third year of the current depression.

The officials in charge of finding "test work" were put to it to find enough, and loans for public works were made. One of the most successful efforts was a sewage and paving enterprise which was seriously handled as a rehabilitation project. Workers were equipped with stout clothing and shoes, in contrast to many workers on relief work whose clothing was often insufficient for the exposure which the job involved. They were given 4 weeks' training and then put upon piecework, with the prospect of discharge for inefficiency, while efficiency meant a chance of a continuous job. Naturally, the numbers employed in this way were limited, not more than 8,000 in all, many of whom became competent to do the new work and permanently shifted to it. Naturally, discharge for inefficiency can be used effectively only on a job that is a good deal more attractive than bare relief. Such jobs cannot be found for all. Neither can continuous work in the new employment be guaranteed to everyone on works that can be found generally for relief purposes. Nevertheless, for as many as can be reached by such a scheme, there can be no question of its infinite superiority to the ordinary haphazard procedure of "made work."

This Lancashire experiment seems to stand very nearly by itself in the high standards of work set and in the genuine rehabilitation features which characterized it. During the depression of 1886, there was a considerable increase of relief work under a circular issued by Mr. Joseph Chamberlain, which "rejected the only points worth having in the Lancashire scheme."[6] The work was to be given out by the Poor Law Guardians in the form of short periods of unskilled-labor projects on which less than standard wages would be paid and for which no standards of output would be set up. Thus it appears that, in avoiding the danger of treating the unemployed too well, those who devise the relief works have commonly fallen on the other horn of the dilemma, and have made them so unattractive that workers who should have the first claim on this kind of relief, namely, the steady workers, seldom apply until they are driven to it and until their industrial status has been permanently lowered. On the other hand, chronic casuals "add it (the relief work) to the list of low-grade temporary jobs by which they subsist."[7]

This dilemma is expressed by Sir William Beveridge in the following words, referring to the difficulties of low-grade casuals:[8] "To give them relief work on conditions as attractive as their ordinary

[6] Davison, op. cit., p. 32.
[7] Davison, op. cit., p. 34.
[8] Sir William Beveridge, Unemployment, 1909, cited in Davison, op. cit., p. 35.

life is to leave no incentive to return to independence. To make the relief less attractive than ordinary life is to make it bad and degrading * * * All these attempts * * * have substantially failed to make assistance less eligible than independence—simply because of the bad conditions of independence. A nation cannot treat its dependents less badly than it treats its citizens. Only when it has humanized industrial conditions can it safely humanize the poor law."

One phenomenon which has appeared frequently has been sabotage on the work, with the result that work which should have had some value, even though of secondary grade, was reduced to substantial futility. Instances are cited in which tools were buried and time spent looking for them. Apparently, the attitude of the workers toward the work was colored by the tradition of the old workhouse test.

It is from the background of this experience that the present English attitude toward relief work must be judged. It is a very different experience from that which we have so far had under the Civil Works Administration and the subsequent relief work carried on by the Federal Emergency Relief Administration. Whether these differences are due to differences in the American situation and in the traditions of American workers, or whether they are simply due to the fact that our experiment has not continued long enough to develop the problems faced by the British administrators, can only be surmised. At present the English are inclined to rely on the system of unemployment benefits, rather than on public works in any form, for the relief of unemployment.

One of the outstanding examples of a public works policy directed to achieving far-reaching purposes and improving the character of the economic development of the country in general, is the Italian development under the present Government. There, as in England, the period in which these works have been carried out has been one of more or less continuous emergency, rather than of intermittent cyclical depressions of moderate magnitude. And while the projects have been of a sort which might have been subjected to fairly definite tests as to whether the economic results were worth the expenditure, there appears to have been no attempt to weigh the results meticulously in these terms, but rather to regard them as socially desirable without very direct reference to their financial cost. One interesting but incidental feature was the setting up of a supplementary fund in addition to the substantial expenditures otherwise provided for, to be used at any time or place where the situation of unemployment might threaten to produce disorders which the legal authorities might find difficult to handle.

Among the outstanding features of the Italian public works program have been ambitious road developments and reclamation projects for agriculture, including the draining of the Fontine marshes. Excavations of Roman remains have also been carried out on a large scale.

Perhaps the outstanding feature of the American experience with relief work in the current depression has been the temporary experiment with large scale employment at very liberal wages, judged by relief work standards, under the Civil Works Administration. This Administration made no serious attempt to make sure that relief work was less attractive than private opportunities which might be open. The emphasis was all on the attempt to give "real work for real wages." The experiment was undertaken for a limited period only, apparently as a means of getting through the winter of 1933–34 at a time when the program of expansion in regular public works had not yet had time to get under way on a large scale. This experiment did at least accomplish one thing which the English relief works have generally failed to accomplish; namely, it did attract regular workers of high grade, including engineers, writers, painters, and other white-collar workers. Needless to say, it also attracted the chronic casuals. The subsequent relief work carried on by the Federal Emergency Relief Administration has, in many cases, not attracted these same high-grade white-collar workers, who still needed relief but preferred to shift for themselves rather than apply for relief work after the termination of the Civil Works Administration. One ideal of relief work is to furnish something better than relief to a minority who especially deserve it—the "elite of the unemployed." This may prove impossible under the conditions imposed by a long siege of unemployment, together with the low wages which are, in the long run, necessary for this kind of work. Under any system, many of the elite will fail to be reached, and many who are not of the elite will be included.

One thing which has been accomplished by the American experiment is the segregation for special treatment of a special class; namely, the young men who would otherwise be drifting around the country as hoboes or tramps, simply because industry could not absorb them. They have been taken into the Civilian Conservation Corps to the number of about 300,000,* and have been given treatment which probably rates as rehabilitation, from the standpoint of their general physical and moral condition, although it does not train them specifically for industrial situations which will be likely to be open for them in the future. This experiment has some kinship with the German Labor camps, although so far as maintaining morale is concerned, there has naturally been nothing corresponding to the Fascist indoctrination which is said to be carried on in those camps.

The American experiment has had the advantage of being free from the English workhouse tradition, but there can be no certainty that this advantage will be anything but temporary, especially if the present crisis should be followed by a fairly long period of chronic unemployment in which the demoralizing effects on the unemployed make it difficult to draw the line between the worker who would be a chronic casual, even under good conditions, and the victim of economic dislocations. We have not repeated the mistakes of the English experience; rather the National Government at least, in its initial experiment, made its mistakes in the other direction, of undue liberality. However, the English administrators in their more recent efforts found it difficult or impossible to maintain wages below the prevailing rates in private industry, while the American experiment in 1934 was apparently moving in the direction of paying the unemployed a relief stipend and trying to find for them some short-time work or other to do in return for it.

It appears impossible to provide relief work for all of the unemployed in a major crisis, and probably impossible to do so in any

* In 1934. The Work Relief Act of 1935 provides for twice that number.

fairly prolonged period of chronic unemployment. The best service which relief work is capable of rendering can be rendered only to a few in our present state of knowledge, namely, to provide industrial reeducations for those whose old jobs are likely to vanish permanently and who will need to find new places. The next best thing which can be done is to carry over workers who are fairly sure to find jobs upon revival on a self-respecting basis which will prevent them from suffering permanent demoralization. This, again, is a service necessarily limited to a selected portion of the unemployed and is enormously difficult to render successfully, even on this limited basis.

C. Public Works as an Antidote to Depressions

The minority report of the British Poor Law Commission of 1905 marked a new stage in the discussion of public works with reference to unemployment. It advocated not relief work of the former sort but rather a scheduling of regular public works and regular governmental purchases in such a way that a larger amount would be done in times when private business was less active, and a smaller amount when private business was more active, with the idea that this would serve as a regulator and stabilizer of the total economic activity of the nation. The work was to be done under normal conditions, the labor being selected according to its qualifications for the work in the usual way and paid current rates of wages.

This idea had been advocated in France in official bulletins in 1898 and 1900 urging public bodies to reserve works for this purpose, and in 1902 had been officially adopted as a purpose to be striven for.[9] In 1911 a permanent committee was appointed to study the forecasting of unemployment and to inform the Minister of Labor so that he might allocate public works accordingly. Further decrees were issued on October 17, 1918, and on January 18, 1919, and at present an attempt is being made to carry out this type of policy, but with results which are as yet doubtful. The recently established Institut de Récherches Économiques is engaged in investigating the results which have actually been accomplished under this policy.

In England, little was done until the depression of 1920–21, when $125,000,000 were granted for public works.[10] The subsequent period in England was rather one of chronic unemployment than one of recurrent cyclical depressions, with the result that the original proposal of holding back public works in good times in order to put them into execution in bad times had little chance to operate. At present England is engaged in a large housing program, but no general drive for expanded public works similar to that in the United States has been made.

The theory underlying the proposal has been developed by Sydney and Beatrice Webb, the Prevention of Destitution, 1911, also by Bowley and Stuart, Is Unemployment Inevitable. The condition contemplated by this theory, in its original form, was one of relatively mild cyclical fluctuations in which not more than one-sixteenth, approximately, of the wage earners were out of work during depressions and in which a typical decline in the total wage bill would not amount to more than 5 per cent. The total amount of public spending (about £150,000,000 per year) was to be from 8 to 10 times the

---

[9] International Labor Office, Report on Unemployment, 1922, p. 119.
[10] Otto H. Mallory, in Business Cycles and Unemployment, pp. 236–239.

amount of the total shrinkage in wages, and was to be steadily maintained through prosperity and depression. Bowley and Stuart calculated that if 3 or 4 per cent of the governmental orders were reserved year by year, to be executed altogether when trade began to fall off, this would counterpoise the cyclical fluctuations, so far as concerned those industries in which depressions were actually met by dismissing workers instead of putting them on short time. They estimated that the rearrangement of not more than 40 million pounds of expenditure during the whole of the decade 1897–1906 would have smoothed out all the yearly fluctuations. This implied the reserving of orders for some 7 years and the increase of spending during not more than 3 years of the decade.

It is worth noting that in England public utilities are more generally operated by Government than in this country, with the result that there is at its command a large volume of capital expenditures for telephone and other facilities, which in this country are in private hands. It is also worth noting that the proposal presupposes that, without any such program, governmental expenditures in general at least remain stable during depressions; and, further, that the program contemplates an increase at such times in all forms of public purchasing, not merely public works in the narrow sense.

The list of expenditures suggested as available for such a program included half the yearly budget for post offices, parks, and Government buildings in general, half the annual provision of stores, such as army blankets, canvas, khaki cloth (of which large stocks were kept) the whole or half of the work of putting wires underground and of installing telephone extensions to small villages, at least half of the work of foresters and the improvement of the Duchy of Lancaster, part of the school building program, the whole of the road building program, naval vessels other than dreadnaughts, and even a considerable amount of Government printing of a historical character which did not require current publication.[11]

The theory contemplated also that the necessary funds could be raised in ways which would come out of unemployed capital, and thus would constitute a net increase in the total volume of spending in the country. The secondary effects of the expenditures were not forgotten, and it was pointed out that even such industries as the manufacture of gramophones would be stimulated by the spending of the incomes which would result from the public purchases. More recently, an attempt has been made to estimate these secondary effects in Professor Keynes', the Means to Prosperity, and by his colleague, Mr. Kahn of Kings College, Economic Journal, June 1931.

In Germany, the definite adoption of the theory and policy of public works as a stimulus to business dates from the first large-scale program of the Brüning government in 1932. Prior to 1929 there were many local projects of housing and other works, largely financed by loans from America, but no concerted program. After the end of the orgy of borrowing from abroad, funds for such purposes were hard to find. The memory of the post-war inflation was a strong deterrent to large plans whose financing would rest on expansion of credit. Some special efforts were made from 1930 onward, but at first their effects were probably neutralized by efforts to balance budgets. A special tax,

---

11 Sydney and Beatrice Webb, the Prevention of Destitution, pp. 116–18.

part of which had been used to stimulate housing, was in 1930 put at the disposal of local governments to meet general fiscal needs. Its benefits to housing were replaced by a subsidy from the general government, but a small one. Some relief work was carried on, but the general policy was one of liquidation.

In 1932, a large program was instituted, financed by credit inflation, under which the banks became holders of some 1½ billion marks of construction bills in about a year and a half, while some three-fourths billion of paper currency was issued.[12] The total amount spent may not have greatly exceeded that spent prior to 1930, but the method of financing represented a very different theory. Under the Hitler government, former fears of inflation are no longer expressed. There is some *pflichtarbeit* connected with the receipt of relief, but the main effort appears to be in the field of regular public works.

In the United States, the general idea of increased public works as a stimulus to business was endorsed by the President's Conference on Unemployment (1921). In the early stages of the current crisis, President Hoover urged both public authorities and private industry to expand construction work as a measure to counteract the depression. Various States have adopted plans looking toward the scheduling of public works in this way (for example, the California act of 1921) with few tangible results. Under the Federal Employment Stabilization Act of 1931, a 6-year schedule of Federal public works was drawn up, with the idea that it might be utilized as a business stimulus. This 6-year program has undoubtedly been of some service in the preparation of projects which were submitted to the Emergency Public works Administration, but the expansion of public works under this administration has gone farther than anything contemplated in the 6-year program drawn up by the Federal Employment Stabilization Board, and has had to rely to a large extent on projects not recommended by that Board. The present emergency has had to be met without the previous accumulation of postponed projects, and it seems probable that major emergencies will always go beyond the scope of any such reserve if public works are expanded sufficiently at such times to make an impression at all commensurate with the need.

The size of the present emergency goes so far beyond the mild fluctuations contemplated by the original theory that it raises a totally different problem, and one to which the methods advocated by the Webbs and by Bowley would be totally inadequate. For one thing, there has been a wellnigh irresistible pressure put upon governments to reduce their current expenses in order to balance their budgets, with the result that it is no longer possible to assume that if government does nothing in the way of public works, these current expenses at least will go on unchanged. We have actually run into the paradoxical situation of expanding expenditures and employment of certain sorts while contracting expenditures and employment of other sorts. This creates a problem which needs to be met before we can be sure that the expanding of public works will represent a real increase of public spending and will fit into a harmonious and consistent budgetary program.

---

[12] Paper read by Carl Landauer, before meeting of Econometic Society, Berkeley, June 1934.

While the expenditures contemplated in this original theory would not be confined to construction, but would be spread to some extent over industry in general through purchases of miscellaneous governmental supplies; still the construction of buildings and capital equipment would naturally receive the greatest stimulus in dull times. This is appropriate, since it is in these fields that by far the largest shrinkage occurs in private demand. And it is largely from these industries that the cumulative effects of the depression spread to industry in general, through the effects of the resulting shrinkage in purchasing power.

One phase of the theory which has undoubtedly not been adequately dealt with is the question of the ultimate effect of public spending on the conditions governing the revival of private demand and private activity. The tacit assumption commonly made seems to be that private revival will come at much the same time and in much the same way in which it would have come in any case, if the government had done nothing. This assumption might be justifiable in dealing with the mild movements which the original theory had in mind; but when it is a question of such major crisis as the present one, and of such huge programs of public spending as the one on which this country is now embarked, the question of the effect on private recovery needs to be reexamined. There are serious possibilities that government spending may actually become an obstacle to private recovery.[13]

D. The Development of City and Regional Planning

The most effective actual work in the field of public works planning in this country has come from a totally different source and has been animated by a totally different set of purposes,·having nothing to do with the ironing out of cyclical fluctuations in industry. It has centered around the movement for city and regional planning and concerns itself with the general advantages of drawing up an organic plan in which the development of a given area will be forecast or guided, or both, and a consistent scheme of public works will be projected and carried out to bring about the desired organic development. The Chicago plan and the New York regional plan are outstanding examples. They have brought about great improvements in the areas covered, in terms both of beauty and of physical efficiency.

Under the present Federal administration this idea of regional planning has been extended to a much larger area and to a more substantial control of its economic life under the Tennessee Valley Authority; this authority is experimenting with the guidance and control of the economic development of the entire Tennessee Valley region, and encountering problems and possibilities which are not found in the development of municipal areas. The outcome of this experiment will write a new chapter in the history of regional planning.

I. ADVANTAGES INHERENT IN THE LAYING OUT OF A PROGRAM AS AN ORGANIC WHOLE IN WHICH SINGLE PROJECTS ARE VIEWED AS PARTS

In the first place a comprehensive program of this sort, extending over a considerable term of years, makes possible the setting of larger goals than would be visualized as attainable under piecemeal methods. The development of the waterfront of Lake Michigan in Chicago is an

---

[13] This will be taken up in Chapter X below (Nullifying Influences).

outstanding example. Single unrelated projects would never have been sufficiently ambitious to achieve the connected system of parks, occupying the entire lake front, which is coming to be one of the great assets of the city of Chicago.

In the second place the service value of constituent projects may be increased by coordinating them in the general scheme. A single dam on the Tennessee River could not develop the amount of power nor combine it with flood control as effectively as does a system of dams in which the units farther upstream serve to regularize the flow through the lower dam and to make possible more regular power development as well as in themselves furnishing additional sources of power at times when the flow is large, and at the same time regularizing this spasmodic large flow sufficiently to avoid danger of floods.

It is commonplace that disconnected navigable waterways, with depths of channel and dimensions of locks unrelated to each other, do not afford an effective means of navigation as compared to a coordinated system, designed for the movement of traffic from one waterway to another, and with minimum depths and dimensions throughout the system, which are sufficient to promote the movement of effective units of transport. Furthermore, waterways cannot be effective unless adequately coordinated with other means of transportation which are necessary to serve as feeders.

In the municipal field, systems of communication, parks, and other facilities, coordinated with a development and location of civic centers and public buildings and the designation of particular areas for industrial uses of various grades, and for residences, schools, etc., serve to bring into being a much more effective whole, as well as preventing different uses of land from conflicting with each other in such a way as to destroy each other's usefulness. Factories, stores, and transportation terminals are necessary and legitimate, but not in residential areas, and residential developments in areas naturally destined to these other uses are an invitation to the destruction of values which have been built up by legitimate investment.

Over larger areas, public works need to be coordinated with plans for land utilization, and for the withdrawal of land from particular uses. And it is obvious that withdrawals of land from agricultural use should be correlated with policies of reclamation which aim to put more land into agricultural cultivation. In some cases, the withdrawal of certain areas from farm use and turning them over to forests makes possible a considerable economy through reducing public roads expenditures serving sparsely settled areas, and also the actual consolidation of town and county governments and the reduction in the number of governmental establishments which have to be maintained.

The greater certainty of the character of community growth which goes with wise and successful planning of this sort tends to reduce the waste of private funds on improvements which are destined to be unsuited to the ultimate character of the locality in which they are made, as well as waste of public funds in public improvements which are destined to a similar fate. Naturally, this presupposes wise and intelligent planning. Crude and unintelligent planning may be no better in these respects than no planning at all, or even possibly, worse. In general, public works must adapt themselves to the necessities of private development rather than attempt to control it completely or to put it in a strait-jacket. The system of streets and avenues on Manhattan Island may be cited as an example of unfortunate and misdirected planning which has increased rather than reduced the difficulties of future generations. With wise planning, however, speculative gains and losses in real estate may be very much reduced, and in some cases the government may be enabled to secure for itself the "unearned increment" which accrues to private property, partly as the result of natural community growth and partly as the result of the direction given to that growth by the scheme of public works. This, however, is a matter of extreme difficulty and involves the buying up of property whose value is to be increased, before the knowledge of the plans which will increase its value becomes public property.

2. OTHER GAINS INCIDENTALLY MADE POSSIBLE

Other improvements not so definitely inherent in planning may also be made possible. Planning may be made to serve as an effective antidote to some of the wastes which arise from the system of distribution of works between localities which has come to be spoken of under the heading of "pork-barrel policies." With a program extending far enough ahead, different localities may see that they are going to get a fair share of the total expenditures, without the necessity of insisting that they shall get what they consider a proper share of each year's budget. Thus it may be possible to concentrate on a single large project for a sufficient time to carry it through to a stage at which it can begin to render service, and then turn to other projects and carry them through, rather than carrying out disconnected and ineffective fragments of all the projects at once, with the result that none of them is carried through to fruition in a reasonable time. This applies particularly to our national waterway expenditures, but the same principle is found at work in many other cases. Once a project is undertaken, it should be pushed forward at an economical speed, and not allowed to drag on for decades, with resulting losses of interest during construction while the project is not in condition to render service.

If a project is scheduled as a part of a long-term program, it becomes possible to choose the most opportune time for carrying it out. Mr. F. L. Olmsted has worked out the principle of "curves of urgency" for public works, of which a simple illustration would be the cutting through of a street which involves the tearing down of existing buildings. From the standpoint of reducing cost, the most opportune time is the time when existing buildings have reached a stage of obsolescence and are about to be replaced. Previous to that time, there is an unnecessary cost involved in acquiring and destroying property which still has considerable service value. On the other hand, if the project waits until the old buildings have been replaced by modern and more expensive ones, then the cost of the project rises suddenly and enormously. In such a case, the opportune period may be extended somewhat by acquiring property in advance and thus insuring that new structures will not be built on it, of such high value as to make the cost of the proposed improvement prohibitive.

If a coherent plan is laid out, the relative value or urgency of single units in that plan may be much more truly judged by those who have to decide what is to be done in any given year, because they will have all the alternatives before them. In the present emergency, many projects have been taken up because they belonged to a class of work with which officials were accustomed to deal and which could be quickly put into execution without too much time spent in making basic decisions, acquiring necessary sites, and drawing elaborate plans and specifications. This is, of course, an inferior and faulty principle of choice, and one which can be avoided by adequate planning and preparatory work.

Furthermore, a well-coordinated plan covering an entire State, for example, may have an opportunity to avoid the evil of throwing into the scales of choice between classes of projects wholly irrelevant considerations of a purely fiscal sort such, for example, as result when States make grants of highway funds to localities, leaving it to the localities to decide whether they will qualify for these grants. This results in the local officials being able to secure the spending of $2 in their areas at a cost of only $1 to their local constituents. Naturally, this results in a strong tendency toward spending too much on this particular class of works at the expense of others which may be more needed. There can be little doubt that highway construction has in numerous localities been carried too far in terms of the alternative purposes for which the money might have been spent, such as schools and sanitation.

In its broad aspects, such planning should make possible a more rational apportionment of the total expenditures of the community between public and private channels. In come cases, the community may avoid certain public expenditures because it is enabled to see more clearly the whole budgetary situation in which these expenditures would involve it, both as to the ultimate cost to which it is committing itself and as to the alternatives which may arise in the future. Unplanned budgets frequently carry items for the first stages of a project, such as acquisition of land, which might never be passed if the whole cost were known. And communities frequently commit themselves to projects which they have reason to regret afterward when more vitally necessary ones come up for consideration after their financial resources have been virtually pledged. On the other hand, the effect of such planning may not be to reduce the total amount of governmental expenditures, but to increase it by showing ways in which the funds may be used to promote the interests of the community and even to increase the values of the taxpayers' property.

Another advantage which may be gained in connection with such planning is the advantage of more systematic financing. When large projects come up for consideration one at a time and spasmodically, they are much more likely to be financed by borrowing, with the result that the community is ultimately saddled with a large burden of debt charges for works which do not directly contribute revenues to defray these continuing costs. But if a program has been laid out which makes possible a fairly uniform schedule of expenditures for a considerable period of years, the advantages of the "pay as you go" policy become much more apparent and much easier to realize. Thus the effect of systematic planning, if wisely used, is likely to be, in the end, to reduce the volume of governmental debt which represents such a large and growing portion of the financial burdens laid upon State and local taxpayers.

3. SOME BROADER PURPOSES OF REGIONAL PLANNING

In the case of such regional experiments as the Tennessee Valley Authority, it becomes far more true than in the case of municipalities that the planning of public works is merely incidental to a plan for the development of life and production in the area. It depends upon the character of the development toward which the planning authority is directing its efforts, and may be used as one of the instruments, but only one, for influencing economic development and causing it to follow the lines which are planned for it. Planning of this sort may be limited to forecasting normal future development within the limits of conventional types of productive organization. For example, it may be a question whether staple farming or cultivation of miscellaneous produce is more suited to the agricultural areas of the region, and at what point manufacturing will find its most natural and favorable development. Problems of this type are difficult and far reaching enough. They become still more so when there are maladjusted industries or industrial groups to be taken account of, and their future development guided into new channels of a different sort, with a view to curing the maladjustments.

Here there is need of a great deal of expenditure for activities of a kind not ordinarily classed as public works, and these activities must be highly experimental in character, involving some uncertainty as to the outcome. Among the experiments with which we are now engaged is the buying up of submarginal lands and the moving of the displaced population, not only to other localities, but in some cases to new and different kinds of occupations or even to novel kinds of economic units. The so-called "subsistence homestead" on which small-scale self-sufficing cultivation may be carried on in connection with various forms of decentralized manufacturing, represents one of these experiments in which the outcome is necessarily far from certain. Governmental aid to cooperative self-help organizations is another example, though one in which the Government is not heavily committed. Its own experiment with relief work in which the workers produce goods for their own consumption is an extension of this self-help principle. Low-cost housing is another field in which experimenting is being done, and, if this is to succeed in reaching the classes for whose benefit it is intended, some ways must be found of furthering that end which are different from what has been done before. This is true because we have had many attempts in the field of low-cost housing without as yet succeeding in overcoming the difficulties which stand in the way of making such housing both self-sustaining and cheap enough to reach the lowest income groups.

It is possible that, with the control over such basic factors as the location of town sites, public acquisition of lands, control of development affecting land values and other factors, which a regional authority of such scope as the Tennessee Valley Authority is in a position to control, more far-reaching results can be obtained than heretofore. Where urban land values have already been built up on a basis of undesirable congestion of population, there are obstacles from which the newer type of authority might be free. It may also be able to carry on the work more systematically and on a large scale, and so obtain economies in actual construction and operation. These are only examples of the types of experimental pioneering which may be involved in the more far-reaching sorts of regional planning and which represent untried possibilities, and opportunities for evolutionary development toward a better economic system.

These three major elements, then, relief work, anticyclical timing of regular public works and expenditures, and general regional planning are all parts of the background with which the United States approaches the problem of planned public works at the present time. These three elements have never been thoroughly integrated. In some respects they are likely to be mutually helpful, and in some respects there are inconsistencies or antagonisms to be harmonized as best they may be

II. HARMONIES AND CONFLICTS BETWEEN THE PURPOSES IN VIEW

To a considerable extent, the elements—work relief, timing of public works and expenditures, and general regional planning—are harmonious with each other. If public works are to be timed with reference to industrial fluctuations, one of the necessary prerequisites is a program such as regional planning furnishes. Thus, where regional planning exists, one of the essential steps has already been taken. It has been the general lack of such advanced programs which has made the localities so bafflingly slow in presenting projects to the Public Works Administration for their approval and financial help. Among the notable exceptions is the city of Cincinnati, which had developed a public-works plan under its city manager, and which has been able to make a much better record than other localities in submitting sound projects for approval. Looked at from another angle, a sudden attempt to make a large increase in public-works expenditures vastly increases the danger of embarking on ill-considered and incoherent projects. It likewise vastly increases the usefulness of an organic plan which affords a schedule of well-considered and coherent projects.

One positive advantage of a program that combines these various elements lies in the fact that while interest in planning to avoid depressions is likely to be spasmodic, interest in regional planning is steadier and more reliable. Further, it may help to carry the whole program through the critical period when depressions seem far away and when planning for them, if it stood by itself, would be likely to lapse. Regional planning is generally accepted as worth while, encounters hardly any material resistance, and is likely to command stronger support than ever in times of prosperity when peoples' minds turn to the great future they see for their community. Programs for alleviating depressions are beset by more doubts and conflicting interests and are likely to have the strongest support only when a depression is actually under way and when it is too late to plan. They are in the class of the things the devil would do when the devil was sick, or of mending the hole in the roof, which cannot be done when it is raining and is not needed when the weather is fine.

The critical period for present plans for dealing with future depressions will be the period of prosperity following the next revival. Not only will people be little inclined to think of the dangers of coming depressions, but material interests will rise up to resist doing anything they believe might interfere with the period of prosperity following a revival. It is in such a period that people are least likely to think of the dangers of coming depressions, and particularly to do anything which might retard the prevailing high rate of business activity, for the sake of conjectured hard times which may never come. In such a time public interest would probably not be sufficient to support a program of postponing public works for the sake of creating a reserve to be used to meet a future depression, if that program stood by itself. But if it were one of the incidental duties

18

of an organization set up to carry out purposes which the public does recognize and does support and which have nothing to do necessarily with preparation for depressions, then the depression-insurance features of the program may have a better chance for survival. Naturally, this presupposes that the organization set up will genuinely serve both purposes. What this means in practice is that it must contain individuals who approach the problem from both standpoints; otherwise, regardless of the purposes stated in the law setting up the organization, one purpose is likely to be sacrificed to the other because the personnel itself is preponderantly interested in one or the other. If a planning organization were solely in the hands of regional planners of the usual type and background, the probability is that measures for the timing of public works with a view to controlling depressions would largely be allowed to go by default, while if the personnel consisted solely of individuals interested in the theory of anticylical timing of public works as an antidote to depression, the reverse would be true.

As has already been pointed out, the natural form in which regional planners cast their programs is that of a fairly uniform schedule of works with expenditures which do not fluctuate materially from year to year. To be asked to stand ready to increase this program or decrease it at comparatively short notice, for reasons having nothing . to do with the community's need for the works, would naturally be regarded as an interference with the smooth carrying out of the projects and might actually interfere with initiating some of them at the most opportune time (from the standpoint of the regional planner) or prosecuting them at the most economic rate. It might involve postponing projects until after the community has developed to a point at which they would be worth carrying out, and thus sacrifice some of the services they might render, or it might involve carrying them out before the community has reached that point and, therefore, incur a burden of interest and maintenance on works which were not yet fully ripe for construction. Thus there would be elements opposed to economy, as well as opposed to the neat and orderly carrying out of the program. However, from this standpoint it is no more disastrous to speed up the program during depressions and curtail it during prosperity, than to curtail it during depressions and speed it up during prosperity, which is what happens under ordinary conditions. Systematic planning is at least no worse than no planning.

On the other hand, there are possibilities of taking advantage of the reduced levels of construction costs and the cheap rates on borrowed capital which prevail in times of depression, and thus actually increasing the economy of the whole program through carrying it out in part as an antidote to business cycles. These possibilities, however, are not large, and may easily disappear altogether in the face of a large expansion of public works, especially if no particular care is taken to avoid inflated costs. This question will be more fully discussed in a subsequent chapter. Suffice it to say here that one pair of purposes which is not at all easy to reconcile consists of (a) the purpose of making the expansion of expenditures in a depression large enough to afford real relief, and (b) the purpose of seeing to it that the expenditures promote private revival rather than retard it, and do not spoil the market by bidding up costs in such a way as actually to deter private investors from resuming their own capital expenditures.

More serious, perhaps, is the probability, amounting to a moral certainty, that no practicable amount of shifting of works from year to year within a 10-year program such as regional planners might draw up, can possibly be sufficient to create a large enough reserve to handle the needs of the occasional major crises in our economic system. Thus, if the program of expanding works in dull times is to be carried out when it is most needed, in times of really serious crisis, it seems inevitable that it must take in works of inferior importance or inferior urgency, or works so far ahead in point of time in the regular schedule as to amount to the same thing. Such emergencies, it seems, must always disturb the plans and ideals of the regional planner, if they are to be adequately met. In considering this difficulty, however, the pertinent question to ask is not merely whether such a situation is unwelcome to the planners, but whether it will involve less disturbance if it is planned for than if it comes without previous planning or preparation. Judging by recent experience, major emergencies can be counted on to bring with them a demand for large expansion of public works. And if this demand falls upon a system of Federal, State, and local governments which are not prepared to meet it, it will inevitably produce worse confusion and inefficiency than if it has been contemplated and prepared for in advance. The situation is a little parallel to that of the War Department official during the Spanish War, who complained that he had gotten his Department working quite efficiently when a war came along and spoiled it. Orders for Government supplies were limited to a few concerns who handled the business regularly and in sufficient volume to give the Government better and cheaper service than if it had been distributed in smaller amounts among a larger number of concerns; but the result was that a sudden and large expansion in the orders for equipment faced almost insuperable difficulties. This was a case in which efficiency in meeting the emergency when it came could be brought about only by measures involving some loss of routine economy during the intervening period of peace. Since the purpose of a peace-time army is to be ready for possible war, the answer to this problem seems obvious.

Another conflict, which is not as serious at it may seem, is the conflict between the economy of the pay-as-you-go system and the necessity for large public borrowing when works are expanded in times of emergency. A system which expands public works in dull times necessarily involves some borrowing at such times, but in minor depressions this would not be a serious matter and would not interfere materially with the natural and salutary tendency of a far-sighted government to reduce the total amount of its debt for such purposes. It could not literally pay as it went in every single year, but it could very closely approximate this standard, and would be much more likely to do so than under the present unplanned system. It would still be under the necessity of borrowing very large sums in major crises, but that necessity, as we have seen, cannot be avoided, and the public credit would be in a much stronger position to meet it, in proportion as it had previously approximated to the ideal of pay as you go.

There is an incongruity, which may not amount to an actual conflict, between the purposes of relief work and those of a planned public works program. The ideal of the public works program is to increase the volume of work done on ordinary principles of selection and payment of employees, while relief work involves some concessions to the principle of need in selecting employees, and usually the payment of less than the market rates of wages. If relief works take over types of projects which might otherwise come under the regular public works administration, there may be a feeling that the government is profiteering on the needs of the employee and getting work done cheaply which it would otherwise have to pay regular market rates for. Possibly one doubtful consolation in this matter is to be found in the fact that relief works, despite low rates of pay, are proverbially expensive in proportion to the results obtained.

It would clearly be difficult to have the two types of work carried on simultaneously by the same organization. The natural system is to keep the organizations separate and allow them to follow different policies. Problems would remain as to what types of work should be regarded as the proper field of relief works, and these cannot be said to have been solved. In general, it seems inevitable that relief works will be confined more or less to projects of inferior grade of importance, but if the organization is sufficiently ingenious to discover forms of work not taken over by other organizations and yet of high value, it would seem impertinent to borbid them to carry on such valuable projects.

In general, it appears that the purposes of regional planning can be made to subserve the purposes of mitigating industrial cycles, and that regional planning furnishes one of the basic prerequisites to planning of the other type. Such conflicts as appear are not so much conflicts between the two types of planning as conflicts between orderly regional planning and the disrupting effects which major industrial crises are certain to bring with them, whether they are planned for or not. At least, the orderly progress of a regional program would not be more seriously interfered with by a moderate increase in the volume of work done during a depression, than it is already interfered with at such times, by the decrease of work which results from shortage of funds and the pressure to balance the budget. Anticyclical timing of public works can go to considerable lengths without introducing any greater disturbance in a regular program of works than is already produced by industrial fluctuations when they are met without previous planning.

III. RELIEF WORK: ADVANTAGES AND DISADVANTAGES AS COMPARED WITH DOLES OR INSURANCE

A. General Characteristics of Relief Work

In the United States, relief of destitution has been a local responsibility, and until the present administration this principle was maintained by the Federal Government. The great burdens imposed by the depression were met by the localities as best they might be. The problem naturally was on a scale of magnitude in which the traditional poor farm meant nothing. Moreover it involved a totally different kind of need from the destitution due to personal causes, with which the poor farm was adapted to deal. Large amounts of out-door relief (to use the British term) became absolutely necessary. In many localities, this was combined with the idea of letting the unemployed do some work in exchange for the relief received, with the result that there was a considerable amount of relief work locally carried on, which was, for the most part, at low rates of pay uniform for all. In short, it was on a relief rather than a wage basis.

With the Roosevelt administration, relief work became a national policy. The first large item of this sort in the program of the administration was the Civilian Conservation Corps, representing a special kind of treatment for a special class. Youths and young men, many of them just reaching the age of self-support and finding industrial opportunities closed against them, were drifting around the country in large numbers after the well-known fashion of the hobo or tramp. The dangers of this situation, particularly to a group who would under normal business conditions have settled down in some regular employment and regular place in society, are so obvious as to need no argument.

As a means of meeting this problem, approximately 300,000 young men were placed in camps, equipped with suitable clothing for out-door work, and set to work building forest roads, making fire barriers and trails, and generally doing a large variety of out-door work which was useful, although not of the sort which would have found a place in ordinary budgets at that time. They were handled by military officers, paid $30 a month and subjected to a certain amount of discipline intended to counteract the demoralizing effects of their previous irregular existence. The total cost of this type of employment has been in the range of magnitude of approximately $1,000 per year per worker. While reports on the experiment are somewhat conflicting, it appears that it has, in general, succeeded in its main purpose. In addition, other camps have been set up as refuges from the road, for the remaining migratory unemployed.

As autumn of 1933 came on, it became evident that the relief problem during the coming winter was to be an unusually serious one. While unemployment had somewhat decreased, under the operation of the National Recovery Administration, the reserves of the unemployed were by this time quite completely exhausted, with the result

22

that the need for relief was the greatest yet faced. In the meantime, the program of public works had not gotten under way in sufficient volume to constitute a factor of major importance. To meet this situation, an avowedly temporary program of relief work was instituted under the Civil Works Administration, aiming at the employment of as many as 4,000,000 unemployed workers. This number was very nearly reached at the height of the program. Average rates of pay varied somewhat, but in general ran between $12 and $15 per week, an amount which turned out to be more than available forms of low-grade private employment afforded in many localities, and which was frequently considerably more than was being paid on existing local work-relief projects. Relief work on this scale was impossible to maintain. The original appropriation of $400,000,000 was exhausted before the date originally set for the ending of the experiment, and it was brought to an end earlier than originally intended. Nevertheless it carried some millions of workers through the worst of an unusually severe winter.

On termination of the Civil Works Administration's activities, relief·work was taken over by the Federal Emergency Relief Administration, under the same Administrator, but on a less elaborate scale. One of the most interesting phases of the new program is the proposal to set relief workers at work on the production of commodities for their own consumption and that of others on relief.

This brief sketch of the American experience serves to indicate that relief work may be a thing of varying character; in fact, that there are fairly distinct types of such work. It may afford special treatment for a special segregated class under conditions separate and different from those of ordinary employment, or it may select particular superior groups of individuals and attempt to find work which suits their capacities, or it may simply attempt to afford a more self-respecting substitute for relief for the better grades of the unemployed in general, or it may be another form of relief, applied generally on a basis of need rather than a basis of industrial quality. Pay may vary from an amount intended to be the equivalent of a fair wage for the type of work done (in which case it is likely to be more than actual earnings in many trades where hours have been heavily curtailed) or it may be a relief stipend based upon something like bare necessities, or it may be something intermediate. In this country, the general object has been, not to make relief unpleasant as in the case of the old English workhouse, nor even in the main to furnish a test of willingness to work, but rather to afford something more consistent with self-respect than an outright dole, on the assumption that most of the workers would prefer work to idle relief if they had the option. In short, it was based on the assumption that they had self-respect which did not require penalties or disciplinary treatment, but only conditions affording some opportunity to maintain it. The civil works experiment was definitely aimed at providing "real work for real wages" and therefore it was in intention as far removed from outright relief doles as the circumstances permitted.

One other condition giving rise to a special need for relief work consisted in the fact that there were many unemployed, often of the highest grade mentally and socially with specialized training and attitudes, who did not belong to the construction industries and who would not be touched by an ordinary public works program. They constituted a group for whom the system of the dole was peculiarly obnoxious and calculated to produce peculiarly serious effects. This was not because it was likely to demoralize them in the ordinary sense of making them willing to rely on charity and relax their ambition for self-support, but rather because their failure to maintain themselves was so keenly felt that it tended to produce nervous breakdowns or other psychological conditions which might be fairly serious.

The production of mural paintings and of calculating machines of the most elaborate and complicated sort are only two interesting examples illustrating the variety of high grade workers for whom occupation was found. To unemployed artists and high-grade technical workers, this employment was a godsend, while it lasted, and the moral effects were wholly beneficial. In general, the fact that regular public works can reach only a limited group out of the millions who are unemployed in a major crisis and that many of the others are of types for whom doles are peculiarly unsuited, seems to argue that there may be a special place for relief work outside the field of public works as a permanent feature of a program for meeting these major emergencies. Even unemployment insurance would fail to include many of this group.

Enough has been said to indicate the general advantages of relief work. And enough has also been said to indicate that it cannot be given to everyone in a major crisis. In this respect, Mr. Walter Lippmann's proposal for affording everyone an opportunity to do some kind of useful work at relief wages, seems to reckon without all of the practical difficulties of the case. Ideally, the moral advantages of work in contrast to idle relief should naturally and logically be reserved (since it cannot be given to everyone) for those to whom it will make the most difference and will do the most good. This argues for limiting it to a selected group from which the chronic casuals and unemployables would be excluded. But such a program is not easy to achieve.

The difficulties and disadvantages of relief work start with the difficulty of finding worth-while things to be done which are not otherwise provided for and which would not mean displacing a worker on regular pay by a worker in receipt of relief wages. This necessarily limits the choice largely to works of inferior importance of urgency. Moreover, while the Federal Government might be willing to carry on works in its own interest on a relief basis, it has particular reason to be chary in the matter of doing things with workers in receipt of relief wages, which a State or local community might otherwise do for itself. The restrictions placed upon projects under the Civil Works Administration were such as to rule out both maintenance and capital additions to permanent improvements, as well as regular operating expenses falling naturally upon the local government. If literally construed, it would seem that substantially everything of value naturally and obviously available would be ruled out. Largely by disregarding or circumventing these restrictions, much really useful work was found. One administrator who may be rather typical substituted for his own purpose a different kind of restriction, namely, whether the work was something which the locality was not able to finance and which there was no prospect of its being able to finance for some years to come.

It was at once an advantage and a disadvantage of the Civil Works Administration that it was looked upon in a different light from relief work in general, with little or no stigma attached to it. This was in harmony with the purpose of the administration and had no disadvantages so far as the workers concerned were of a superior type, but in the case of others, drawbacks appeared. The fact that white-collar workers registered in large numbers under the Civil Works Administration but many of them failed to transfer registration to the subsequent relief work indicate that the Civil Works Administration met a need for this superior class which ordinary relief work did not meet. On the other hand, it is testified that Negro domestic servants in the District of Columbia gave up private situations in order to "work for the Government", with a feeling of added dignity. This was, of course, an evasion of the purpose of the enterprise, an evasion of a sort which could not be wholly prevented under the circumstances of quick action and the handling of large numbers of applicants, which, under the circumstances, was inseparable from the liberality of treatment which was afforded. Such a problem suggests a need for different treatment of different groups, possibly even under different administrative units. Such differential treatment is not easy. Every additional unit gives rise to troublesome and time-consuming wastes in the process of determining where a given applicant belongs, with frequent possibilities that a worthy applicant may be passed from one unit to another and fail to get prompt relief when it is urgently needed.

In general, it seems that the advantage of relief work, from the standpoint of the morale of the workers, tends to disappear as the work becomes too obviously improvised tasks of little inherent value and as the wages are too obviously relief in a thinly-disguised form. When the point is reached where the value of the work is obviously negligible, or nearly so, and it appears that the worker is conferring a favor on those who employ him by making the job last as long as possible, so as to save them the difficulty of attempting to find some fresh work, it is time to consider whether the advantages of work relief as compared to outright doles has not completely disappeared.

These difficulties and disadvantages all tend to become greater as the work is continued for a longer time and as it is done on a larger scale. It is obviously harder to find worth-while jobs for 4,000,000 workers than for 1,000,000, and harder to find them for 2 years than for 2 months. For example, the Civil Works Administration art project seems to have been justifiable as far as it went, but the painting of murals in school buildings could not go on indefinitely.

Moreover, the farther it went the more glaring would be the inconsistency between murals not urgently needed and the inability to pay teachers to keep regular classes going. The reductio ad absurdum would, of course, be the painting of murals in a school which was closed for lack of funds. This presumably has not happened and is only interesting as a suggestion of the inherent difficulty of the situation, growing partly out of the idea of balancing the regular budget while going in debt for emergency outlays and partly out of spendings in the same area by different governmental units, one of which has reached its limit while another has credit and is willing to use it. The point is, not that such work should not be done, but rather that current regular services should not have to be injuriously curtailed.

Another disadvantage is the fact, already mentioned, that such work is proverbially expensive in proportion to the amount accomplished, in spite of low wages. It would be interesting to study the experience of the Civil Works Administration and see to what extent it may have avoided this disadvantage. If relief work does not attempt to reach all the unemployed, but only a selected fraction, it may select workers for their fitness for the particular work at hand (subject always to the limitation of not taking workers already employed). If selection is entirely on this basis, a fairly good working force may be built up. But with relief wages above the level of cash relief (as they should be) there is a strong incentive to select workers according to need, especially if the work relief fund comes from the Federal Government and the burden of maintaining those not reached by it falls on the locality. Local administrators then can hardly fail to select workers with large families who would otherwise put a heavy drain on the local relief funds. Moreover, many of the persons who are of the highest type and farthest from the unemployable class are not physically fitted for the kinds of work available, and a mixture of people of this sort with chronic unemployables has its disadvantages as a working combination.

As a form of relief, relief work is more expensive than outright doles. For a government committed to a policy of public-works expansion this would not naturally be a serious disadvantage, since the excess goes into channels affording stimulus to business and is not wasted from the standpoint of the whole program. But the total amount required may exceed what the Government is prepared to spend; it will certainly exceed it in any major crisis. It is reported that approximately 1 person in 6 in New York City was on relief early in 1934 and with responsibilities of this magnitude the Government cannot afford the luxury of paying uniform wages, which would necessarily be in excess of minimum needs for some, if they were adequate to minimum needs for others. The cost of materials, while not large in this type of work, is still a matter which desperately straitened budgets cannot undertake without the danger of exceeding the limits of the Government's credit. It appears that, in major emergencies, relief work must be limited in its scope, and that large masses of the unemployed must come under some system of idle relief.

The experiment, recently announced, of including in relief work the production of goods to be consumed by the otherwise unemployed workers themselves, is one which may prove to be of great significance and should be watched with the utmost interest. The logic of such an experiment is obvious. In fact, this is the only obvious method by which a volume of work can be found of whose usefulness there can be not the slightest doubt, and which automatically increases with the increase in the numbers of those who need it. We have not yet found methods of making effective the "right to work" for all members of our society; yet that right is so basic that no system which fails to secure it can possibly meet successfully the critical examination of the present age. When the private system fails to furnish an opportunity for great masses of workers collectively to produce the subsistence which they need, it is only logical that that opportunity should be otherwise afforded.

The many local self-help organizations which have spontaneously sprung up all over the country give abundant evidence of the force of this principle, although their very local character prevents them from setting up an effective and self-sufficient system for the production of all of the necessities for the people concerned. The Government has been giving some aid to these local organizations, and this policy should clearly be continued, and both kinds of experiment be closely watched.[1] There are many difficulties in the way of fitting any system of self-sufficing production into the scheme of an economy whose main principle is that of business interprise, especially when it is expected that the self-sufficing form of production will serve in a secondary or reserve capacity, going into operation only as the system of business enterprise fails to keep the population fully employed and fully supplied. These questions will be somewhat more fully discussed in chapter XIV. For the present, it is worth noting that this form of production represents a field of great and unexploited possibilities for enlarging the scope and transferring the character of relief work.

B. Unemployment Insurance or Reserves

Unemployment insurance, like relief work, is a thing which takes more than one form, and may be so handled as to increase or reduce the differences between it and outright relief. The government may or may not contribute to the regular maintenance of the system, although if the system is to be maintained through major crises, the government has to come to its support in one way or another. Benefits may be in proportion to wages, or may be equal for all, or may be on the basis of need. The right to receive a benefit may hinge merely on being out of work, or there may be an additional need test. The system may cover all forms of unemployment, seasonal as well as cyclical, or it may be administered with the provision that benefits do not begin until after the individual has been unemployed for a length of time representing approximately the usual seasonal loss of time in his particular trade. There is always a waiting period, before benefits begin, and this may be longer or shorter. There is almost necessarily a limit of time beyond which the fund will not pay benefits; a limit which may or may not vary with the amount of premiums which have already been paid in for time actually worked before unemployment began.

Some of these differences in policy go so far as to alter rather fundamentally the essence of the system as contrasted with other methods of relief. For instance, where a need test is established, or where benefits are paid in accordance with need, or both, the system loses its peculiar character and its peculiar advantages in contrast to outright relief. These advantages hinge on the fact that the support during unemployment comes as a matter of contractual right, based upon contributions in which the worker himself has paid a share.

Germany has relied on the principle of insurance for some time, and the British have gone definitely over to the system, to the extent of abandoning any considerable reliance upon relief work. Out of their long experience with relief work they appear to have become convinced of its disadvantages and to feel that the system of unemployment benefits avoids these disadvantages while still preserving the main desideratum of a more self-respecting system of provision than outright relief. The stigma of charity is avoided, and the English

[1] Since the above was written, these local organizations have apparently developed little, while the Federal Government has itself taken up production of goods to be consumed by the otherwise unemployed.

appear to have found the payments less demoralizing than the make-shift attempt to find more or less nominal work. While evasion and malingering inevitably constitute a problem, the weight of testimony is to the effect that it has, on the whole, been successfully prevented and does not constitute a major disadvantage. of relief.

One of the more serious possible disadvantages, from the standpoint of helping toward regularizing private employment, is the probable effect of the benefits in stiffening the resistance of the workers to wage reductions when such reductions may be needed in order to enable demand to revive sufficiently to absorb the supply of workers. So far as statistical evidence goes, it does not show that in England the system of out-of-work benefits has prevented a deflation of wages. As to whether it has prevented the deflation from being as heavy as was needed in the economic situation there can, in the nature of the case, be no very convincing proof.

From another standpoint, unemployment reserves may be regarded as a means of stabilizing purchasing power, seeing to it that it does not fall off to the full extent that production falls off in an industrial decline. In this way some of the cumulative effects of an industrial decline may be minimized or prevented by doing what amounts to transferring purchasing power from good times to bad times. But in this connection the administration of the reserves faces a very difficult choice. If it invests the reserves in various forms of income-yielding securities, of long or short term, as it would naturally do in the attempt to make possible larger benefits in proportion to contributions, then it faces the fact that it is systematically buying investments in a dear market and selling them in a cheap market. Losses would inevitably result. Furthermore, the throwing of securities on the market, or the contraction of investments in short-term paper, would both have effects tending to increase the depth of an industrial depression. This fact has already been noted in connection with the reserves kept by corporations, which have been used in the stabilization of interest and dividend payments. Where the reserves are handled in this way purchasing power as a whole is not transferred from good times to bad times, but only purchasing power distributed to certain classes of consumers. This distribution is stabilized at the expense of concentrating the fluctuations in the field of funds devoted to the purchase of investments and fluctuations in this field may have just as serious consequences as fluctuations of consumers' incomes and expenditures. These difficulties can be met by a wise experimental policy in which a proper proportion is found between ordinary investments, governmental investments, and possible outright maintenance of cash balances.[2]

It goes without saying that in this country, which appeared, in 1934, to be on the verge of adopting unemployment insurance in some form or forms in the several States, all these problems should be studied, together with the experience of other countries. It appears clear that the system can be made far more satisfactory than outright charitable relief and better in its effect on the people concerned. It also seems that a well-managed system of this sort is superior to the forms into which relief work of a general and long-continued sort is likely to degenerate. On the other hand, it seems

[2] Cf. Alvin H. Hansen; The Flow of Purchasing Power in Economic Reconstruction, N. Y., 1934, pp. 210-237, esp. pp. 219-236.

to be definitely inferior to the best and most successful forms of relief work, especially those which succeed in finding work of a sort for which the worker is particularly suited, or those which are able to bring about definite rehabilitation of the workers.

It clearly makes a vital difference to a policy of relief work itself, whether there is also a system of unemployment insurance in force, and what its character is. A system of insurance would remove the urgent need which leads to the cruder and less successful forms of relief work. On the other hand, it might still prove practicable, where some clearly useful form of relief work is available and also workers who are clearly suited to it and willing to perform it, to work out some kind of combination in which workers entitled to benefits might substitute relief work and thus possibly reduce the burden on the insurance fund. Of course, workers employed on regular public works would have the same status as other employed persons, and would be contributing to unemployment reserves, not drawing upon them. This has, in some cases, led to the practice of taking workers into public work just long enough to get the necessary stamps on their employment books, and then throwing them back upon the insurance fund. This is, of course, a makeshift which should be scrutinized in terms of its effect on the whole policy. There are evident problems to be met in fitting together public works, relief work, and unemployment insurance.

But so long as the system of unemployment insurance is not universal in its coverage, there will undoubtedly remain scope for the operation of relief work, though presumably on a diminished scale which may make possible better results. The whole question of the place of relief work, including making goods for personal consumption, should be thoroughly investigated in the light of the experience of this emergency, and also with reference to fitting into a system where there is unemployment insurance as well as a system in which this does not exist.

C. Outright Relief

As in the case of insurance and relief work, there is more than one system of relief itself. The system of grocery orders has been widely used in this country, as well as assuming payments of rent. It seems to be the experience of workers in this field, however, that, even where this system is used, some cash payment is a virtual necessity, even though the payment may be extremely small. And the self-respect of the recipient is much less injured if the family is given a cash payment and the responsibility and opportunity of spending it to his best judgment.

However, the particular problems of administration of cash relief do not concern this report. It is concerned only with relief as an alternative to employment on public work. On that basis, the outstanding facts can be stated quite simply. Outright relief costs fewest dollars per person relieved, and even in its best form it is the least beneficial of all the ways of handling the problem. And in spite of this, it becomes necessary to fall back on it to care for the many cases who do not fit into the other schemes for handling unemployment. Naturally, a fairly comprehensive unemployment-insurance system would obviate the greater part of this need.

D. Conclusion

The probability is that in the near future we shall see some continuance of all these measures and shall have a chance to adjust their relative place in the scheme according to the results of experience. It appears probable that insurance will come into use, spreading gradually or rapidly according as to whether the Federal Government does or does not apply heavy pressure in that direction, and that the field of work relief will dwindle unless experiments in the direction of producing commodities for the workers' own consumption prove reasonably promising. In the latter case such work may come to constitute an important, if not a large, section of our economic system. Provision should be made for continuance of experiments in this direction.

IV. VARIETIES OF ECONOMIC DISLOCATIONS

A. Importance of the Question

It should go without saying that any program for the utilizing of public expenditures in such fashion as to furnish an antidote for business dislocations should be based on the clearest possible understanding of what those dislocations are and so far as possible, the causes to which they are to be ascribed. Not merely the kind of dislocations, but their size is important. As already noted, early English advocates of this kind of public expenditure policy had in mind fairly regular ups and downs in general business, which were so mild that unemployment in a depression was not more than some 5 percent greater than in prosperity. At present we can only envy the simplicity of the problem as it appeared to these early writers and the ease with which they were able to show that proper timing a minor part of the regular government expenditures could neutralize such mild cycles without great disturbance to government work or to government finances.

It is obvious that the kinds of disturbances we have been witnessing in the last 20 years are of a totally different order of magnitude and call for much more strenuous measures. The earlier writers could contemplate laying out the schedules of work which would normally be due in the next 10 years in any case, and merely changing the timing of such outlays as could be shifted without great inconvenience. The amount of shifting possible under this type of program would be totally inadequate to combat the more recent and violent disturbances. If anything amounting to a remedy, or even a partial remedy, is to be looked for, it will require more radical policies.

It is not merely important to have in mind how business actually behaves during these disturbances, so that we might show what it is we are trying to counteract, but also what the causes are which bring these distrubances about, so far as we can diagnose them. Further, it is important to know whether or not a public-works policy actually tends to neutralize the causes of disturbance or whether it is a mere palliative which may even get in the way of the natural remedies, such as they may be, and make the underlying condition worse rather than better.

B. General Character of Business Movements

Invaluable as it is to draw on the results of the statistical laboratory in analyzing business movements, it is equally necessary to be forewarned as to what the statistical laboratory does to these various and heterogeneous movements of men, steel, concrete, wheat, credit instruments, and all the rest. The laboratory makes a composite picture of things which are actually separate—interdependent but never merged—and then having made this composite picture which it may express in a single line on a chart, it then examines the movements of the line and separates out different components of the move-

31

ments which are never separated in reality.[1] Thus the statistical
laboratory makes both mergings and separations which represent
abstractions rather than the facts as business originally experiences
them.

The general business curve is made up of records of different industries, different regions or localities, and different industrial groups,
none of which are ever all moving in the same direction. Many of
them seem to show tendencies toward timing different from the others
and different from the composite of general business, although the
general business curve reacts on most of them so that even if their own
natural movement is much longer, that long movement will be broken
up into shorter units, at least in many cases. In particular, construction, which is at the center of this report, seems to show some tendency
to move in longer cycles than general business while at the same time
showing some rise and fall in response to the general business curve,
even when that does not fit in with its own movement. Neither an
abstract construction cycle nor an abstract general business cycle
which ignores the particular idiosyncrasies of construction gives an
accurate picture of what happens in the world where roads and bridges
and school houses are actually being built.

C. The Shorter Type of Business Cycle

The most clearly marked cycle movements of the composite picture
we call "general business conditions" are comparatively short cycles
varying in the United States from 2 to 5 years in duration, with an
average of approximately 3⅓ years, and varying fully as much in
amplitude and severity as they do in duration. This report is no
place in which to attempt a comprehensive theory of these business
cycles, but a few of their outstanding characteristics have a really
important bearing on the problem of using public expenditures as a
remedy.

1. OUTSTANDING GENERAL CHARACTERISTICS.

First and most obvious is the movement of prices. Here a thing
which may be hard to remember at the present time is the fact that
the ordinary cyclical movement of prices is comparatively mild,
almost negligible for ordinary consumers' goods of the perishable sort.
The main fluctuations come in wholesale prices and especially in the
prices of durable producers' goods, and consumers' goods of the most
durable sorts. These comparatively mild ups and downs are super-
imposed on fairly long and fairly slow upward and downward movements, broken by an occasional cataclysmic change which is usually
traceable to war.

These price movements illustrate very well the way in which everything in this picture is at once a result and a cause. The price movements create disturbances in business—shifts of income between
wages and profits, gains and losses on inventory, and corresponding
tendencies toward liberal advance buying or the opposite policy of
hand-to-mouth purchase. But while the price movements create dis-

---

[1] This statement applies only to a slight extent to the studies of the National Bureau of Economic Research. This Bureau has refrained from constructing its own curve of general business conditions, using
this composite concept only in determing the dates of the turning points marking recession and recovery.
Its series for specific factors, such as pig-iron production, eliminate seasonal movements but not secular
trends, and are thus closer to the unmodified facts than the usual curves employed in business-cycle analysis.

turbances, it also appears that attempts to keep prices rigid in particular cases make the disturbances worse rather than better. Where there is a tendency for prices of construction materials to fall, that is a symptom of weakened demand, and a policy of keeping prices rigid in face of that weakness does nothing to help demand revive but rather prevents it. Thus, while prices help to transmit disturbing influences, they are symptoms of more underlying causes; and a policy which aims to go to the root of things will have to deal with the more underlying factors.

2. SHIFTS IN THE RELATIVE DISTRIBUTION OF INCOME

Along with the movements of prices and the corresponding movements of volumes of production goes, of course, a change in the total national income, but this change affects different groups of shares differently. Business profits show very intense changes, while on the other hand, the actual distribution of this class of income in the form of interest and dividends payments is steadied, with the help of reserves, to a rather remarkable extent. It is natural that interest payments should remain fairly steady, since so many of them are on long-term obligations and a heavy shrinkage in this class of disbursements could come only through default or reorganization. It is, however, somewhat remarkable that dividend payments actually continued to increase after the beginning of the 1929 recession in business, and for about a year did not fall below the level at which they stood when the recession first appeared, in midsummer of 1929. Thus the movement of distribution of interest and dividends is sluggish and retarded. Mild or short depressions do not register fully, while a long and severe depression, which exhausts corporate reserves and brings about defaults and reorganizations, makes heavy inroads on this class of income. Wages do not fluctuate as much as business profits, but ordinarily fluctuate much more than the actual distribution of interest and dividends. While both wage rates and volume of employment respond to expanding business, the wage earners' total income at such a time does not increase as fast as the total income of industry, with the result that the percentage share going to labor decreases.

The effects of these shifts in the distribution of income are too complex to be fully traced in this study. It is clear that the high profits of prosperity do not represent a general scarcity of goods, but rather arise largely from disproportionate movements in different financial magnitudes affecting income and expense in such a way that the remainder fluctuates intensely. There is also ground for considering, at least tentatively, the proposition that the growth of profits during the boom represents an absorption of purchasing power which will not be fully spent, of which much less than the general average will go for consumption, and much more than the general average will be saved or invested, with the result that actual consumers' spendings cannot increase as fast as the total dollar magnitude of production, while savings increase faster.

It is not certain that it is desirable for consumers' spendings to increase proportionately in a time of boom expansion. There is ground for advocating, instead, a stabilization of income disbursements, tending toward a stabilization of spendings. The actual behavior of interest and dividends represents such a stabilization, as far as it goes. Perhaps the chief criticism of it is, first, that it reaches the class of consumers which, on the average, needs it least, and secondly, that it is done at the expense of increasing the instability of investment expenditures. Thus the management of the financial reserves results in aggravating rather than mitigating some features of the industrial disturbance.[2] It has been argued, for example, that liquidation of reserves in order to maintain dividends aggravated the slump in security values which began in 1929 and which went so far that it became a source of secondary and cumulative effects, weakening the credit structure by shattering the values of collateral. One may conclude that while changes in distribution and corresponding changes in the proportion of income actually spent play an important part in business cycles, attempts to control the cycles through altering the distribution of spending power are not easy or simple and may have effects tending to defeat the end in view.

3. INTENSIFIED FLUCTUATIONS IN DURABLE GOODS

Both in terms of physical production and prices, the most intense fluctuations occur in the field of durable goods, including construction and all forms of fixed capital investment. The possibility of this sort of intensified movement is inherent in the nature of durable goods, since the time when new goods are bought or old ones replaced is to a large extent optional and may depend on moods of optimism or pessimism as well as on more substantial considerations. Furthermore, a sudden increase or decrease in the demand for a finished product or service creates a condition in which, if the amount of durable structures and equipment required is to adjust itself quickly and perfectly to the changed demand, the current output of these durable structures and equipment must change much more intensely than the output of the ultimate product or service. Thus, in this field of durable goods, there is a tendency to concentrate, let us say, 2 years' expansion in 1, when demand has started to grow beyond its normal relation to existing capacity, and this condition is naturally followed by a corresponding slump.

Perhaps the most serious feature of this kind of movement is the fact that it brings about a corresponding expansion and contraction of general purchasing power, resulting in increases and decreases of the total demand for goods of all sorts, durable and perishable alike. In this way the effect is transmitted cumulatively, multiplying itself and spreading to business in general. Thus it operates to bring about the well-known vicious spiral of decreased production and decreased spending power in times of depression. The figures do not seem to show whether there is any movement of ultimate consumers' spendings which initiates a business expansion or a business contraction. Spendings seem to move in harmony with incomes, and the conclusion is that a decline in general spendings is, in the main, a result of a decline in incomes, resulting in turn from a decline in production. From this standpoint the movements in the production of durable goods, following as they do a more fluctuating course than the movement of consumers' spendings for the ultimate products concerned, seems to be a peculiarly strategic source of disturbance.

[2] Cf. discussion of unemployment insurance in chapter II.

The field of construction is, of course, a large and important section of this durable-goods field, and public works constitute a considerable and increasing part of it. Construction, in general, not only shows the kind of intensified fluctuations which have been discussed, but also shows a definite tendency to lead the general curve of business. It also shows some tendency to move in longer cycles of its own; for example, in the period between 1922 and the present there has been one long cycle of construction reaching its peak at approximately the time of the mild depression culminating at the end of 1927. This fact may account for the extreme mildness of that particular depression. Thus there may be cases of mild general depression in which the construction industries are not depressed at all, but are above normal.

As for public works, they show a very general tendency to follow the ups and downs of business prosperity, more especially the larger and longer movements. But public works in any given locality are likely to be governed by special conditions and may not follow the general business curve at all closely. The effect of minor fluctuations of business is so delayed and confused that it is sometimes hard to identify. The effect of business fluctuations on public revenues is spread out in time, owing to the fact that some kinds of taxes feel the effect promptly and others feel it only after a considerable delay. As a result the milder fluctuations of business have little effect on public revenues for the current year and little discernible effect on public expenditures. Such effect as there is appears, in general, to be a retarded one. So far as public works follow the general business cycle, they appear to lag, rather than to lead, as does private construction. Thus they tend, as they are ordinarily made, not to initiate business movements, but to strengthen somewhat the cumulative effects of these movements after they have gotten under way, especially the larger and more serious ones.

4. MOVEMENTS OF CREDIT

Movements of credit are probably, in the main, not an initiating cause of business fluctuations, responding rather to the demands made on the credit institutions by expanding or contracting business. But they do constitute what is probably an indispensable enabling condition of the kind of expansions we have been speaking about, as well as an intensifying factor in expansions and contractions. Mention has been made of the tendency for the demand for durable goods to expand faster than ultimate consumers' expenditures during a revival, and also faster than incomes. If expenditures for durable goods were limited strictly to the funds which consumers have saved out of their current incomes, these cumulative expansions could hardly take place at all, or at most, would be very much milder than they actually are. But the possibility of drawing funds from an elastic reservoir of credit means that expenditures can increase faster than incomes, these expenditures giving rise in turn to increased incomes and so, for a time at least, to still further expansions of spending.

This proposition has its bearing on any attempt to counteract the cycle by the use of public works. If the government simply takes funds by increased taxes of a sort which would reduce the incomes available for spending, the result is likely to be, for the most part, a mere shifting of spendings from one kind of goods to another, not a net increase. It is only so far as the funds for public works come either out of credit expansion (or a reduction of credit contraction) or out of individual incomes which would otherwise be saved and not invested in the purchase of actual productive equipment, that a public works program can really have a stimulative effect on the total volume of business.

5. CONJECTURAL MOVEMENTS IN RELATIVE VOLUMES OF SAVINGS AND INVESTMENT AND RELATED QUANTITIES

Though figures are not conclusive on this point, it seems probable that, while savings increase during prosperity, capital expenditures increase faster, and while savings shrink during business recessions, capital expenditures shrink more sharply. Thus capital outlays during a boom come in part at least out of credit expansion, while during a recession savings are accumulated which do not find an immediate tangible outlet but which go in part to cancel past inflation, or at any rate, constitute in themselves a deflationary movement. Connected with this is the fact that productive capacity during a boom is expanding faster than total purchasing power, from which it would seem to follow that it is outgrowing its own market, so that expansion at this rate is bound to come to an end. And when this happens, the result is not merely a cessation of general expansion but an actual decline due to a falling off of current work on new construction. A further proposition seems to follow, having a definite bearing on a public-works program, namely, that an expansion of incomes does not promptly produce an equal expansion of spendings. During the boom, spendings tend to exceed incomes, and not to be limited by them, while during a depression, which is the pertinent stage from the standpoint of a public-works program of the kind we are considering, savings are being made which are not fully spent. In either case there is reason to doubt whether an increase in incomes would bring about an equally large increase in spendings, since in either case spendings are not accurately governed by incomes.

6. IRREGULARITIES IN THE CYCLICAL MOVEMENTS

If these cyclical movements were perfectly regular, both in time and in severity, a public-works program could easily be adjusted to meet them; but if this were the case private business also could meet them and prepare for them far better than it does. It is precisely the irregularities which create the uncertainty on which the basic character of the problem hinges. Some movements are short and some are long, some mild, and some violent, some show a large increase and a small decline, and others a small increase and a heavy decline. Some depressions show a quick rebound and others a long prostration. Moreover within the upward and downward movements of a single cycle, there are set-backs and temporary reversals which always give rise to some uncertainty as to whether the movement has reached its end or whether it will shortly be resumed.

Thus it is never possible to predict with accuracy either how far a current movement will go or when it will come to an end. For this reason it would be impossible to initiate a public works program which would take, let us say, 6 to 9 months before work actually got under way, in such a fashion that the employment would begin at just the time it was needed. It is even impossible to determine with accuracy in just what stage of a cycle industry is at the present moment. One must wait some months before one can be sure that an upward movement is going to be sustained and is not merely one of those numerous false revivals which frequently punctuate a decline and are followed by still larger downward movements. Thus, even if preparatory measures were so perfect that contracts could be let and work could begin with an absolute minimum of delay— say in a few weeks—still it would not be possible to start an expansion of public works simultaneously with the beginning of a downward movement of the cycle of general business. Fortunately, perhaps, that is neither necessary nor desirable.

More serious, perhaps, is the fact that the magnitude of the effort made by the Government cannot be accurately gaged to the magnitude of the depression in private business, which it is aimed to combat, without a very serious lag. A public works program of uniform magnitude, put into effect mechanically whenever the existence of a depression should be certified by the proper authorities, would never except by coincidence be exactly adjusted to the need for it. This difficulty will be dealt with later when we come to consider different types of public works programs.

D. The Different Phases of a Cycle

1. THE DECLINE

As has already been noted, the beginning of a decline is probably not so much traceable to an initial decline in consumers' spendings as to the fact that industry has reached a state of overcapacity with the result that the demand for further construction falls off. This state of overcapacity is often referred to as if it were, in and of itself, the central cause of a depression. Certainly it does create difficulties for business management. The existence of excess capacity tends to develop cutthroat competition and to make it more difficult to maintain profits. Cutthroat competition of a sort may occur even during the later phases of an expansion, taking shape not in reduced prices for products, but in increased prices for materials and labor. It is a well-known fact that prices of materials tend to rise faster and farther than prices of finished products. These prices probably reach an inflated level from which they must come down in order to make possible sustained business activity under the prevailing profit system. But these difficulties would not be fatal in and of themselves were it not for the scondary effects in the shape of a decline in the volume of construction. It is this result of a condition of over capacity which furnishes the real reason why it leads to a general contraction of business.

This principle has a direct and important bearing on what a public works program can and cannot do to combat a depression. Can it, if promptly initiated, prevent a decline in private business or can it merely fill in the decline and tide business over until private sources of demand revive? This is an important question. The answer seems to be that while public works can fill in the decline in private activity they cannot prevent it. They may, however, reduce its magnitude by reducing its cumulative effects.

Let us suppose that the volume of consumers' purchasing power were supplemented by government outlays as fast as private sources of incomes declined. This would maintain the private demand for consumers' goods, but if productive capacity were already fully equal to this demand, or more, there would still be a positive decline in private capital outlays, lasting until the postponing of replacements and of new construction created a gap to be filled. Until such time, the burden of filling the gap, if it were to be filled at all, would fall upon public expenditures. What could be done would be, first, to prevent a decline in the production of consumers' goods and secondly, to forestall the more extreme intensification of the decline in private demand for producers' goods due to (1) the actual decline in consumer demand and (2) straitened finances and the difficulty of raising funds, which result in the postponing of maintenance and replacements even beyond what the condition of consumption demand would indicate.

Thus the peak of private production cannot be maintained or quickly restored, but the bottom of the decline can be sustained somewhat. One result might be that the next succeeding boom would be milder. This would be especially true if the expansion of public expenditures during the depression were followed by a corresponding contraction during the next expansion of private business.

The sum total of public and private production can be maintained on peak levels only on two conditions. One is that the Government not merely shifts its expenditures from prosperous to depressed periods, but actually expands the total. The second condition is that the funds to finance this expansion shall be raised in such a fashion that they do not come out of private incomes which would otherwise be spent for tangible goods and services. Over short periods this can be accomplished by inflationary borrowing, but the service of the loans must ultimately come out of taxes. Hence, a long-term program of this sort, such as is needed for the purpose of sustaining business indefinitely at peak levels, must rest for its success on the discovery of forms of taxation which will not come out of spendings. The possibility of such forms of taxation will be discussed in chapter VI, in connection with the progressive-expansion type of public works program. For the present it may suffice to note that it represents a difficult problem and that the probabilities seem all against its being successfully solved on a large scale.

2. THE PROCESS OF DECLINE

The main conditions of a tangible sort have been already noted. They consist in a more or less simultaneous general decline in production, incomes and consumers' purchasing, but with these stages of the process farthest from the consumer showing, if anything, the promptest movements. In particular, durable goods show far greater fluctuations, both in physical volume and in price, than perishable consumer goods. In this movement, construction shows the violent movements characteristic of durable goods, but with an especially strong tendency to lead in the shorter business cycles combined with a tendency to move in longer cycles of its own. It is also interesting to note that, during the milder cycles, bank credit does not show a marked positive decline on the down swing of the general business curve, but merely a cessation of expansion, while general business is mildly contracting. It is only the more severe business contractions which are accompanied by an absolute contraction in the volume of bank credit. This is evidence, so far as it goes, that limitation of bank credit is not the crucial determining factor in a typical business decline. The indication is that such a decline cannot be stopped or reversed merely by offering credit more freely. Something needs to be done to make the market absorb more credit; to create an effective demand for it. In other words, the way to produce industrial expansion is to expand industry, since it is from expanding industry that effective demand for credit comes.

A public-works program fits into this picture in that it tends to neutralize one of the central causes of contraction; namely, a shrinkage in construction. It does this, not by giving rise to larger private demand for construction, but by substituting a public demand. And it is probably not possible to do very much more than this by any method, if once the conditions leading to a depression have been allowed to come to a head.

In mechanical terms, such an increase in public expenditures has the most positive action of any of the general classes of remedies, acting directly to increase the flow of purchasing power into precisely the field where the shrinkage is greatest. And the Government is in a position, at such a time, to use its credit to raise funds for such a purpose, and so, in part at least, to make up for the failure of private industry to use all the credit which the banking institutions have available at such times. Capital expenditures by government presumably have the same effect as capital expenditures by private industry, so far as concerns the increased flow of purchasing power which comes about when the people who have received these public expenditures proceed to spend their incomes. Whether such public expenditures have all the utlimate effects in stimulating private business that private capital outlays typically have is a difficult question which will be taken up later. The answer appears to hinge on the effect of these public expenditures on private capital outlays, and on this point there are conflicting views.

Be that as it may, however, the immediate and direct effect is clear—far clearer than the corresponding effect of the attempts to increase purchasing power by the methods of the National Recovery Administration codes, whereby the burden falls first upon the employer and may then be shifted through price-raising mechanisms which may easily have the effect of limiting output rather than expanding it. As far as it goes, the public works remedy acts directly to counteract that industrial shrinkage from which other shrinkages spread and ramify, and in that sense acts upon the causes of industrial contraction, though it does not remove those causes.

3. DEPRESSION AND THE BEGINNING OF REVIVAL

One of the questions about which students are not agreed is whether a depression tends to cure itself or whether it waits for some outside impulse to start business moving upward. So far as the milder depressions at least are concerned, it seems that there are certain curative forces at work. Stocks of goods in the hands of dealers have grown larger than the depressed condition of trade warrants, and in the attempt to reduce these stocks the dealers curtail their purchases more sharply than their sales have been curtailed. This in itself tends to intensify the force of the depression, but when the stocks have been once reduced sufficiently purchases tend to rise again to a point where they equal sales, and this has a slight tendency to initiate a revival, provided sales themselves are not still shrinking.

As to sales, many people at such a time are continuing to buy goods in spite of being temporarily deprived of income, drawing on their reserves for the purpose, with the result that, for a considerable group of consumers, expenditures for consumption goods are in excess of incomes, or do not shrink as much as income has shrunk. Thus, if the depression is not too severe or prolonged, a limit tends to be set on the shrinkage of consumers' purchases and of the production of consumers' goods. After a time, postponed replacements and obsolescence tend to bring about a revival in the demand for capital goods from the abnormally shrunken levels characterizing the bottom of the depression, and thus the cumulative forces of revival are given a chance to begin to operate once more. Thus a mild recession may produce its own cure, although, naturally, the process will be stimulated if meanwhile some favorable event of an outside character has come into the picture.

All this depends, however, on the possibility of completing the reduction of dealers' inventories before consumers have exhausted the reserves on which their continued buying power depends, and also on a revival in capital expenditures due to obsolescence and postponements before these consumers' reserves have been entirely exhausted. A depression as severe and protracted as the one we have just passed through results in exhausting the reserves of the great mass of the unemployed, while the tremendous shrinkage in the demand for products means that a very considerable part of industrial equipment is no longer needed for production, and may become unserviceable through obsolescence without creating any effective demand for new equipment to replace it. Thus a sort of stalemate seems likely to arise in which the usual forces of recovery from a mild depression cannot be counted on to operate, and an outside stimulus of some sort is needed.

Even in such a case, demand does not shrink to zero, and if we wait long enough there will be need of capital replacements, some of which at least will not be blocked by the difficulty of finding available funds, but will actually be made. But it is by no means safe for the industrial system to wait indefinitely for a revival to come about in this way. The social damages are too great and the danger of irreparable disaster is too serious.

A further factor arising from the more extreme depressions consists of a shattering of the basis of credit in the shape of the values of securities used as collateral and the prospective earnings of business units. Where the depression is accompanied and intensified by an excessively heavy decline in prices due to causes outside the regular course of business cycles themselves, this difficulty is naturally intensified. The burden of fixed debts increases as prices fall, and the aggregate burden may even become greater while industry is paying off large amounts of its nominal debt measured in terms of dollars.

The conclusion is that an outside stimulus, such as public works can afford, is peculiarly needed in the case of the more severe depressions. This suggests a certain caution in the use of public works as a remedy for depressions in general. If it should prove, for example, that the efforts which government can make without exhausting its financial power are no more than sufficient to counteract the milder depressions, and if government should follow a policy of doing its utmost whenever a depression appears, then it may be in danger of finding itself with its resources exhausted in the initial stages of what may turn out to be a serious crisis, and thus unable to furnish further aid at just the time when that aid is most critically needed.

To anticipate some of the conclusions of this study, it may be said that the power of government, acting through a public works policy alone, does not appear sufficient to neutralize all industrial fluctuations and bring about a condition of complete stability. For this purpose, there is needed not merely the efforts of government, but also some effective planning and coordination within industry itself, by methods which are not yet worked out. The problem is such a serious one that we shall undoubtedly continue to try to develop such methods. It goes without saying that both government and private industry will find the milder cycles easier to deal with than the more severe ones, but it also appears that the more severe cycles are likely to exhaust the resources and cripple the efforts of private industry more completely than those of government, with the result that governmental efforts would be the only resource on which we could fall back in the more severe crises, and therefore should not be exhausted in dealing with lesser ones. Thus it is peculiarly important that, even for those lesser depressions which government might by itself be able successfully to counteract, government should not assume the whole burden, but should use its utmost efforts to bring about such an organization of private efforts as may ultimately be relied on to bear the major part of the burden in the milder cases.

E. Possible Longer Cycles

Some of these shorter business cycles show a large rise and a small decline, some a small rise and a large decline, while in some the rise and decline are fairly evenly balanced. And more serious crises are separated by longer intervals than the ordinary period of a single shorter cycle. Thus various students of business cycles have found evidence of cycles of approximately 10 years, and even 20 to 25 years, underlying the shorter movements. These longer movements show some of the characteristics of the shorter cycles, but in some respects they are different and these differences seem to bear definitely on the use of a public-works policy as an antidote.

If these longer movements have any uniform laws and causes, it is hard to explain them in terms of a mere concentration of capital expansion, financed largely by expanding credit, such as a public-works policy might directly serve to counteract. If there is an undue expansion of capital facilities in these longer movements, it would seem that it must depend not merely on credit expansion but on a volume of actual savings so great that our existing economic system has not been able to find out the right uses to make of it. As a result, the problem of the distribution of income with a view to increasing the amount used for consumers' purchases is a much more pertinent one with reference to these longer movements than with reference to the shorter cycles.

Furthermore, it is obviously far more difficult for a public works policy to be systematically carried through one of these longer movements. Certainly the type of policy which proposes that we should not change the total amount we spend for public works, but merely change its timing, would be very nearly helpless in dealing with these longer swings. Public works, the need for which is already in sight, may be postponed for 2 or 3 years or may be built 2 or 3 years before the need becomes urgent, but no one is going to postpone the building of needed roads, schools, sewage disposal plants, or other public facilities for 7 or 8 years in anticipation of an emergency which may possibly never come. And to postpone them over a term of 15 or 20 years would be still more clearly out of the question. If public works are to deal with the major emergencies, which come at intervals of 10 years or more on an extremely uncertain schedule, we must face the necessity of being prepared, at intervals, which cannot be fully foreseen, to expand public works beyond the range of projects which would be included in any regular 5- or 10-year schedule of ordinary needs.

F. Noncyclical Disturbing Factors

Some mention has been made of outside causes which may intervene to affect the course of business. These causes are of almost infinite variety and range from major to minor importance. The most far-reaching, and the one from which we are now suffering most severely, is the factor of war and its after effects.

There is some evidence that a major war tends to be followed, first, by a short industrial revival with a short recession following, and then by a longer revival culminating, after a decade or more, in a major depression. This was certainly the pattern in the United States following the World War, and similar patterns have been found following other major conflicts.[3] But the particular effects of a war cannot be dealt with in summary fashion by any such typical curve, since its after effects, particularly in the field of international trade and financial relations, may take such a variety of forms.

War is also sometimes used as an example of the tremendous reserves of productive power which a country possesses and which can be drawn into activity by an unlimited policy of public spending, financed largely by credit, and accompanied by inflation. The argument is that a similar policy would be successful in what is sometimes called "war against depressions", if only we had the resolution to follow it. The comparison is suggestive, but there are also many differences to be taken into account.

One obvious difference is the fact that in 1917 the United States had a negligible Federal debt and stood ready to increase it to any extent that the needs of the conflict might involve, leaving the questions of ultimate financial adjustments to be settled when the conflict should be over. The whole psychology of the moment was one calculated to override financial cautions and timidities. At the outset of the present depression, this country still had fully two-thirds of its burden of Federal war debt, while the growth of State and local

---

[3] Col. L. Ayres: The Economics of Recovery, esp. p. 17.

debts had balanced such repayments as the Federal Government had made, and the total burden had remained approximately constant. Under these conditions any proposal to expand spendings on the war scale would have started from a point a great deal nearer the limits of our public credit (indefinite as these may be), while the prevailing mood of the economic community was one in which financial apprehensiveness was naturally uppermost and courage to undertake unknown financial responsibilities at a low ebb.

One hopeful thing which may be gathered from the consideration of the effects of war is the conclusion that the disturbances resulting from the World War, both internal and international, are quite sufficient to explain why the depression which began in 1929 was so unusually severe and prolonged. To mention only one major circumstance, the fall in prices which accompanied this depression was itself a post-war phenomenon and out of all proportion to those declines in prices which normally go along with business cycles. This decline in prices, concentrating as it did with peculiar force on certain staple international commodities, resulted in complete prostration for agriculture, which had already used up its reserves in the struggle against adverse conditions from 1920 onward. And many other industries were only less seriously affected. Thus, the claim that the present depression is a preliminary symptom of the final break-down of capitalism loses much of its force, because there is another explanation so obvious and so apparently adequate. But it does not lose all of its force, so long as war persists, and so long as its economic consequences appear to be increasingly serious.

Another set of disturbing factors consists of changes in supply or in demand affecting particular industries. To a considerable extent these may neutralize each other, but if they set up serious disturbances, such disturbances are likely to spread cumulatively. The collapse of agriculture is a major example, but many lesser ones might be found. It appears that there has been a shrinkage in the demand for men's clothing lasting over several minor business cycles. This may in part be an adjustment to the development of the automobile, and in that case may be offset by increases in spending for other things than clothing. But at any rate it represents an unpredictable disturbance affecting this particular industry.

It may be that the construction industry itself is facing some such downward tendency, relative at least to past trends of growth. No one can be certain, and counteracting forces may be discovered. It is generally accepted, however, that we are facing a period of declining growth of population. And if this is true, it means that the volume of construction needed to supply fresh additions to the population on our previous scale will shrink something like as sharply as do the early additions to population. And if this tendency were not counteracted by other tendencies toward more liberal housing accommodations per family, larger productive equipment per worker, etc., it might mean an absolute shrinkage of a permanent and rather serious sort for the construction industry. At any rate, the future trend of population growth, and all the implications it carries with it, are among the most basic factors to be taken account of in any long time planning, either for our economy as a whole or for that section of it which comes under the heading of public works.

G. Progressive Changes, and Their Possible Disturbing Effects

1. THE INCREASE OF DURABLE GOODS

Not only short cyclical movements and irregular and occasional disturbances, but also regular progressive processes of growth and change may need to be considered in attempting to canvass the probabilities as to what kinds of economic dislocations we are likely to find ourselves facing in the coming generation. This is true for two reasons. In the first place, these progressive changes may alter the character of the shorter business cycles or of any longer ones which may be found to exist. And in the second place, these progressive changes may call for adjustments which our economy does not succeed in making as fast as they are called for, with the result that we may fall into dislocations of a more chronic sort than anything we have yet experienced.

As to the shorter cycles, their industrial manifestations have been seen to center in the production of durable goods, and this class of production is showing a large increase, both absolutely and relative to goods of other classes. A larger and larger part of our national production consists of goods of a type whose creation can and will be concentrated in periods of active business, or postponed in periods of stagnation and the pessimism that goes with it. Thus there is reason to expect that, unless we succeed in finding effective means to combat the tendency, these cycles may grow more severe in the future than they have been in the past.

Not only their severity, but their timing, may be affected, though it is hardly possible now to predict what the character of the effect is likely to be. Different kinds of goods last different lengths of time before they tend to be replaced owing to wear, obsolescence, or other reasons. And a concentration in the production of new goods has a certain tendency to be followed, after the lapse of the normal replacement period, by a less sharply defined concentration in demand for replacement. Adverse conditions may, however, counteract this tendency. If, for example, we are thinking of industrial equipment, the normal time for an increase in replacements may come when demand has suffered so large a shrinkage that there will be more than enough productive capacity to supply it, even if replacements are postponed for a considerable time.

Or if we are thinking of automobiles, the length of time any given individual uses a car before trading it in for a new one becomes a matter of habit with the individual, but is far from being a necessity; the old car may very well be used twice or three times as long if the budget contains no spare funds for a renewal.[4] The result may be to build up a potential demand, like a coiled spring waiting to be released by a touch of prosperity and to add to its cumulative effect. The average age of automobiles increased materially between 1929 and 1933, and the average age of cars in the hands of their first purchasers probably increased much more. Clothes, on the other hand, not only do not last as long, but are more typically worn out by the first purchaser, and thus afford less margin for postponed replacement.

Perhaps the most definite conclusion that can be drawn from these considerations is that a relatively decreasing proportion of our pro-

---

[4] Some pioneer work has been done in the anaylsis of this whole factor of the timing of replacements by Thomas M. McNiece. See "Rhythmic Variations in Industry," Mechanical Engineering, November 1933, pp. 659-666.

duction consists of goods for which the need for replacement is prompt and insistent, and which can be counted on to bring an effective demand into the market after a certain period of depression, before the critical point at which the reserves of unemployed consumers become exhausted. If this be true, there is probably an increasing likelihood of a depression passing the critical point and leading to a more prolonged and serious prostration.

2. THE INCREASE IN PRODUCTIVE POWER

The mere increase in productive power carries with it more problems of readjustment than we are accustomed to recognizing in this country, where the work of developing an unexploited continent has automatically opened up so many avenues of utilization, and where export markets were always open for any surplus beyond domestic needs. Increases in our power to produce different goods do not automatically proportion themselves to the capacities for expansion in the demand for these different products; in fact, there are definite tendencies to the contrary. Agricultural productivity in terms of output per worker has substantially kept pace with productivity in manufacturing—in fact, slightly exceeded it, during the period 1889–1925.[5] The possibilities however, of expanding demand are proverbially far more limited in agriculture. The result was that the number engaged in agriculture remained stationary during this period, and since the war has actually declined, while the numbers in manufacturing increased 89 percent. More important is the fact that even this adjustment was not enough to avoid a crisis in agriculture with reactions on the other sections of the economy as the purchasing power of farmers collapsed. Agriculture has been a chronically sick industry since the World War and a source of weakness to the rest of our economic structure.

The absorption of increased productive powers in manufacturing has been assisted by the development of numbers of new commodities, some of them of major importance. Thus the development has not had to depend wholly on increasing the demand for commodities of familiar types. If it had been so limited, the probability is overwhelming that the total production of goods would have been less than it has been. It would be a rational thing for a society so situated to choose a smaller output of commodities and more leisure than if it had a greater and more enticing range of commodities to choose from. The trouble is that under our form of the system of business enterprise, the leisure would not be deliberately chosen by those who received it, or so distributed among the population as to be a blessing by lightening the burden and strain of the economic struggle. Quite the contrary; it would be a specter instead of a blessing—total idleness coupled with total loss of income, forced on part of the people while the others worked very nearly as hard as before. And as a result, there would be even less output of commodities than under the supposed rational choice of "less goods and more leisure", because the unemployed and those dependent on them would have lost their power to buy the things they urgently needed.

There is no need of laboring the fact that unemployment is not the same thing as desirable leisure. The point is that our machinery

---

[5] Leo Wolman, in Recent Economic Changes, pp. 452–53.

for converting increased productive power into useful and well-distributed leisure is very clumsy and normally works at a very slow rate. This is added to the fact that the machinery for converting increased productive power into increased output of goods is not simple and calls for more far-reaching adjustments the faster the rate of material progress it is called on to assimilate. The rate of progress is now very rapid, and the development of scientific research into a firmly established institution, organized, and well financed and equipped, appears to guarantee that there will be no great falling off in the future.

There seems to be greater certainty and stability about such things as the development of new steel alloys or substitutes for rubber than about finding a new way of putting these materials into some shape that will make human beings happier. Yet if this last process does not keep pace with the other, we may not be able to assimilate the results of increased productive power as fast as it comes into being.

In short, mere material progress, if it proceeds beyond a somewhat uncertain rate, may create dislocations in our economic system because we cannot make the necessary adjustments fast enough. If dislocations should arise from this source, they might naturally be not cyclical, nor occasional, but chronic. There is, of course, no proof that such a thing must happen; merely adequate prima facie grounds for believing that it may happen. Mere technical progress seems capable, lacking the necessary adjustments, of bringing on a state of chronic inability to use all our labor power. This is something that goes beyond the labor turn-over that regularly accompanies progress, beyond the temporary displacement of particular workers from particular jobs, and beyond even the difficulty some of these workers may have in finding other positions if they are beyond the age at which employers readily take on new help, or if they cannot adapt themselves to the requirements of new kinds of work. The experience of various countries after the World War showed that chronic unemployment is possible owing to failure to make rapid and difficult adjustments—though in their case the difficulty could hardly be said to have arisen from an embarrassment of productive riches. And our own recent experience has given a rude shock to whatever remained of the belief that we are immune to the economic ills that beset Europe.

The conclusion is, not that we are necessarily headed for a state of chronic collapse, but that, among the possibilities which we may have to meet, and hence should be wise to be prepared to meet, are conditions of unemployment lasting a great deal longer than cyclical depressions, or temporary emergencies produced by outside causes. With regard to the bearing of this on public works policy, there are two possibilities, and two corresponding types of policy. One is that public works should be limited to dealing with strictly temporary emergencies, and the other is that a public-works policy of a different and more sustained sort may have a useful place in dealing with the more enduring kind of difficulties.

The policy being carried out by the Public Works Administration during 1934 was clearly adapted only to the temporary emergency, and would have to be abandoned if the emergency should prove to be continuous over a long term of years, since no government can go on indefinitely borrowing billions for non-self-liquidating works. A more enduring policy must necessarily be financed by taxation. These two types of policy will be discussed later; for the present it is enough to note that the policy followed should have a rational relation to the causes of the difficulty it is aimed to combat. One possible cause has been discussed; namely, growth in productive efficiency at too fast a rate for industry to make the necessary adjustments. Other possible causes remain to be dealt with.

3. OVERSAVING

One theory holds that a rich and individualistic country tends consistently to save too much of its income, and spend too little for consumption, resulting in the piling up of a mass of productive facilities capable of producing a great deal more than consumers are ready to take off the markets. According to this view, the function of public works is to rectify the balance by increased public spending, the funds being raised in such a way as not to decrease private spending materially, but rather to come so far as possible out of sections of the national income which would otherwise have been saved and invested in surplus facilities for private production. According to this view, the need of some such measure to rectify the balance between saving and spending is a continuing need, calling for a continuing increase in the average rate of public spending, in addition to any temporary increases or decreases from this average rate which may be needed to combat temporary conditions of depression or of unhealthy boom in the capital-goods industries.

As a full explanation of the present world-wide depression this theory does not seem adequate. This depression covers not only capital-exporting countries, especially the United States, in which a good case for oversaving could be made, but also capital-importing countries in which the existence of such a condition would be difficult or impossible to establish. In fact, students in some of these countries are urging that too little saving rather than too much is the source of difficulty. Possibly these apparently conflicting views may be brought closer together in a somewhat more complete theory.

Oversaving would not create depression so long as the savings continued to be spent for tangible goods in ways that created employment and a corresponding distribution of incomes. The trouble would seem to be that when capital equipment reaches a certain state of surplus relative to demand for goods, further savings cease to be so spent. This might come about rather suddenly, bringing about a reversal from prosperity to depression, or it might conceivably come about rather gradually, resulting in a continuous or progressive excess of savings over investment. It appears, then, that the direct source of the trouble lies in a shortage of investment rather than an excess of savings in and of itself. In bringing about this condition, an excess of savings may or may not play an important or decisive part. In a relatively poor country, normally importing capital, the shortage of investment might easily be diagnosed as due to a shortage of savings, especially during the depression itself. And in a country situated as is the United States, an excess of savings, particularly during the previous period of prosperity, might well have played an important part in bringing about this condition provided it could be held responsible for the excessive investment which took place during the prosperous period.

This last point is important, because investment during a boom is financed not only by savings but by credit expansion. And there is at least a possibility that a reduction of savings and an increase of consumers' spendings during the boom would have resulted, not in less investment, but in more, financed by a still greater expansion of credit. At any rate, it seems evident that in attempting to control this situation, it would not be sufficient to control savings alone; control of credit expansion would also be needed.

Another objection to the oversavings theory comes from those who hold that there cannot in the long run be too much accumulation of capital—that if there is a temporary excess, interest rates will fall, reducing the incentive to save and increasing the incentive to invest, and thus bringing about an equilibrium once more. With this view there are several difficulties.

One is the fact that interest rates are somewhat sticky, not moving freely enough to keep pace with changes in the actual yield of additional investments of capital in industry, especially if these are figured on the basis of yield to industry as a whole. On this basis, true surplus capacity installed in boom times yields nothing, though single enterprises may profit by increasing their share of the Nation's business, and are able and willing to pay high rates for capital. This leads to the second difficulty, namely, that fairly high rates of interest do not deter business from overinvestment in prosperous times, nor do low rates of interest suffice in themselves to raise investment to normal figures in dull times when the prospect of profits from additional investment has vanished. The third difficulty is the fact that changed interest rates, within the usual range of such changes, do not have any great effect in stimulating or retarding savings. In fact, they may even have the reverse effect to the one that is required to bring about equilibrium. For a lowering of interest rates results in raising the market values of existing investments, and creates a profit from appreciation on the holding of outstanding securities, aside from the cash earnings they yield from current production. Thus it tends actually to attract savings into this field. There seems, therefore, to be insufficient reason for expecting the automatic machinery of the market to bring about the desired perfect equilibrium and prevent any possible oversavings.

While it may be true that we cannot have too much capital, provided we make ideal use of it, it appears clear that we do not make that ideal use. To do so calls for new methods of production, new products, new occupational adjustments, and a deal of industrial pioneering in discovering the right ones. A great deal of this is successfully done, but apparently not fast enough to absorb added capital as rapidly as we create it, and without waste. The limiting factor seems to be not our power to accumulate capital but our power to make the difficult adjustments necessary to absorb it. If these adjustments could be speeded up, oversaving might be impossible; but as things are there seems good prima facie ground for thinking that oversaving exists, relative to the power of absorption possessed by our economic institutions. The conclusion is that, if something like chronic unemployment should appear to threaten us, the remedies suggested by the oversavings theory would be worth investigation and possible experiment. Whether a permanent expansion of public works should be tried as one of these remedies will be discussed later.

4. OTHER CAUSES—CONCLUSION

Change in the rate of population growth, already discussed as a disturbing factor, might well have been discussed at this point as an enduring trend to which our adjustments may be inadequate or tardy. It may accentuate the difficulty of usefully absorbing a rapid increase in capital, as well as possibly, though not necessarily, leading to a relative decline in the construction industries over a long period.

Another long-run trend appears to be a change in the conditions of international trade and the international division of labor. The post-war period has witnessed a violent movement toward national self-sufficiency, amounting to a disruption of previous trading relations; but underlying this is probably a long-run tendency toward greater similarity in the type of economic development of the various regions of the industrially developed world, as well as a constant extension of this area of industrial development. As a result, some of the forms of national specialization giving opportunity for large amounts of international trade are probably destined to diminish in scope. Surpluses above domestic demand may become more serious matters; the need of developing a domestic market for domestic products more imperative; the penalty for neglect or failure more severe.

To sum up, there are grounds for including chronic dislocations among the difficulties we may be called on to meet during the coming generation. There is, of course, a limit to the profitableness of time spent contemplating evils that may never come to pass; nevertheless the wise general prepares for as many contingencies as possible. And in this realm, recent experience has shown that mental preparedness is a terribly sluggish affair, and the hastening of it enormously important, aside from the question of making definite choice between specific plans. The least we can do is to guard against committing ourselves to policies whose success or justification hinges on the assumption that our difficulties are cycles or disturbances of a short, self-curing sort. There is always the possibility of troubles whose roots lie deeper.

H. Present Prospects

1. CONDITIONS UNFAVORABLE TO REGAINING 1929 LEVELS OF BUSINESS

While prophecy is proverbially risky, still, if one must hazard a conjecture as to the immediate future, one way or the other, it would certainly seem safe to conclude that business will not quickly regain the levels of 1929—not in the first revival and very likely not in the one following. Chief among the reasons for this skeptical conclusion is the fact that the wave of prosperity which burst in 1929 appears to have been in part due to temporary conditions; we were not only busy in making up what had been lost during the war in the way of construction and supplies of durable goods, together with the cumulative effects which follow any such process; we were also playing a peculiarly profitable part in the economic reconstruction of Europe;

that is, it was profitable for the time being.   Europe was for a time, paradoxically enough, the most profitable kind of customer, because she bought our goods without paying for them.   Europe needed goods and also needed loans, and was not for the time being in a condition to send back large volumes of commodities in payment.   This country had a surplus of loanable funds, and was eagerly ready to produce the goods which Europe needed.   Thus our industry was in the position of commanding a large foreign market without losing any corresponding section of the home market by reason of commodities imported in return for our exports.   This probably afforded a greater stimulus to industrial activity in this country than if we had received payment for our exports in terms of goods in the normal way.

We were, in a broad and general sense, lending abroad the funds with which our own goods were purchased; and this naturally raises the question why we could not have gotten rich just as fast if the funds which went abroad and then came back to buy American goods and take these goods abroad, had been spent in this country in the first place, by the Americans who originally possessed them.   There is probably no exact way of proving the answer to this question. But if the funds in question had been invested as capital in this country, the chances are that a condition of over-equipment would have appeared much more rapidly than it did and would have led more quickly to a crisis and depression.   Or the enormous stock market boom might have come just that much sooner, and also collapsed sooner.

The change from a debtor country to a creditor country on a huge scale, coming with no intervening period of adjustment (for whatever the war was, it was not that) called for something like an economic revolution in this country which this country was not prepared to make.   A sudden shift from the huge export surplus to a huge import surplus would have meant, not wealth to this country but almost certainly poverty.   It would have meant unemployment, with loss of purchasing power in the domestic market, and the cumulative results which follow such conditions.   It was almost a necessity for us to go on exporting more than we imported for some time at least if we were to avoid the disastrous result of a too sudden readjustment of our economy.

This temporary equilibrium of lending and selling was broken in 1929, and there seems to be no prospect that it can be fully restored. Such a condition certainly could not last forever.   Out of the depression came increased trade barriers and decreased possibilities of export trade, together with a decreased field for the making of loans abroad. The fact that the process of lending and exporting is still going on, though in new directions and on a reduced scale, serves to indicate the extreme difficulty the American economic system experiences in adjusting itself to anything different.   And this difficulty will not vanish, but will have to be met as the necessary readjustment to our creditor status cannot be indefinitely postponed.

If the current revival should carry physical production up to the 1929 level, there is still the question what that would mean in terms of employment.   Improvements have been made since 1929, enabling a given output to be produced with less labor, and many more probably stand ready for introduction when confidence revives sufficiently and when the condition of the capital market makes it possible to raise the necessary funds. Thus, unless there is a shortening of hours in industry which continues beyond the intended term of the National Recovery Administration, there may be a considerable amount of unemployment even after the current revival has gone as far as it can.

One factor which may be merely temporary is the fact that the difficulty of finding work has caused a good many individuals to join the search who would not otherwise have been in the labor market— wives who have had to support the family because their husbands could not get jobs, or others in a similar situation. In addition, there are many who have remained in school or otherwise held off from the market, but will be seeking jobs as soon as a revival becomes established. Thus there may temporarily be an abnormally large potential supply of labor. If a system of general unemployment insurance or similar out-of-work benefits should be established while unemployment due to the depression is still very heavy, there might be a tendency for this temporary increase in the labor supply to become permanent. That is, people who were not normally in the labor market but had been temporarily drawn into it might find that they could draw out-of-work benefits merely by keeping their status as potentially employable workers. This might be more profitable than merely retiring into the home, when the normal wage earners regain jobs. It is said that some workers in England, who had been drawn into industry by the war, have been kept on the rolls in this way, although they would not normally be among the gainfully employed at present.

To sum up, there is doubt whether industrial activity will quickly return to the 1929 level, while even if it does this rate of industrial activity will probably result in less employment and more unemployment than in 1929, unless work spreading or other measures are taken to prevent it. There is one thing which may falsify this prediction, namely, if the United States should solve the extremely difficult problem of developing domestic purchasing power, and bringing about the actual use of that purchasing power in ways which will more than make up for obstructions in the export markets. And this is not a simple matter—not merely a matter of raising money wages and then allowing industry to raise prices sufficiently to offset the increased wages to its own satisfaction.

2. EXPANDING DOMESTIC MARKETS—HOUSING AS AN ILLUSTRATION

The problems and difficulties which are involved in expanding the home market can be seen in an acute form in the case of the market for housing. At present there is not a shortage of houses but a nominal surplus, for the simple reason that families with shrunken incomes have had to double up or move into smaller quarters. This is, presumably, a temporary condition and this false surplus will diminish or disappear with revival of business activity. In terms of more normal developments, there is still one large element in the situation which serves to limit effective demand for new housing construction. Very nearly all of the new housing space actually built is built for the class of comparatively well-to-do or the more than well-to-do; and this class composes only a minority of the population. Other classes live to a very large extent in quarters which were originally built for families of larger incomes, but which have deteriorated. Some new housing of a cheap sort is built for the more prosperous among the laboring groups, especially in smaller towns and outlying districts where detached two-family frame houses or bungalows are found. Philanthropic low-cost housing projects typically reach and benefit either white collar workers or the upper levels of the manual working groups. For the great mass of low-paid laborers there is hardly such a thing as new construction. They live entirely in deteriorated properties, many of them close to the line of forced abandonment.

In other words, new construction of housing is limited to a very small section of the total market. The reason is the very simple one that only those who are fairly well off can pay the costs of new building or make it profitable for a prospective landlord. This is partly a matter of low incomes and partly because the costs of building have not come down commensurately with the cheapening effects of mass production of manufactured commodities in general. And a study of the causes of high building costs will reveal many elements, no one of which in itself is all important. Therefore no one remedy by itself can cure the situation. And that is one reason why it is not likely to be quickly cured under individualistic principles which depend upon one remedy at a time, applied by one individual or one economic unit and limited to the matters which it has under its control.

There is no possibility of raising incomes sufficiently to enable common laborers to pay the costs involved in new houses with really satisfactory accommodations, so long as costs remain as they are. Wages and land values are stubborn elements of cost. High prices of materials and other elements may be attacked with some success, and the use of public funds could reduce interest charges. The economies of mass production may lower costs, but probably not enough in themselves to bridge the gap between costs and buying power. If all of these factors were successfully attacked at once, the result might be to open up to the construction industry an enormously increased market. And in working for that market it would be meeting one of the most serious needs of the American people at the present time.

The problem is not simple, and the part which public construction might play in it is not simple. But there are evidently great possibilities of expanding demand, and possibilities which there is an urgent need for developing, not only because workers need the work but because families need the improved housing.

3. SUMMARY OF PROSPECTS

To sum up our present prospects, one may conclude that there are not likely to be any violent revivals or collapses in the near future. A slowing down of the rate of growth of our population, the less favorable conditions of foreign trade, and the caution remaining from the experience of 1929 to 1934 all argue against any great exuberance of revival. On the other hand, unless and until revival does go to rather exuberant lengths we are not likely to have again a crash of a magnitude approaching that of the last one.

For one thing there is little likelihood of another huge and catastrophic drop in prices, covering the world at large. This was a phase of the post-war economic readjustments or a result of post-war economic dislocations, and having once happened, it is not likely to be repeated in the near future. According to the views of Colonel Ayres, we have now gone through the secondary post-war depression and so completed the round of major disturbances which are normally to be expected as the sequels of a serious war. This of course does not prove in itself that there are no troubles ahead. History never repeats itself completely, and there are plenty of economic difficulties remaining in the whole situation, whose potentialities have not by any means been exhausted. All of which brings us back for consolation to the fact that the world has not so far to fall at present as it had in 1929 and, therefore, is not likely to suffer a great major crisis.

Those considerations seem likely for some years to come to outweigh the effect of the increasing importance of durable goods in our economic system, which tends, as we have seen, toward making fluctuations more violent. Ultimately, more violent movements will probably appear again, unless in the meantime successful means of control are developed.

Thus, if our economic system is in danger, we shall probably have some sort of a breathing space in which to attempt to save it; the "final crisis of capitalism" is not likely to come within the next 5 years. What may come during that period is a disquieting growth of chronic or semichronic unemployment in the light of which the public-works policy of the coming decade will need to be formulated.

The program suited to these conditions must be above all things adaptable. It must include a choice of policies to meet different conditions rather than one stereotyped program suited to conditions of one sort, and incapable of change if conditions change without notice. Such a policy must manage to maintain itself in a situation in which future normal trends are uncertain and in which it is not possible to tell how much of the unemployment prevailing at any given time will vanish with the next cyclical revival and how much is due to more permanent causes. It will even be impossible to tell promptly and certainly whether industry is just starting a cyclical decline or pausing during a cyclical advance, and, after the decline becomes an assured fact, it would still be impossible to arrive at any working certainty as to how far it would go or how long it would continue. Under these conditions possibly the most significant index will become the index of unemployment (with difficulties some of which have been indicated) since unemployment always represents an evil to be dealt with, whatever its causes.

A. General Grading According to Value or Urgency

There is no universal formula for measuring or otherwise determining the precise value of public works, or even their precise order of value, relative to each other. Different processes have to be used, according to the nature of the works in question. In some cases, where the works render a definite economic service as a means of production, their economic value can be estimated in money terms. Where possible this should be done. But in many cases it is not possible, and even where it is possible there are likely to be complicating elements of a sort that defy precise measurement. The values concerned include the cheapening of transport through better roads, conservation of natural resources for future generations, preservation of health, recreation, and the intangible values of a harmonious and aesthetic setting for buildings, landscaping and access to the world of out-of-doors.

Practically all the essential principles involved can be seen in the case of roads. In the first place, better roads serve to reduce the cost of travel and of transportation which will be carried on in any case. This becomes essentially a matter of balancing the capital cost and maintenance expense of the improved roadway against reduced operating expenses and the value of time saved in the moving of traffic. While simple in principle, such a calculation presents difficulties.

It calls for a canvass of the volume of traffic, made with due regard to fluctuations and to the conditions of peak load which may determine the point at which additional capacity in a highway is needed. It may be that the peak load is of a different sort from the ordinary commercial traffic whose economic value is easier to reckon, consisting chiefly of pleasure traffic during holidays. Circumstances like these would have to be taken into account. Furthermore, the calculation involves estimates of maintenance expenses and of the life of a highway before renewals will be necessary, all of which may be uncertain if the type of highway is one which has not been tried out for a considerable period under service conditions. Highway authorities are continually experimenting with new kinds of roadbeds and surfaces, one of the important problems being the search for a structure of moderate cost which can be used for minor roads where the density of traffic would not justify the cost of concrete or bituminous macadam, yet which will furnish a better surface than the ordinary dirt road and will be reasonably durable under moderate motor traffic. Incidental problems include investigation as to what types of traffic are responsible for the greatest damage to different types of road surface, and the adapting of the road structure to the traffic, as well as adjusting the traffic to the economically practicable road structure by limiting maximum loads or by other forms of regulation.

Another type of problem arises where it is proposed to reckon as one of the benefits of the highway the increase in value of lands along its route. The objection has been raised to this procedure that the increased value of the land is a form of capitalization of the current service benefits rendered by the roads to the inhabitants, and that, if these service benefits have already been counted, then the increase in land values can be added without counting the same benefits twice. Thus the added value of lands is a doubtful criterion, but it may serve to catch some of the benefits resulting from improved highways, over and above those which can be directly measured in the fashion we are now discussing.

A different question arises in connection with additional traffic which has developed as a result of highway improvements and which would not have moved otherwise. This presents a still more difficult problem of measurement. In many cases it means simply that things which would have been done in any case are now done in ways which involve the use of this particular roadway; in other words, it becomes a question of competition between rival methods involving different means of transportation. In this case the whole value of service rendered by the use of the new road is not a clear gain, but only the net saving brought about by introducing the new method of production. It would be easy to spend a million dollars on a road which diverts traffic from other roads or from railways, although the actual saving on the traffic diverted is not worth the expenditure of the million dollars. The criterion here is, so far as possible, to bring about an even basis of competition between different methods of production, so that the one which survives shall be the one which involves the lowest total cost, including the cost to the user of the highway and also the cost to the community of building and maintaining it.

In the case where new service is genuinely developed, the value of this service is sometimes reckoned at the difference between the cost over the new highway and the cost over older types of road. This involves too high an estimate. The fact that this service was not developed under the older methods of transportation means that it was not worth the cost involved in such methods, and, therefore, the net gain, when the lower cost of the improvement makes possible the moving of new kinds of traffic is less than the full difference in cost by by the two methods. Half the difference has sometimes been taken as a fair average figure to represent the net gain from genuinely new service.

So far as the new service represents travel for pleasure or any other ultimate consumption good, its real value can be only imperfectly reflected in money estimates. Families on pleasure trips are now able to cover more ground and to reach places formerly inaccessible, but, on the other hand, the fact that so many people are able to reach these places means that the very advantages of seclusion, privacy, and wildness which made them attractive, are measurably reduced. Furthermore, the value of the roads for pleasure purposes depends a great deal upon the character of the road and its immediate surroundings. The road lined with billboards and cheap refreshment stands has a very doubtful value for these purposes, and one of the promising things in the highway policy is the efforts which are being made to improve this condition.

Another difficult problem consists of the balancing of values as between those who use the roads for traffic purposes only and those who live on them, or the character of whose environment is determined by the type of road existing. It is interesting to note how a strip of concrete highway may be favored by those who can use it but do not have to live on it, and opposed by those whose residences are located on the particular strip.

Maximum advantage, in terms of all these kinds of values, measurable and immeasurable, depends not upon single roads, but upon a coordinated system of transportation in general. As to roads, what is needed is a system of traffic lines involving a minimum of interference with residential and scenic values, possibly laid out in wholly new locations where the traffic is sufficient to justify this. It also includes secondary roads following the same principle, so far as possible, although such roads will be unable to avoid towns and residential districts to the same extent. And it involves rural roads in which a reasonably efficient road surface may be combined with preservation of the character of the countryside. Finally, there is need for a coordinated system of all methods of transportation, by rail, highway, water, and air.

One of the values which has not been mentioned so far is the value of safety. So far as concerns damage to property by accidents, this can be fairly definitely measured. Injury and death to individuals also involve economic costs which can at least be roughly estimated, although methods of estimating the economic cost resulting from the loss of a human life are still in a rather crude state. Insurance companies have made attempts in this direction, and the present writer has attempted to make an improvement on the usual method used in such calculations.[1] The cost resulting from the loss of a human life depends upon age, economic status, and the number of dependents, if any, who are left to be cared for. A figure of $7,500 is a fairly representative one to cover these purely economic elements represented in the loss of income to survivors. However, the value of a human life to the person who loses it is one of the things which is naturally of first importance in the ordinary judgment on this matter, and it is something which these calculations necessarily leave entirely out of account. It is a literally incalculable element. Thus the question comes down to a matter of how much we are ultimately willing to spend in order to save human life, when the question comes up in the form of the cost of safety provisions on highways, and the effect of such provisions on the annual toll of accidents. The same question arises in the case of injuries. Economic losses may be estimated, but the direct value of a sound body, in and of itself, to the person concerned is something which connot be measured.

Thus it appears that there are certain fairly calculable values, and others as to which the only test is the test of how much an enlightened public is willing to pay when the issue is put before it as clearly as plans and statistics permit. An intermediate standard, if it can be called a standard, consists in putting the question in the form: "How much would the individuals who receive the benefits be willing to pay for them if they had to pay as individuals for each separate benefit received?" Putting the question in this form may shed some light on the ultimate judgment, but the answer can never be a definite sum. It can at best serve as a check on some of the vaguer and less justifiable ideas as to the value of public works which sometimes lead to wasteful expenditures.

On the cost side, a special consideration arises when the carrying out of public works is undertaken as a means of putting otherwise

---

[1] See Economic Costs of the World War to the American People, ch. XIII, esp. p. 220, and appendix B.

unemployed resources to work and getting something out of them in place of nothing. Here the fiscal cost of the work has to be balanced against the social cost of idleness, or at least against the fiscal burdens of public relief which would have to be borne in one way or another if employment were not afforded.

If the public expenditure involves secondary effects—as it normally does—resulting in increased incomes for the members of the community over and above the amount of the Government expenditure, this is a further offset to the cost. However, these benefits do not accrue if the effect of the public works is merely to substitute public spending for private spending which would otherwise have been carried out. Private spending has just as many secondary effects as public and very likely more, under ordinary conditions. These diffused benefits of public works may properly be taken into consideration, but they need to be taken with a proper view to the conditions that determine whether these diffused benefits would actually be achieved or not. If the public works are paid for with borrowed money, the cost takes the shape of a continuing debt charge, and the true social burdens involved in this debt charge are the things to be weighed against the benefits resulting from the works carried out. Such a debt charge, on a debt held by domestic bondholders, is not a net economic loss to the community, but rather a transfer of wealth from certain groups of citizens to others, and the net social burden involved consists largely in the hampering of industry through the effects of levying and collecting the necessary taxes. Thus it constitutes in itself a difficult problem in social economics. In the face of all these difficulties, simple fiscal calculations must continue to be used, with the proviso that they may need adjustment, but that radical adjustments should not be made unless sufficient cause is shown in the particular situation involved. Ordinary economic prudence should continue to take as its point of departure the calculations of whether the works concerned are worth the amount of money spent, in the usual fiscal terms.

In a general way, it seems practicable to divide public works according to their value into four main classes. The precise boundaries between these classes are naturally somewhat vague, but in a given case there is typically not too much doubt in what class a given project belongs.

Grade A.—Works which properly belong in a rational 5- or 10-year program, conceived according to customary standards of good judgment as to the value of the works and the total amount which the community can afford to spend on them, may be classed as "grade A." It is with grade A works that the program of reducing business fluctuations advocated by the Webbs and others would deal. Among these, distinction must be made between those which are urgent, or whose timing cannot be changed without materially impairing the usefulness of the results, and those which can be postponed or anticipated relatively easily. The more urgent works furnish the basis for what may be called the "minimum economic program" for any given year, while optional works furnish the basis for what is called, in this study, a "supplementary program."

There are likely to be limits on the possibility of postponing works of grade A without too great a sacrifice of the values to be received from them, and as a result optional works may become urgent if they have been postponed, for example, as much as 3 years. On the other hand, if a given project is postponed past a certain critical point, conditions may change so that it will no longer be economically worth while to carry it out at all, or for a considerable time in the future. Reference has already been made to the idea of "curves of urgency" developed by Frederick L. Olmstead, Jr., and to the example of the changing value of existing structures which may need to be torn down, as these structures depreciate and are ultimately replaced by more expensive ones.

In connection with the works whose timing in a 10-year program is optional, there will probably be some which could be anticipated but not postponed, and in general the amount of possible postponement and of possible anticipation may not be equal. Political conditions being what they are, it is likely to be found easier to anticipate works which are due in the future than to postpone those which are fairly ripe for construction during the current year.

Grade B.—There are many projects whose values are not clearly and demonstrably inferior to those in grade A, but which would not be included in a program of customary scope. In many cases the question whether they should or should not be included may be controversial, with room for differences of judgment between enlightened people. Some of these projects, if once inertia could be overcome and they could be carried out, might prove to satisfy wants which would assure their continuance and thus make their way into grade A. Some projects are of only slightly inferior importance, and while they might not be considered worth their cost on ordinary principles, would be well worth their cost after deducting from it the reduction of evils and burdens resulting from unemployment which might be avoided if these projects were carried out at appropriate times. In some cases it may be doubtful which specific projects belong in grade A and which in grade B, the less doubtful factor being the total amount which the community feels it is justified in spending according to budgetary principles during a term of years. Thus the line between grade A and grade B may be defined by a total amount of expenditures rather than by a list of specific projects.

Grade C.—This included projects of substantially inferior value, justifiable only as a substitute for relief where a large burden of relief would have to be undertaken in any case.

Grade D.—This includes projects whose value in themselves is so low as to be almost negligible, but which may be resorted to where a definite amount of relief work has been determined upon and where no better projects can be found. In some cases, the Civil Works Administration seems to have descended to this level, although on the whole and considering the circumstances, the worth of the projects selected seems to have been rather surprisingly high.

B. Particular Characteristics Bearing on Project Choice

1. TIME REQUIRED TO COMPLETE PROJECTS

Some projects may be finished in a few months, while others, like the completion of navigation improvements or works of flood control on a large river, may require 10 or even 20 years to complete the whole system at ordinary rates of prosecution of the work. Single dams or large public buildings may require 1 year or several years for completion. The greater number of projects undertaken by the Public Works Administration have been relatively small units requiring only a short time for completion. Where new projects are undertaken in the attempt to expand public works during a depression of ordinary magnitude and duration, it is natural and proper that these should be chiefly of this sort. Otherwise, they would not be likely to reach the stage of maximum employment of labor until too late to render much help to the current situation. In fact, they might serve chiefly to give an additional stimulus to the next period of industrial prosperity at just the time when such a stimulus will do more harm than good. On the other hand, where projects are already under way, which are likely to take 5 or 10 years to complete, it may be possible to speed up the current rate of expenditure, or to retard it, without very seriously affecting the date of final completion and without seriously increasing current costs.

2. RELATION OF PROJECTS TO AN ORGANIC PROGRAM

Some projects stand by themselves to the extent that, if they are carried out at any given time, the results will have value, while others are so organically related to a larger program that until the whole program is substanitally completed, the single works will have little value, or only a small part of the value which they are designed to have in the ultimate whole. On the whole, works which are physically separate but functionally parts of an organic program may be carried out at varying times without seriously affecting the usefulness of the whole result. On the other hand, if they are carried out earlier than contemplated, there is no direct service value gained as a result. Choice of projects for emergency programs must be made with the characteristics in view.

3. AMOUNT OF MAINTENANCE INVOLVED

Projects may or may not commit the community to burdens of future maintenance, and the long or short life of the works may determine whether the community is committed to such maintenance for a long or short period ahead. If it is a question of anticipating future works, the cost is less if the maintenance expense is small. The type of program which aims merely to shift public-works expenditures from prosperous to depressed periods is best served by anticipating projects which have a low maintenance cost, especially if the program goes beyond the scope of grade A works. It is only the type of program which aims at permanently enlarged public spending which would welcome additional works carrying a high maintenance cost for the future.

4. EFFECT ON PRIVATE EXPENDITURES

Projects may involve a reduction in future private expenditures through rendering a service which individuals would otherwise have to pay for. The well-established example of this is the public school, while libraries, free public clinics and similar services belong in the same class. Such services are often rendered free on the ground that they are necessary and that many persons, if required to pay for them, could not get them at all, or could not get them on anything like an adequate scale; or public-works projects may stimulate additional private expenditures (public parks stimulate vacation trips), or they may call forth, and absorb into the public pocket future private expenditures which would otherwise go into the pockets of private individuals furnishing competing services for a price. This is commonly the case, directly or indirectly, with projects classed as self-liquidating, such as public housing programs.

5. EFFECT ON PRIVATE CAPITAL OUTLAYS

Projects may tend to displace or to stimulate further capital investment from private sources, as well as further current expenditures.

6. PROPORTION OF OUTLAY GOING TO DIRECT LABOR

Projects may differ in the proportion of expenditure going directly to the laborers engaged on the work and employed directly by the agency which carries the work out. In this respect, however, differences between broad classes of works appear to be rather moderate, at least within the limits of grade A works and in the absence of extraordinary measures limiting the use of machinery. The type of works carried out under the Civil Works Administration has shown a much higher percentage of the funds going to direct labor—about 75 percent.

7. RELATION TO FUTURE SELF-MAINTENANCE OF WORKERS

The result of the work may be to afford future means for independently self-sustained labor. An example would be subsistence homesteads, assistance given to "self-help organizations", and possibly, to a certain extent, the policy of employing workers in producing commodities for the consumption of the workers themselves. Works ordinarily classed as grade C may be of the highest social importance if they accomplish this end in a sound and useful way.

C. Conclusions

Judgment as to the classification of particular projects cannot be made by a general policy-forming body, but must be left to those acquainted with the character of the particular work making up the program. There will always remain the unavoidable difficulty that selection of projects for a comprehensive program must be made by those not so intimately acquainted with the character of particular works as are those actively engaged in the service of the very many separate departments whose needs have to be reconciled. The body which makes the first selection embodied in a recommended program should be of such a character as to be able to weigh the testimony to the departmental agencies and to determine with good judgment in what respect their verdict should be taken as final (e. g., the date when shifting shoals require the relocation of a lighthouse) and in what respects their proposals may be cut without serious damage to the value of their services. The ultimate authority of legislative bodies necessarily remains, but the recommendations of a board should carry, in most cases, decisive weight by virtue of the character of the board and the evidence on which its findings are based.

A. The Contraction Side of Timing

Any policy of spending more on public works in dull times than in prosperous ones naturally presupposes that during prosperous periods work will go on at less than the average rate; and any such policy of the grade A type presupposes that during prosperous times work will go on at less than a long-term normal rate, in spite of the fact that these are the periods when funds are most plentiful and the natural tendency is to spend liberally. Advocates of a planned program therefore typically propose machinery for the limiting of expenditures in good times, although one variety of program would make definite provision for expansion only, leaving contraction to more automatic forces.

Definite provisions for limitation of outlays in good times commonly hinge on the adoption of a 5- or 10-year program of works, involving a budget of so much per year on the average, and a provision that a certain percentage of this work shall be deferred, to be carried out either when some designated index shows a depressed condition or when such a condition is certified by the properly authorized body. Coupled with this is frequently the provision that appropriations for the full average yearly program shall be made and part of the money remain unspent, with a further provision authorizing any necessary borrowing to make such authorization surely effective it would need to be reserved out of the debt limit of the governmental unit concerned.

Some consider it hopeless to expect legislative bodies (which cannot be authoritatively bound by any such program) to remain within the limitations of such a scheme. The political official is anxious to make a record of accomplishment for his administration, and to point to as many public improvements as possible which have been carried out during his term of office. Thus, if there are available funds, there is an almost overwhelming pressure toward the using of those funds for public works during a current administration and against postponing any of them for possible use in conjectural future emergencies. This is one of the strongest reasons for thinking that anticipation of public works is easier than postponement. It remains to be seen whether an administrative machinery can be set up which will be sufficiently devoted to a long-run timing program in the interest of reducing business fluctuations, and sufficiently powerful in the whole administrative situation to overcome this political obstacle. Those who despair of overcoming it fall back on the proposal that work should be expanded in time of depression by means of comparatively short-term borrowing which would have to be quickly amortized, with the expectation that the burden of amortization, carried in the budget in succeeding years, would automatically limit expenditures during these years.

The first method, if practicable at all, seems appropriate to a grade A program limited to minor depressions. Major emergencies will always exhaust any reserves which may be accumulated in this way. A glance at the relevant figures is quite convincing on this score. Few, if any, of the advocates of a timed program have expressed the hope that more than 50 percent of the normal long-term budget of expenditures can be shifted from one year to another. When expressed in those terms this amount of shifting does not appear very large, but when looked at in another way it appears so large as to be practically impossible of achievement and certainly a maximum representing ideal performance. It would mean that in a year of depression, following a prosperous year, public works expenditures would be expanded from 50 percent of the long-run normal to 150 percent; in other words, an expansion amounting to 1 whole year's expenditures at the normal rate, or 200 percent of the minimum rate at which works were carried on during prosperity. In terms of the proportion of the total annual dividend expended in this way, this would mean increasing the percentage from approximately 2 percent to approximately 6 percent.[1]

In terms of employment, this would mean an expansion in the numbers directly employed, in the general range of magnitude represented by 800,000, with a corresponding expansion of indirect employment on materials and auxiliary services somewhat smaller than the expansion in direct employment.[2] Added to this is the secondary effect resulting from the spending of the income by the persons who receive it, the amount of which during the first year may be roughly estimated at approximately three-fourths of the primary stimulus.[2] Thus we should have a total expansion amounting to possibly 7 percent of the national dividend, or possibly 2¾ millions of workers employed, out of a total working population of between 45,000,000 and 50,000,000. If the program lasted longer, the secondary effects, under favorable conditions, might be somewhat larger.

When this is compared with the shrinkage of the national income and of employment during a major crisis, it becomes clearly evident that it can only neutralize a fraction of the shrinkage. During the current crisis, actual employment has shrunk not less than 25 percent, not reckoning with the large amounts of part-time employment, while the national dividend has shrunk by a much larger figure. If we took a 25 percent shrinkage of the national dividend as representing a major crisis, such a public works program would neutralize something between one-third and one-fourth of it. This is far from negligible and would be well worth a great deal of effort and expense if it could be achieved. All that is argued here is that after a public works program of the grade A sort has done the utmost of which it is capable under the most favorable conditions conceivable, there still remains a great deal to be done, and the major part of the industrial shrinkage resulting from the more serious crises will remain to be dealt with in other ways. If such crises are to be met by continued expansion of public works, they must be met by going beyond the limits of any accumulated reserves of works placed in a 5- or 10-year program and covered by advance appropriations.

---

[1] Based on figures given by Wolman: Planning and Control of Public Works, especially pp. 108–115; also on King's estimates of the total income of the United States.
[2] See discussion of cumulative effects of public expenditures in ch. IX.

B. The Expansion Side of Timing

Here the vital question at issue is not merely how far but how promptly public works should, or can, be made to expand during a business recession. Obstacles to quick expansion are well known, including the legislative procedure of appropriation-making, or authorizing borrowing and carrying it out, of selecting sites and acquiring land, of drafting and examining plans, receiving bids and letting contracts. Furthermore, on projects of considerable size, it frequently requires at least a considerable part of a year before the preliminary stages of the work are out of the way and a stage is reached where a large volume of employment can begin. There is frequently an interval of 3 months between the submission of budget estimates by departments and the passage of the Budget. Where bond issues are required, these may, as in the case of the New York State government, have to be submitted to a popular referendum, involving a further delay, although interim borrowing may be possible. W. N. Loucks has itemized the steps involved in the starting of public improvements in the city of Philadelphia, with the time intervals involved. As an example of his conclusions:

"The usual or reasonable time required to complete the joint procedure of authorizing a loan and authorizing and starting a project which has to be submitted to the art jury and which is to be paid for by that loan is about 218 days in the case of a councilmanic loan, and about 257 days in the case of an electoral loan. These reasonable times become 190 and 229 days, respectively, for projects which need not be submitted to the art jury * * *.

"The reasonable maximum time interval for the completion of the joint procedure of authorizing a loan and authorizing and starting a project which has to be submitted to the art jury and which is to be paid for by that loan is about 464 days in the case of a councilmanic loan and about 556 days in the case of an electoral loan. These maximum times become 404 and 456 days, respectively, for projects which need not be submitted to the art jury. Such time intervals would result only from a complete combination of unfavorable circumstances at each of the steps.[3]

One of the great difficulties consists in the confusion of separate local governing bodies which frequently exists (Chicago being the proverbial horrible example) and often prevents any concerted action on a uniform plan.[4] Even centralized purchasing agencies hardly exist in the large cities, and thus opportunity is lost for systematic planning in the field of purchasing or ordinary supplies, which contains possibilities for the same sort of scheduling as a timed Public Works program. Where Federal grants and loans are part of the procedure, a further delay is involved for the scrutinizing of projects and the carrying out of the various steps involved in the issuance of the subsidy.

Aside from all the obstacles to prompt expansion arising from the mechanical nature of administrative machinery, one which is perhaps equally basic is that arising from the attitude of local public officials, which in turn is very largely dictated by their responsibilities to local interests. The tendency is very strong for them to carry out public works as the need for these works is felt by their

---

[3] William E. Loucks, The Stabilization of Employment in Philadelphia, 1921, pt. III, pp. 150-151.
[4] Despite this handicap, the development of the Chicago lake front plan indicates that progress is possible.

constituents, and not to allow considerations of public policy with respect to the business situation at large to enter into the question of timing their activities.

This attitude is not to be set down as a case of mere ignorance and inertia. It is probably more basic than that and more difficult to remove. It is probably a very fair expression of the actual interests of a single constituency in a single piece of public work to be carried out for the benefit of that constituency. Secondary effects on the state of business activity in general are diffused widely over the country, with the result that if a particular community spends money, let us say, in 1935, which it would not otherwise spend in that year, for the sake of benefits to the general business situation; it will be spending money to benefit a large number of other communities, and it is very likely that comparatively little of this general business benefit will actually remain in the particular community making the expenditure. That community will have the public works to show for the money, and possibly not very much in addition. It is only those officials whose responsibilities are Nation-wide who have a really effective interest in the timing of public works for the benefit of the condition of general business. Local officials must probably be reached, if they are to be reached at all, by definite and tangible financial incentives, such as cheap loans or grants. And this, as we have just seen, adds one more element of delay to the program.

Things can be done to speed up this process include advance financial authorization, advance selection of projects involving preliminary examination of engineering features, advance surveys of those at all likely to be soon adopted, and possibly, in some cases, drawing up of plans and specifications in advance where projects are fairly certain to be carried out within, let us say, not more than 2 years in any case, and where there is little chance of changing technique or other changing conditions making it necessary to do the work over again. There are rather strict limitations on this last step in preparation. To draw up blueprints and specifications for a sewage-disposal plant or a school building 3 years in advance would merely invite the necessity of throwing the work away and starting fresh. Nevertheless, the city of Cincinnati, under a city manager system of government, has been able to expand work rapidly in the current emergency, largely by virtue of an advance program, coupled with the carrying out in advance of a great deal of the engineering work.

With the best that can be done in these respects, new projects cannot be gotten under way quickly on the arrival of a depression. Since some time must elapse after the peak of prosperity is past before it can be certain that a recession is actually under way, it is all the more impossible to catch such a movement in its early stages and check it before it gathers headway by the starting of new public works projects.

One proposal, in the light of this difficulty, has been that the rate of prosecution of projects already under way should be greatly speeded up. This would involve spending existing appropriations at a rate which would exhaust them before their time was up and would, therefore, need to be accompanied by supplementary appropriations rapidly passed. The amount of additional work which can be promptly secured by this means may be a material help, but it is likely to be rather narrowly limited.

This proposal has been accompanied by the idea that even a relatively small amount of additional expenditures, thrown in with sufficient promptness, might check the advance of a depression and prevent its cumulative effects from getting under way. This appears to be a more than doubtful hope. It seems to imply that it is possible to maintain private business activity at something very close to boom levels by a relatively small public expenditure thrown in at the right time. We have seen in chapter III that a cyclical depression usually results from a condition of over-expanded investment in private productive equipment, which means that, even if the total volume of consumers' demand were maintained by adding public to private spending, private demand for further capital equipment would fall off until the excess should disappear through obsolescence or the growth of normal demand, or both. The cumulative effects of this shrinkage might be counteracted, so far as concerns total employment, public and private both, by a sufficient volume of public spending, continued during the interval until the excess of equipment disappears. This is likely to be at least 18 months in the case of an average mild recession. Thus a prompt and small burst of public spending seems to have little chance for forestalling the progress of a recession by a reaction which removes the causes of the private shrinkage and restores strictly private activity to its boom level. Larger and longer continued expenditures seem necessary

Another difficulty with this program is the fact that it involves the attempt to maintain business activity at a boom level which, for business as at present constituted, is supernormal and cannot be maintained. This does not mean that we must give up all hope of raising our level of productivity above past boom levels by utilizing the productive forces which still remain unused even at such times. But in order to do this, the proportions of things in our economic life need to be altered in ways which can only be worked out experimentally, and which go much deeper than an increase in public works or the prevention of a shrinkage in the construction industry as a whole. It becomes, among other things, a problem of altering the distribution of incomes in such a way as to increase the proportion spent by consumers.

A permanent standard of living at the level represented by any of our past booms would call for a different distribution of efforts and expenditures from that which actually prevailed during those booms. It is something we have never experienced. It is a paradox that the maximum consumption we have ever attained was only attained because we were at the same time diverting more of our productive effort to capital equipment than we could possibly keep on diverting for that purpose indefinitely. Thus a program which attempts to maintain something close to boom levels of activity, without having solved these long-run and far-reaching problems of readjustment, is probably impossible for that very reason.

Hence it seems sounder and more practicable to allow that part of the program which consists of expanded public works to wait until business activity is shown to be below that somewhat vague level classed as normal. By this time the cumulative effects of depression will be under way, though not the most serious ones arising from major crises. The program will then bear the burden of neutralizing these cumulative effects, but as we have seen, it is probably not possible to avoid this necessity in any case by merely forestalling them.

In the period after a recession has begun and before activity has declined below normal, or before unemployment has increased to a point constituting a minor emergency, probably the most useful thing which could be done would be to put under way all those final preparatory measures for expansion which it is not practicable to keep constantly up to date. The Public Works program should be in the condition of a peace time army with a standing force under arms, an organized national guard ready to be called to arms quickly, and plans for larger mobilization. What is suggested for this first move corresponds roughly to the mobilizing of the national guard, but without giving them their marching orders. Blueprints and specifications could be drawn up for projects which have been accepted as part of the 5- or 10-year program and which would be in line for execution as soon as a minor emergency should be established. Everything could be prepared for the inviting of bids and the issuing of contracts. If the downward movement should be halted without passing into the stage of even a mild depression the matter could stop there, and the additional work need not be carried out. In that case, some of the preparatory work might have to be done over again at a later date when the projects were actually executed, and this would involve some slight additional cost, but the gain in preparedness for prompt action would be well worth this minor risk.

At the other extreme from the proposal to expand works immediately at the beginning of a decline stands the view expressed by Prof. S. H. Slichter of Harvard that the most useful thing a public works program can attempt to do is to hasten and strengthen a revival after a depression has reached its bottom.[5] This rests on the judgment (a) that it is impossible to check a recession in the first stages, before its cumulative effects have come into play and (b) that these cumulative effects are too strong to be neutralized by any public works policy which it is practicable to put into effect. This proposal means the abandonment of the attempt to use public works as a stabilizer of business. In fact, as applied to minor cyclical movements of comparatively short duration, it would be very likely to accentuate the fluctuations by initiating works which would reach the stage of large additions to employment at just about the time when private business itself was expanding too rapidly. Moreover, those minor depressions can be fairly well trusted to run their course and eventually end in a revival of the customary sort, without the aid of a public works policy.

The real usefulness of such a program would come in cases where a recession has reached unusually serious proportions and has gone so far as to paralyze the normal resources of private recovery. In such a case, Government spending may be substantially the only means left for initiating a revival and avoiding a dangerous period of prolonged paralysis. Thus, if Professor Slichter's view were adopted, the policy of expanded public works might best be confined to the occasional major crises.

⁵ S. H. Slichter, The Economics of Public Works, Amer. Econ. Rev., March 1934, pp. 174–185.

This carries implications as to the type of program suitable to such use. The grade A program, so far as it hinges on the postponement of projects embodied in a 5- or 10-year schedule, would be unsuitable, for reasons already pointed out. Projects of this grade cannot be held back as long as would be required. Future projects of this same grade might be anticipated, but the amount of work so furnished would not be sufficient to handle such a very serious situation as is presupposed by this type of program. Thus a grade B program would be necessary. The earlier stages of the depression should then be utilized for the preparatory work necessary to enable the grade B program to be put promptly into effect.

On the whole, it does not seem wise to adopt this point of view unqualifiedly, nor, especially, to abandon without a determined trial the hope of reducing the seriousness of industrial fluctuations by an expansion of public works which does not wait until business is prostrate and unable of itself to initiate a recovery. An intermediate policy, or rather a combination of the two, seems the proper one to attempt. This means that the initial stage of a recession would be occupied with final preparatory measures for setting in motion the expansion side of a grade A policy, which should be put into effect as soon as business is definitely below normal. This might be so successful in reducing the minor fluctuations that they either would not constitute a serious burden, or could be handled by the help of stabilization policies carried out within the structure of private industry itself. This might be accomplished without exhausting the reserve powers of Government available for dealing with more serious emergencies when they might arise.

When the grade A program is actually put into effect, preparatory work should be pushed to enable a larger program of the grade B sort to be put into effect promptly in case, despite the grade A program, recession should continue and reach the stage of a major emergency. This, again, involves some work which might bear no fruits, and which might be wasted in case the major emergency did not actually appear, or did not appear for a number of years. This would not be a serious matter compared with the advantages resulting in the way of prompter action when the emergency does appear. It is analogous to military preparedness involving the drawing up of plans, most of which will never be used.

C. Expansion Without Contraction; A Progressive Increase in Public Spending

One view holds that the proper function of public works is not to furnish an intermittent stimulus when private activity shrinks, followed by a corresponding shrinkage when private activity expands, but rather to absorb permanently an increased amount of the spending and producing power of the country in order to correct an enduring tendency to maldistribution of effort. This view rests on a particular theory of economic dislocations which has already been briefly discussed (ch. IV). According to this theory the real source of stagnation, or the more serious source, lies deeper than temporary bursts of expansion of capital facilities which proceed in excess of current savings and are financed largely by credit expansion. This real source of trouble is held to lie in a persistent tendency of savings to expand faster than industry can absorb them in useful forms of capital equipment, consistent with a stable and healthy industrial development. As to this theory, it is almost certainly wrong in what it denies or tends to neglect, while in what it asserts it is probably at least partly right but cannot be proved with the evidence at present available.

Temporary bursts of capital expansion do use credit inflation and go beyond the amount of current savings—so much appears reasonably certain. In fact, it is difficult to see how a rapid industrial expansion can come about without credit inflation in some form or other, though it is not healthy nor probably necessary that this credit inflation should flow wholly or mainly into expansion of industrial capital. The purchasing power to buy current production comes mainly from the incomes yielded by productive processes carried on in the immediate past. If this were the only source, rapid increase in production would be well-nigh impossible; and rapid increase in dollar volume of production would be quite impossible. To bring about rapid increase some further source of purchasing power is necessary. If the expansion is to be greater than the ratio of normal increase in the circulating medium, the further increased purchasing power requires either further credit expansion or a reduction in prices, but a reduction in prices is likely to make trouble of a different sort. A slow downward tendency of prices is not inconsistent with industrial expansion, and is probably the healthiest condition for it, but a rapid decline in prices is a condition in the face of which business cannot expand, as it is now constituted. Hence a rapid expansion of industry seems to require an expansion of credit.

But if there is to be, over a long period, an expansion of industry greater than the ratio of normal increase in the circulating medium, it can hardly be financed by an endless supernormal expansion of the credit machinery. It must rest on a more enduring basis such as would be furnished by a slow downward trend in the price level. This condition might be favored by eliminating, if possible, the concentrated bursts of expansion in capital equipment and the corresponding bursts of credit expansion. But this would still leave the problem— frankly unsolved at present—whether the normal flow of savings, even if not supplemented by credit expansion, furnishes more capital than industry knows at present how to absorb. Perhaps this question is too hypothetical to be particularly significant, since the "normal" flow of savings under these conditions would be different from the average flow under actual conditions. A more practical question might be whether the average flow, modified as it will presumably be in the future by periods of credit expansion and contraction, has a tendency to exceed the amount of useful investment our system can find for it. As already indicated, the probable answer is "yes", but evidence necessary to proof is not at present available.

The most prominent proposal identified with this theory calls for an initial and very large expansion of public works as a means of getting out of the present depression, financed by inflationary borrowing, followed by a permanent enlargement of this type of public spending, financed by forms of taxation so levied that the additional revenue would come mainly out of savings and not out of income which would otherwise be spent for consumption. It is the latter phase of the program which is here in question, and the crux of this is the possibility of raising large amounts of added revenue in the way proposed.

For this purpose two types of taxation have been suggested, one centering in more steeply progressive income taxes, the other in an attempt to tax savings directly. This latter proposal, in the only form which the writer has seen, appear complicated, inquisitorial and unworkable, leading to more and more difficult extensions in the attempt to stop the leaks, escapes and evasions which would inevitably spring up. As to the income tax proposal, it appears that when one starts with an income tax which is as highly progressive as the system in the United States at present, further large increases in revenue cannot be obtained without making the additional burdens regressive rather than progressive in their incidence.

It is the individual income taxes which are in question; and a Federal program of the proposed sort could hardly be achieved without making it necessary to double the normal yield of this part of the Federal tax system by increases in the higher brackets, involving only a slight decrease in consumption. In the very highest income brackets, it may be fair to assume that practically all of the income beyond that covered by the next lower brackets is saved. But the tax on these highest brackets could not be doubled, and any practicable increase would yield relatively small revenue. If one proceeds to the more moderate income brackets—say from $10,000 to $100,000— tax burdens could be very greatly increased and yield very substantial added revenues, but it seems certain that only a minor part of this added revenue would come out of savings, and this becomes increasingly true the farther down one goes in the scale of incomes. And any part of such taxes which comes out of consumers' spendings would have no effect in shifting the balance between consumers' spendings and savings, which is the purpose of the whole plan.

Under these conditions, there appears to be only one chance, if any, for raising the necessary revenue in the necessary way. It might be done if there were an enormous increase in the incomes out of which the taxes would have to come, an increase that would not merely wipe out the shrinkage that has taken place since 1929, but one that would raise incomes well above the predepression normal. The part of the proposed program bearing on this is the first part— an emergency Public Works program much larger than the present one, and financed by expansionary borrowing. To achieve such results as are called for would require a program of not less than 10 billions, coupled with secondary effects considerably larger than could be confidently expected. If the first part of the program failed, the second could not hope to succeed.

Thus it appears that the scope within which this proposal could be successful is confined within rather narrow limits. Within these limits, it might be useful, but its effect would appear to depend more on making the revenue system more progressive in its incidence than on the particular forms of public spending to which the revenues are devoted. There is no reason, from the standpoint of this theory, why it is any better to spend money on roads than on statistical research or health service, or any better to spend it on schools than on the salaries of teachers to carry on the work of education.

The crux of the problem, from this standpoint, appears to be a matter of redistribution of incomes rather than of a particular form of public spending. And the problem of redistribution of incomes is undoubtedly a broader one than can be adequately dealt with by methods of taxation alone. This appears to be a problem of national planning in the large, rather than a problem of public works in the limited and conventional sense, although it may involve some permanent expansion of public works and corresponding public consumption as over against private consumption, as one phase of it, which should be kept in proper proportion to the other phases.

One feature of this proposal is that public funds should be spent on non-self-liquidating works rather than self-liquidating ones, because the self-liquidating works compete with private industry in the markets for the consumers' dollar and tend to aggrevate a condition the core of which consists in too large an amount of resources being devoted to producing things to sell to consumers, compared with the flow of consumers' dollars available to buy the products. The proposal amounts to a large increase in free public consumption not paid for in the form of prices. This encounters the stubborn difficulty that the free consumption must be financed out of taxes, and the taxes must come out of the flow of production which passes through the markets and is paid for by prices. Thus, the base of taxation would be narrowed at the same time that the amount necessary would be increased. This fact accentuates the difficulty already indicated of raising large amounts of additional revenue in ways which would not defeat the purpose of the proposal.

The limit on the percentage of our total national dividend which can go in the form of taxes without materially handicapping and reducing the volume of private business is admittedly an indefinite and elastic one. But it appears fairly certain that the percentages which have been reached in England and France, for example, since the World War, have passed that limit, while the present percentage burdens in this country are probably within sight of it. Thus, it does not appear wise to count on any large or radical improvements in our industrial system from a permanent increase in public spending, financed by taxes.

A. General Limitations

We have already seen that certain types of public works must be carried out when they are "ripe", while others are more elastic as to the time when they can be carried out. Some of the particular elements limiting the policy of timing have been indicated. The precise amount of shifting that is possible within a grade A program is elastic, depending on the degree to which the people are willing to submit to a postponement of desirable projects, or to bear the interest charges of constructing them ahead of the natural time. Students of the problem have frequently taken as a rule of thumb the assumption that one-half of the work in a grade A program could be either postponed or advanced for a year or two. Needless to say, no actual experiences have gone that far, and therefore there is no experimental basis for testing this rule of thumb. Careful examination of the specific projects in such a grade A program, carried out by engineers and others familiar with the problems involved in each particular field, and with an understanding view of the desirability of adjusting the timing, so far as possible—even at some cost— would yield a useful check on rough general estimates. Such a study has not been made, and the rule of thumb may be judged to be an optimistic estimate of the possibilities.

Another possibility, not resting on changes in the time when projects are undertaken, consists of altering the speed at which current projects are carried out. Here also there is a presumption that changes would involve some cost, because the natural speed is presumably an economical one. Projects are naturally carried out as rapidly as may be, to reduce interest during construction, up to the point at which costs would be increased by crowding an undue amount of labor on the working front, or by the necessity of rapidly building up a working organization which must be quickly disbanded again, or of investing in large amounts of mechanical equipment which will not be needed long enough to justify their cost. There are undoubtedly cases in which very large projects, such as waterway channel improvements, are carried on more slowly than would be economical, owing to limited funds available, combined with the policy of distributing the expenditure of these funds over different States and districts. For such projects, speeding up would mean economy.

Another limitation, which would sometimes be important, consists in the limited available labor supply or available supply of materials of a particular sort and in a particular locality where construction work may not have fallen off as much as business in general. This condition is likely to occur chiefly in mild, rather than in severe, depressions. In a major crisis there would be no shortage of labor or materials.

On the other hand, it is urged that construction carried on in times of dull business can be done more cheaply, owing to lower wages, lower costs of materials, possible lower interest charges, the willingness of workers to work harder, and of contractors to accept narrower

71

margins on their bids.   Attempts have been made to measure changes in construction costs, which indicate some lowering during general business depressions, although the amount appears very slight.   The possible savings are probably greater than the indexes show, inasmuch as the indexes do not measure the last two sources of savings.   And so far as wages are measured by union rates, the deflation of wages is undoubtedly underestimated.   On the other hand, a large program of Government works is morally certain to stiffen the resistance of these elements of cost to the normal forces of deflation.   Thus, while a private enterprise, such as the Dennison Co., may be justified in its conviction that it gets construction materially cheaper by doing it in dull times, it is probable that business in general would not be able to get the same saving if it followed the same plan, and morally certain that Government could not get it.   Thus, the net effect of a program of concentrating public works in times of dull business might actually be an increase in costs, because the program would probably tend to prevent any considerable deflation of wage and material costs, while still incurring the additional costs which are involved in carrying out public works projects at an unnatural time or at an unnatural rate of speed.   That is, this would be true unless something were done to prevent it.

To combat this tendency to higher costs would require concerted negotiations and arrangements in which the construction industries would make concessions of a definite amount in return for additional employment at a time when there is unusued capacity of labor and construction equipment.   It is an interesting coincidence that the day on which President Roosevelt signed the housing bill (June 28, 1934) was also marked by the announcement by the National Retail Lumber Dealers Association of price reductions of approximately 10 percent on lumber and building materials.   The reports available do not state how this price reduction was brought about.   But it seems evident that not only the commodities covered by this one association, but many other elements of cost need to be deflated if the housing program is to be thoroughly successful in achieving its end. This proposition may have very far-reaching implications.

Deflation must be brought about.   One method would be to break the power to resist deflation, which seems now to reside in trade organizations, systems of price leadership, etc., and restore a more thoroughly competitive situation.   However, for other purposes, such as those of the National Recovery Administration, there may be a continuing need for organizations in the construction industries which are sufficiently powerful to control competition, including competition in prices.   One obvious corollary is Government control of prices, but this is not a thing to be lightly entered into.   It may be, however, that such organizations as already exist may be used for purposes of bringing together representatives of the trades, who may then be induced to make reductions in prices by agreement without going to the length of setting up permanent agencies for price control in general.   Naturally, such arrangements would be very difficult to bring about.   If successful, they could greatly increase not only the economy but the general usefulness of a Public Works program as a stimulus to private industrial recovery.   They would avoid the very real danger of the bidding up of costs by a Government program to a point at which they act as a deterrent to the resumption of private construction at a time when a stimulus rather than a deterrent is needed.

B. Political and Administrative Difficulties

The greater part of public works in this country is carried out by States and localities, and the difficulty of bringing about concerted action on any uniform policy is obvious. Even if localities are willing to cooperate, many of them, in bad times, are unable to collect their regular taxes, and their credit is in no condition to stand the burden of large additional borrowings. Even where their credit is essentially sound, statutory debt limits may stand in the way. As we have already seen, the regular procedures for the undertaking of public works are time-consuming and cumbersome. The most available weapon for bringing about concerted action is financial help from a central authority, but this adds more necessary procedure to be gone through which may bring still further delay.

The conclusion is that the success of any timing policy is absolutely dependent upon preparatory measures which will take as many as possible of these steps in advance, and leave the actual starting of work dependent, so far as may be, upon a rather simple administrative procedure. This would naturally start with an administrative determination of the existence of a previously defined degree of need, carrying with it the decision to set in motion financial measures already available and engineering plans already either completed or carried some stages toward completion. For meeting major emergencies, the credit of the Federal Government seems to be the only reliable source of funds; and one of the vital needs is the preparation of arrangements with the States and localities whereby the Federal Government should not only be prepared to grant this credit, but the States and localities should be prepared to accept it and use it. Since this preparatory work would cost them something, they may need to be induced to do it by some continuing financial assistance to the preparatory work of the State and local planning organizations which would need to be set up.

While, by spring of 1935, 45 of the States had State planning boards, these boards for the most part had relatively limited budgets. The members are largely unpaid, technical assistance has been financed by the National Planning Board and subsequently the National Resources Board, and actual studies conducted under these boards have been largely financed by Civil Works Administration and subsequently by F. E. R. A. funds or as relief work. City, county, and regional planning [1] is in a very similar situation. Out of 739 city planning boards reporting to the National Planning Board in 1934, 57 percent had no funds for the current year, while 80 percent had less than $1,000. On the other hand, 200 State, regional, and local planning boards made use of relief workers, employing 10,300, with applications involving several thousand more were pending as of May 15, 1934.[2] This is only a small part of the total volume of relief work employed on Federal, State, and local

---

[1] The New England Regional Planning Commission and the Pacific Northwest Regional Planning Commission are furnished with technical staffs by the National Resources Board, which also finances office expenses. Universities and certain public groups have cooperated and loaned equipment and personnel in limited amounts.

[2] Eleventh circular letter of the National Planning Board, pp. 4, 9.

surveys and statistical projects. The total number of white collar workers so employed was estimated at approximately 150,000 in 1934.

Thus, in general, it may be said that most of the States and localities which have introduced planning had not in 1934 assumed the financial burden it involves. Reports to the National Resources Board early in 1935 show a tendency, however, toward increases in funds available.

The question remains whether in better times they will be willing to assume the burden. In such times the money will be easier to find, but the need will be less obviously urgent. The natural course of action in this matter is to wait and see if a realization of the importance of this work will not induce States and localities to give it adequate financing. Naturally, if Federal financing is offered it will be relied on. If the States and localities will not bear the burden of their own accord, the Federal Government has a sufficient interest in the matter to justify it in taking the load, so far as that may be necessary. But that is a matter in which it is wise policy to go extremely slowly, not merely from the standpoint of saving dollars for the Federal Budget, but from the standpoint of conditions necessary to the effectiveness of the program.

It is essential to whole-hearted State and local support of planning measures that the States and localities should feel that these are their measures and not merely something which they are doing because Washington wants them to do it. Once the feeling is established that, in furthering the ends of planning, State and local bodies are merely giving Washington something it wants and is willing to pay for, a condition will be established under which it will be almost hopeless to expect any but perfunctory performance. Washington has an interest in State and local planning, but its successful promotion depends on the development of State and local interest also.

The nature of the preparatory measures needed hinges on the character and objectives of the planning which they are to serve. If the sole objectives are those associated with physical or regional planning as ordinarily conceived, preparatory measures will center upon seeing that projects are chosen such as will fit into an organically consistent and maturely considered program. From this standpoint, deliberateness of procedure is rather an advantage than otherwise, and the result of planning from this standpoint might be to increase the number of bodies through whose scrutiny projects must pass, and so actually increase the obstacles to any quick enlargement of the program, at least if it goes beyond the scope of projects already passed upon. This might be illustrated by the most recent proposed Massachusetts planning law.

If such a plan contemplates a steady rate of expenditure as an objective to be seriously striven for, and not merely followed when convenient, certain further measures are called for. Public revenues will not automatically provide for the requirements of a stabilized spending program; some way of making possible stabilized spending is necessary if a regular program of public works is to be carried out. This is not, of course, merely a matter concerning public works only, but should be regarded as a part of a comprehensive program for making possible stability in public expenses and public services in the face of fluctuating revenues. Measures of this sort have already received serious study.[1] Proposals to this end include measures for greater stabilization of revenues, the accumulation of fiscal reserves and borrowing. As to the accumulation of fiscal reserves in times when revenues are ample, it appears: First, that the principle is sound if the reserves are wisely handled; second, that methods of investing the reserves and realizing on them require much thought; and third, that this method alone cannot completely stabilize the flow of funds available for current expenses. In addition, it appears that any program of effective stabilization must necessarily contemplate temporary borrowing when revenues are not sufficient to meet expenditures under the stabilized program.

It is worth noting that the problem of maintaining outlays for current services is more difficult than that of maintaining public capital expenditures, and is not less important. Borrowing for durable public works is an accepted procedure of "sound finance", whereas borrowing for current expenses represents an unbalanced state of the budget which is regarded as unsound, though admittedly sometimes necessary. More recently, different ideas have been suggested as to what constitutes budget balancing, among them being the idea of balancing the budget over a term of approximately 3 years, or over the term of a business cycle, rather than over a single year. It is being urged that an implacable determination to balance the budget at all costs during every separate year is not good public

[1] A special report on these matters has been prepared by J. W. Sundelson and appears as an appendix to this document.

finance. As for borrowing, it has already been noted that advance authorization may be necessary for prompt action, while localities may require some system of elastic debt limits. Some of the problems involved in elastic debt limits will be briefly discussed in chapter XI.

Is it possible, with the help of such preparatory measures, to insure the possibility of stabilized expenditures? The answer is probably that it is never possible to predict with absolute confidence what will happen in the face of one of those major emergencies, always unique and unprecedented in some respect or other, and therefore never completely predictable, which may intervene to upset the working of any plan, no matter how thoroughly laid. So far as concerns the ordinary requirements imposed by the minor fluctuations of business over a shorter business cycle, the problem is relatively easy. These short business cycles ordinarily involve no very substantial fluctuations in public revenues, and such fluctuation as there is can be easily taken care of. On the other hand, merely to maintain a stabilized budget of expenditures through a major crisis might be too much of a strain for existing fiscal machinery, even with improvements which are now being recommended.

As a general principle, it may be laid down that stabilization of at least the essential current services comes first in importance, and expansion of public works in time of depression comes second. One is tempted to put this in more absolute form and say that, until stabilization of essential current services is provided for, no attempt should be made to expand public works in dull times. But such a hard and fast formulation encounters the difficulty just mentioned; namely, that no one can be sure whether existing provisions are or are not sufficient to stabilize expenditures through a major crisis of the future, whose seriousness and special characteristics cannot be foreseen. Thus, all that it is possible to lay down is that, before undertaking programs of expanding public works in times of depression, there should be sufficient provision made for the maintenance of regular current governmental services to afford a reasonably adequate prospect of success in meeting any but the most unusual and most serious strains.

Such provisions for stabilized spending would not afford a positive remedy for depressions, but would at least avoid making them worse by adding the effects of shrinking public outlays to those of shrinking private expenditures. It would be a distinct improvement over the existing system and would represent a benefit not to be despised. Furthermore, unless stability in general current expenditures of government is first achieved, there is little or no point in talking of remedying depressions by increasing expenditures on public works. To spend more money and to take on additional workers in one section of the budget, while cutting appropriations heavily and laying off employees whose salaries come in another section of the budget, seems a strange and inconsistent method either of increasing employment or of bringing about a desirable total amount of expenditures. It amounts to keeping the desire for economy and the desire for increased spending in thought-tight compartments and attempting to satisfy both at once. There are, of course, reasons for such a policy which are not so completely senseless as this characterization indicates, and the whole matter will be discussed at greater length elsewhere (chapter XI).

If means have already been provided whereby expenses can be stabilized, let us say, during a moderate depression, then it may be in order to think about a further step and to plan for increasing those types of expenditures which can most properly be concentrated in particular years for reasons of general public policy. The very facts which make public works the most appropriate things to expand, if there is to be expansion and not contraction, constitute reasons why current expenses are not the most appropriate thing to contract, if there is to be contraction and not expansion. If shortage of revenues absolutely requires a contraction, then from the standpoint of making the best use of the community's money (and not from the standpoint of fiscal formulas and rituals) we should by all means postpone the construction of public works of minor urgency, which can be built a year or two later with no great loss, rather than cut down on services of education, health, and police, which cannot be made up at all.

Public works, then, are the logical things to expand if there is to be expansion, but not otherwise. If fiscal conditions make an expansion of total spendings quite impossible, then essential current services should be maintained, and fiscal means should be devised which would make this possible. If fiscal resources of States and localities make a shrinkage of their expenditures imperative, while the Federal Government has credit resources which it can use for an expansion, means should be found to maintain the essential current services of the States and localities, even if this involves unorthodox forms of Federal aid. And if all devices fail to ward off the necessity of a shrinkage in total expenditures on behalf of States and localities, it is still undesirable that this shrinkage should fall in concentrated form on current services, while public works are expanded.

In terms of the real strain put upon the finances, the various possible programs stand in the following order, starting with the one involving the least strain. First, stabilizing current expenditures in a mild depression and avoiding a shrinkage in public-works expenditures. Second, stabilizing current expenditures during a mild depression while putting into effect a supplementary public-works expenditure already laid out in an elastic program of the grade A type. Third, stabilizing total expenditures, both of current services and public works, during a major depression. Fourth, increasing total expenditures during a major depression. Thus it is harder to maintain a stabilized budget during a major depression than to finance a moderate expansion during a minor depression, in terms of the real strain put upon the total financial resources of the community.

However, in terms of orthodox canons of fiscal practice, it may be easier to expand public works in a major depression, while allowing current services to shrink, than to maintain current services under such conditions, simply because orthodox canons of fiscal practice approve of borrowing for permanent works and do not approve of it for current services, even though the permanent works are not of a revenue-yielding sort and do not afford any better security for the loans than any other form of wise and judicious expenditure. It appears that the orthodox canons of fiscal practice are in need of modification in the light of the underlying economic realities, in order to make possible the most useful distribution of expenditures during emergencies.

The conception of maintaining essential current services, or of maintaining the level of expenditures on these services, may need some more precise definition in cases where the levels of prices and wages are changing. When these changes are no greater than they usually are in mild business cycles, governmental salary scales do not change, and the maintenance of service and maintenance of expenditures for that service remain substantially identical. But when there are larger changes in prices and wage scales, then some further adjustments may be called for.

First, salaries may be reduced in the same proportion as the reduction in the general price level, with the result that services are maintained and what we may call real expenditures, as distinct from money expenditures, are also maintained. Second, salaries may be cut more severely, while maintaining the same amount of public employment in terms of numbers of employees and time worked. Thus, real expenditures may be reduced somewhat, while maintaining the volume of services. This may, in some cases, be regarded as a necessary evil. Third, economies may be made, such as the consolidation of departments and bureaus, or other economies which permit the maintenance of service with a reduction in the total amount of employee time. This is, of course, in the long run, not an evil at all, although in terms of the stimulative effects of increased spending during a depression, its value is a minus quantity. Fourth, less essential services may be curtailed. This also may be a necessary evil, and is, even more than the third policy, a negative quantity from the standpoint of the stimulative effects of increased public spending during a depression. Fifth, some of the most highly essential services may be curtailed. This is undesirable on all possible grounds and is justifiable only if the fiscal emergency is such as to threaten a genuine collapse of the public credit, with resulting bad effects on the possibility of industrial revival.

Assuming that provision has been made for the maintenance of current services, so far as the uncertainties of the future permit, it becomes proper and desirable to plan for the expansion of public works in times of depression. For this purpose, further measures of preparedness will be necessary. Beginning with the schedule of approved projects, it will need to be differentiated so as to mark off certain projects for postponement in good times and prosecution in dull times, and in addition at least a first reserve should be set up consisting of projects not approved for the grade A program but coming first in line if a larger program is to be followed. Advance engineering work must be done, so far as practicable. Advance acquisition of land will be useful where not too costly and will remove the uncertainty that attends the emergency procedure of entering upon land by condemnation and starting work before the price to be paid for the land has been determined. Actual appropriation of funds, not to be spent until the emergency arises, and corresponding borrowing authorizations, would also help to clear the way of obstacles. Last, but not least, comes the administrative procedure for determining the need for expanding spendings. Here a certain dilemma exists between the need for an objective standard, such as would be furnished by a perfect business index, and the fact that no single index can furnish an infallible and all-sufficient guide to such a policy.

Among the types of indexes which might be used are a general business index, a construction index, and an unemployment index. Furthermore, since conditions vary so widely in different parts of the country, local indexes would be needed for the guidance of local units of government, or of the Federal Government if and when it grants funds to stimulate local public works.

The typical general business index is weak in that it combines a medley of physical and financial quantities, and may not give a clear picture of underlying conditions in terms of any one criterion. The employment index has at least the advantage that there is no doubt as to what it is trying to measure, and the quality of such indices is improving to an extent which affords hope that they may soon be reliable enough to be depended on for such a purpose. An index of general employment may be the most important single guide to the need for increased public spending and public employment, but it should never be used without incidental reference to the state of activity and employment in the construction industries which would have to do the work and receive the funds. Local conditions might cause unemployment at the same time that construction activity was above normal, locally. In such a case, increased local public works would hardly be appropriate. On the other hand, a Nation-wide depression, both in general business and in construction, might justify carrying out some public works in localities which were relatively unaffected. In such a case, financial support would naturally come from the Federal Government and employment could not appropriately be confined to workers in the locality in which the works were carried on. Such considerations as these argue the need for elasticity and judgment in the use of indices.

How far the development of special indices should be carried is a matter which cannot be properly determined in advance, but must be left to be handled by the governmental bodies which have the responsibility for determining when industrial conditions are such as to call for emergency expenditures. As to the general character of these governmental bodies, it is gradually taking shape, with variations from case to case which can best be left to work themselves out, by the test of experience, under local conditions. Until recently, the preparation of State and local projects to take advantage of Federal loans and grants necessarily proceeded, in the main, without the benefit of advance planning. The State and local planning organizations are mainly concerned with outlining the needs of the communities, and, among other things, drawing up programs of desirable public works for the future, though their studies range over a broader field than this. In the public works field, they are not directly concerned with the administrative questions of providing for a future flexible program of public works, to be expanded when private business falls off, and vice versa. This feature of the system remains to be worked out and may call for the setting up of a different type of body, or the giving of new functions to existing officials directly concerned with the administration of public works. The corresponding Federal body in the public works field may need to be of a somewhat different character from State and local bodies for the reason that it will be concerned to a larger extent with allotment of funds to States and localities and so will be farther removed from the actual prosecution of the work.

IX. CUMULATIVE EFFECTS OF PUBLIC EXPENDITURES

A. Indirect Primary Employment and Production

The employment created by public works has been classified as follows:

1. Primary: (a) Direct, employment of workers on the spot in carrying out the work; (b) indirect, employment in producing materials and delivering them to the site of the work and in other services contributing to the work.
2. Secondary: Employment resulting from the expenditures of all those among whom the original public outlays are divided as income. This includes wage earners and receivers of rent, interest, and profits, since a given dollar of public works expenditures goes to all those varieties of ultimate recipients.

As a rough rule of thumb it may be laid down that, under ordinary working conditions, the amount of indirect primary employment is about equal to the amount of direct primary employment. However, where the volume of direct employment is deliberately swollen by reducing the use of machinery, this ratio would no longer hold, and the volume of indirect employment would naturally be less than the direct employment.

As to the amount of the construction dollar which goes to labor, the well-nigh universal estimate made by students of this problem is 80 percent. In fact, the uniformity with which this estimate is followed is so striking as to create a suspicion that some original estimate has been repeated by many writers without independent checking. The present writer has made some rather rough calculations, indicating a range between 70 and 83 percent, 70 percent representing prosperous conditions when profits are liberal and 83 percent representing conditions when construction companies as a whole were reporting no net income at all.[1] These percentages are based on the figures of total labor income reported in National Income, 1920–32 [2] and thus includes salaries as well as wages. The amount going as profits to the construction enterprises seems to have varied between about 17 percent in 1929 and nothing in 1932, while 30 to 41 percent goes into the form of labor income in construction and the remainder goes for the production of materials and for all the incidental outside services which contribute to the process and here to be paid for ultimately.

Probably less than half of this remainder goes to plants engaged in the actual manufacture of construction materials and equipment, the rest going to extractive industries, transportation, public utilities, mercantile, legal, and financial services. The Federal Employment Stabilization Board estimated that in 1929 there were 703,300 persons

[1] The Bureau of Public Roads in a study entitled "Where the Highway Dollar Goes", February 1932, states that nearer 85 percent than 75 percent is traceable ultimately to labor. It seems probable that the general construction figures would be lower than the figure for roads.
[2] Prepared by the National Bureau of Economic Research, for the Bureau of Foreign and Domestic Commerce. The study was made by Dr. Simon Kuznets.

employed in 20,569 plants engaged in the production of construction materials and equipment. (Based on 1929 Census of Manufactures.) For the same year the study of National Income, 1929–32, estimated that 1,528,000 workers were actually engaged in construction industries. In interpreting this figure one must take into account the fact that there are large volumes of construction carried on by industries on their own account which do not figure in the reports of the industries engaged in construction as such. Thus, the estimates for the total volume of construction contained in an unpublished study of the production of durable goods, made by Simon Kuznets, are approximately twice as large as the corresponding figures for the construction industries proper contained in the study of National Income, 1929–32, made by the same investigator. Thus the total number of workers engaged in construction of all sorts must be estimated to be very much larger than the figure of 1,528,000, and it is the larger figure which has to be compared with the figure of 703,300 persons employed in the production of construction materials and equipment. Thus it is clear in any case that the volume of employment in the actual manufacture of construction materials is much smaller than the amount of direct employment on the site of construction work. If the figure given by the Federal Employment Stabilization Board were as comprehensive an estimate as the others, it would argue that it takes four men directly employed to furnish work for one man in the actual manufacture of materials. However, the estimate of employment in materials-manufacturing is undoubtedly less comprehensive than the other figures. One may conclude that this portion of the indirect employment falls somewhere between one-fourth and one-half of the direct employment.

The writer has roughly estimated what becomes of the money spent for materials and indirect services, using the estimates of National Income, 1929–32, and assuming that the money is distributed among the groups labeled: Mining, electric power and gas, manufacturing, transportation, communication, and miscellaneous, in the tables presented in that study. On this basis the following results were obtained:

Indirect primary employment

	1929	1932	Assumed normal results of 1 billion dollars expended
Gross income of construction industry (millions)	$6,971	$1,700	[1] $1,000
Workers employed, direct (thousands)	1,538	673	370
Labor income, direct (millions)	$2,620	$689	$400
Labor income (direct percent of gross)	38.6	40.5	40
Gross per worker	$4,560	$2,820	$2,702
Labor income per worker, direct	$1,730	$1,023	$1,651
Estimated profit of construction industry	$1,184	None	$100
Estimated gross going to materials and indirect serivces	$3,167	$1,011	$500
Estimated indirect workers (thousands)	1,600	640	311
Estimated labor incomes, indirect (millions)	$2,240	$720	$355
Estimated indirect labor incomes (percent of indirect gross)	70.7	71.2	71
Labor income, direct and indirect (millions)	$4,860	$1,409	$735
Labor income (percent of gross)	70	83	75.5
Workers employed, direct and indirect (thousands)	3,128	1,313	681

[1] Arbitrary.

NOTE.—First 6 lines from national income, 1929–32; seventh line, estimated (figures not segregated in national income, 1929–32); rest of table, estimated on basis indicated in text.

The conclusion is that under ordinary conditions indirect employment is somewhat less than direct (not twice as great, as the first estimates used by the Public Works Administration assumed). In 1932 it required a gross expenditure of $2,820 to give direct employment to 1 worker for 1 year. Conditions imposed by the codes might raise this figure a trifle—let us say, to $3,000. The actual amount so far expended under the Public Works Administration program, on what seemed to be the most typical projects, is clearly less than this amount per worker employed.[3] This leads to the natural conclusion that the provisions for minimizing the use of machinery have increased the amount of direct labor and correspondingly reduced the proportion of indirect labor to direct. One may roughly estimate that, under these conditions, indirect employment is not more than three-fourths of direct, and might possibly be as low as two-thirds. The figures on which this statement is based are the estimates of actual expenditures made by the Division of Economics and Statistics of the Public Works Administration covering work done through April 1934.

Different types of work covered by these estimates differ radically. For railroads, $88,470,974 furnished 58,067 man-months of direct employment, or at the rate of $18,688 per man-year. This large amount clearly means that most of the employment furnished by this expenditure was indirect. On other non-Federal projects, $16,706,991 furnished 112,950 man-months of employment, or at the rate of $1,776 per man-year. This total is complicated by the fact that not quite all of the funds were furnished by the Federal Government. Some localities accepted Federal grants, but raised their own loans. Therefore this figure does not represent the full cost of this amount of employment. For Federal projects, $279,788,281 furnished 1,684,169 man-months of employment, or at the rate of $1,992 per year. This is probably the most representative figure, but even this remains doubtful because it presumably does not include the amount which would ultimately go as profits to contractors when the jobs were completed. Probably $2,300–$2,400 would better represent the final cost. On relief highways, $6,680,655 furnished 127,326 man-months of direct employment, or at the rate of $630 per man-year. This represents not only low wages for the workers directly employed but also a very low percentage of indirect employment. Under the Civil Works Administration, approximately three-fourths of the total outlays have been reported as going to direct labor, at wage rates which appear to have varied from $15 to $12 per week, approximately. This would represent, very roughly, a total expenditure of $800–$900 per man-year of full and continuous employment. The indirect employment would be only a small fraction of the direct, and the precise amount cannot be estimated, owing to the fact that materials were furnished by other agencies than the Federal Government. In the Civilian Conservation Corps, the cost per man was about $1,000 per year, of which $30 a month went as wages and the remainder covered subsistence as well as materials. Thus, the proportion of direct to indirect employment varies widely according to the class of work. However, the total amount of primary employment (direct and indirect) furnished by $1,000,000 spent on public works is fairly uniform, except for undertakings in the class of work-relief where wages are much lower than on regular public works.

[3] It should be kept in mind that this publication was prepared in the summer of 1934.

Anotner difficulty arises from the fact that some of the outlay, including part of what is ultimately traced to labor, goes into depreciation and other reserves, which will ultimately result in expenditures for replacement of equipment or for other purposes, but possibly only after a considerable length of time. Normally, the amount which one company is putting into these reserves is matched by replacement expenditures and similar outlays which other companies are making. During a depression, such expenditures are below normal while the policy of discouraging the use of machinery naturally tends toward a low rate of actual expenditures for maintenance and replacement. The conclusion is that some of the indirect employment represented in the above figures is likely to be postponed for a considerable length of time.

B. Secondary Effects: The Problem

The problem of secondary employment or secondary volume of expenditures is far more difficult and conjectural. A fair estimate can be made of the number of workers who share in the original dollar spent for public works, and no statistical evidence is needed to prove that whatever part of that dollar the workers do not get, someone else does. But the problem of secondary effects is almost entirely a matter of conjecture and deductive theorizing. One basic reason for believing that secondary effects exist is the fact that business cycles exist, since the way in which the business cycle gathers momentum in its swings seem to afford fairly convincing evidence that an original expansion or contraction of expenditures has produced secondary effects returning on itself time after time and multiplying its own effects in the process.

Such general corroboration can never be regarded as absolute proof, since the nature of the original impulse can never be isolated with absolute certainty of demonstration. There is one historical instance in which the original impulse seems to be fairly well defined, namely, the effect on the United States of the war purchases of the Allies during our period of neutrality. Here these war purchases were apparently the decisive force which lifted the American economy between 1914 and 1916 from a state of mild depression to the highest level of physical and financial production which it had ever attained. The main point for our present purposes is that the increase in our domestic production was considerably greater, even on a physical basis, than the volume of foreign purchases which presumably it called forth. It is possible, we may conclude, for a given cause to produce an effect considerably larger than itself.

It is also significant to note, as a possible necessary condition, the fact that in 1915–16, the United States was building large amounts of additional plant capacity in the industries serving the production of munitions. If we had already possessed sufficient plant capacity to meet in full the demands of the Allies, it would seem that the same volume of foreign purchases would not have produced as large an effect as it did. Whether it would have produced an effect larger than itself, if there had been no plant expansion in this country, is an interesting question on which it seems hopeless to get conclusive evidence from statistics.

It seems, then, that we have a certain amount of rather general evidence indicating that an increase of expenditures may have cumulative effects. The general behavior of business cycles affords further evidence that these effects do not go on forever. There are obvious reasons why production cannot expand to infinity in any given business boom, because it becomes physically impossible to expand production that far, while the necessary expansion of credit would reach a limit a great deal sooner.

But why do expansions often stop short of these limits? It is not quite so obvious why a contraction of industry does not go on until everyone is unemployed—or rather, until the existing system of private business enterprise, working under the scheme of prices, profits, and losses, loses all its power of employment. We know that it has never yet lost all that power, and, in ordinary depressions, sel dom loses as much as 20 percent of it. These general facts suggest. (1) That economic expansions and contractions have cumulative effects; and (2) that these cumulative effects tend either to exhaust themselves after going a certain distance or to give rise to counteracting forces. But why and how?

The Government spends a dollar. Those who get the money spend it again, and those who get it from them spend it once more, in an endless series. Why, then, would it not be possible, as Mr. Kahn of Cambridge has suggested with regard to an hypothetical limiting case, to employ one man on road-making and thereby give secondary employment to all the rest of the population? If it required, on the average, a month for the money spent in employing this one man to be spent again and for this increased spending to bring about increased income in the hands of others who will in turn spend it, then in the first month there would be spent 1 month's wages plus material costs, etc.; in the second month, two; in the third month, three; and so on.[4] Then the hiring of one road worker could absorb 2,000,000 unemployed, or any other number.

But (as Mr. Kahn did not trouble to point out, rightly regarding the entire case as fantastic) to absorb 2,000,000 unemployed in this way would take 2,000,000 months, or 166,666 years, during which time the Government must be financing the employment of this one road worker (and his descendents to 5,000 generations) by strictly inflationary financial methods, borrowing funds for the purpose which industry would not otherwise use, and continuing to borrow in excess of the budget of interest and debt repayments, by just the amount of the expenditures on account of this one worker.

When one considers the question of interest and repayments in connection with such an inflationary spending policy, it becomes clearly out of the question to project any estimate of its inflationary effect beyond, let us say, 10 years. And when one considers the condition that the funds borrowed by Government must be funds which would not otherwise be used by private industry, it becomes rather irrelevant to project the estimate of future stimulative effects beyond, let us say, the next industrial revival, which may come in 2 or 3 years.

It may be because this theoretical endless increase does not seem to correspond with experience that students of the subject have constructed theories of endlessly dwindling impulses, whose total effect does not go beyond a finite sum and is substantially reached in a comparatively short time. The leading exponent of a theory of this sort is Professor Keynes.[5] There are, in fact, two main theoretical approaches to this problem. One is based upon a series of successive receipts and spendings of income, in which not all of the increased receipts are spent. The other is based upon the approach via the volume of the cirulating medium and its "income-velocity" of circulation. These two approaches will be taken up in the two succeeding sections.

The two theories appear to yield different results. However, one may be sure that if each of them is regarded merely as a method of approach to the problem and is followed out as such until all of the complicating and conditioning factors are taken account of, results obtained by sound use of the two methods cannot well disagree, since each will ultimately have to take account of the facts and forces considered by the other. The disagreement in the preliminary formulations of these two theories is the result of the employment in each case of simplified assumptions which do not do full justice to the complexity of the facts; and especially the result of assuming that certain conditioning factors remain constant when these factors actually vary. This difference between the two formulations is not necessarily a contradiction, and by comparing the two a better idea may be obtained of the results which are actually to be expected.

C. Secondary Effects: the Successive-Spendings Approach

This approach is built upon the assumption that, out of an original dollar spent by Government in ways which involve a net addition to the total spendings of the community, only a certain part is respent by the recipient in ways which go to increase industrial activity within that same community. Of that fraction, only a fraction is spent again in the third cycle, and so on. If the fraction remained the same through these successive cycles (as it presumably would not do) then the result of the original spending by Government would be an endless series of further spendings, dwindling in size in such a way that the total sum to infinity would be a definite and finite quantity. For example, if only one-half of the dollar were so respent the first time, one-fourth the second time, and so on, then the total secondary effect arising from an original expenditure of $1 would be limited to 1 additional dollar, the great part of which would be realized by the time the money had circulated from consumer to producer and back to consumer four or five times.[6] The total effect, then, would be twice the amount of the original expenditure, which would then, to use Professor Keynes' and Mr. Kahn's terminology, be increased by a multiplier of two. If two-thirds of the dollar were respent each cycle, then the total effect would be $3 and the multiplier would be 3. If three-fourths were respent each time, the multiplier would be 4 and so on. This is graphically expressed in chart 1.

[5] See J. M. Keynes: The Means to Prosperity, London, 1933. See also R. F. Kahn: The Relation of Home Investment to Unemployment, Economic Journal, June 1931; Public Works and Inflation, Jour. Amer. Statistical Assn., March 1933. See also M. Mitnitzksy in Social Research, May 1934. Studies have been made within narrowly limiting assumptions by W. N. Loucks and Frank G. Dickinson. See Loucks, The Stabilization of Employment in Philadelphia, Philadelphia, 1931, pp. 161 ff., especially p. 166; and Dickinson, Public Construction and Cyclical Unemployment, Annals, Sup., September 1928. Mr. Loucks is dealing with effects in Philadelphia of local works only; hence the diffused effects on business outside Philadelphia constitute a very large leakage, and others are ignored. Dickinson deals with the effects of the spending of wages only, for the first secondary cycle only, on the assumption that they all go to manufacturing industries (these being the only ones with suitable pay-roll statistics). Neither of these two methods is appropriate to a comprehensive study.

[6] In speaking of the money as circulating, one is using a convenient figure of speech. No literal money needs to move through all these stages. What is thereby expressed is the process whereby the effect of an increased flow of money at one point is transmitted, causing an increased flow at another point.

No such mechanical formula can do justice to the many variable conditions affecting the problem.   In the first place, the only kind of expenditures which can work in this cumulative way are inflationary expenditures, those which represent a clear addition to the flow and not a mere transfer of spending from one person to another, such as happens when the Government spends the taxpayer's money which the taxpayer would otherwise have spent himself.   When large amounts of money are raised, it is never possible to be sure they represent a clear addition of this sort.   If Government borrows the money, someone lends it, and that someone may have less to spend. If the borrowings come partly out of credit inflation or out of savings which would otherwise stand idle, then just that part of the expenditures can have an expansive effect on industry.

In a depression, it may be quite easy at first to raise all the funds in an inflationary way, but as expansion proceeds, conditions change, and ultimately the limits on inflationary public borrowing make themselves felt.   At this point, if not before, further expenditures cease to have any effect in the way of cumulative expansion.   In addition to this limitation there is a more obvious one arising from the fact that inflationary expenditures can go on forever without defeating their own end by so weakening the credit of the Government as to depress industrial activity by the resulting loss of confidence on the part of business men.   The question which of these limitations will become effective first, depends on conditions.   Thus if a policy of inflationary spending starts on a huge scale from a starting point in which credit is already none too strong, the weakening of credit and confidence might set the effective limit on the policy.   Ordinarily, however, it appears that other factors would set a limit before this point of credit exhaustion was reached.

There may be cases where the spending of $1 brings about the spending, not of 1 nor of part of 1, but of 2 or more, in the second or third cycles.   This happens when the demand for goods calls forth a still larger demand for durable means of production, which is also financed in an inflationary way.   However, in time of depression, there is little chance of expenditures acting in this fashion.

Any attempt to estimate these secondary effects quantitatively by this method hinges on three main questions.   First, how much of the expenditure on public works is inflationary?   Second, how long is the cycle from the spending of increased money income by an ultimate recipient to the next resulting spending of increased income by the next ultimate recipient?   Third, how great are the "leakages" representing uses of this money which do not, or do not immediately, result in a stimulus to the actual volume of production?

As to the first question, it may fairly be assumed that, in a strongly marked depression, funds spent for public works will be borrowed, and the borrowings will not take capital which would otherwise be used by industry.[7]   At such a time, more savings are being offered than industry can find use for.   Later, as already pointed out, this may not be the case when industry revives.   Thus borrowings which the Government may carry out in November may conceivably not begin to limit the effective supply of industrial capital until the follow-

[7] 1. Dr. Carl Landauer, who has been studying the experience of Germany in financing public works, concludes that in that country the public borrowings utilized funds which would not otherwise have been used by private business.   Statement in paper read at meeting of econometric Society, Berkeley, June 1934.

ing August, or even later. If, however, the Government has taken all of the unused lending capacity of the credit system, then industry will not find any available to furnish a basis for the activities of revival, when revival is ready to take place. Some observers think that the credit system is in approximately this condition at present, and that the possibility of a spontaneous private revival has thus been forestalled and prevented by the Government's efforts. This does not seem to be true at present, as the banks have large surplus reserves; but the possibility is something to be closely watched, and represents a condition to be guarded against. If this condition is once reached, public spendings not only can have no further cumulative effects of a secondary sort, but no stimulative effects at all, primary or secondary. The conclusion is, then that expenditures financed by borrowing may be stimulative to substantially the full amount spent, so long as the borrowing stops materially short of the unused capacity of the credit system.

In computing the net increase in public spending due to public works, there is one offset to be deducted, resulting from the fact that, by increasing the volume of employment, Government avoids the necessity of paying a certain amount for relief. Even those who are not receiving relief from the Government may be receiving help from other private organizations or individuals or are living on their own reserves, and some of this private relief must be classed for our purposes as inflationary (reducing unused savings or increasing debts). The total amount of all of this cannot be exactly estimated, but an allowance of 25 percent of public works expenditures, representing relief of one sort or another which is made unnecessary, would seem to be a fair one.

The average relief payment per family as reported by the Federal Emergency Relief Administration in November 1933, was $18.22 per family per month.[8] The average percentage of expenditures representing avoidance of relief may be very roughly estimated at 30 percent for Civil Works Administration expenditures, 10 to 15 percent for Public Works Administration, 10 to 20 percent for Civil Conservation Corps, and possibly 5 to 10 percent for the diffused secondary expenditures resulting from these various primary ones. We may assume, then, that something like three-fourths of every dollar spent on public works at such a time represents a real added fiscal burden, beyond what would otherwise be assumed. But if the relief expenditures would also have had to be financed by borrowing, then they would also have had a stimulative effect upon business which would be very nearly identical in amount and character with the stimulative effect resulting from public works expenditures themselves. Thus the important thing is the total amount of expenditures financed by expansionary borrowing rather than the amount spent in any one particular way.

As to the period of circulation, it may be assumed that wages are spent, for the most part, within a week, and begin to result in increased wage payments to other workers in a fairly short period. Interest and dividend payments may be received, on the average, about 2 months after they are earned, but are slower in being spent. On this basis it would seem that an average cycle of 2 months would be a conservative estimate. This is a much shorter cycle than the

⁸ See article by Gertrude Springer in Survey Graphic, May 1934, p. 249.

cycle representing the average period of the flow of purchasing power from ultimate income recipient to ultimate income recipient as expressed in the circuit velocity or "income velocity" of money. This velocity has been estimated at approximately 1.6 per year by Prof. James W. Angell.[9] On this basis we should have a cycle of 7½ months, on the average, for money to flow from a consumer through all the exchanges involved in producing the goods he buys, and to get back to an ultimate consumer again. However, this velocity does not remain constant at 1.6 per year, and there is convincing evidence that it increases greatly with industrial revival and falls with industrial depression. In that case, an average velocity of 1.6 may be entirely consistent with a speeding up of business, such as would result from the transmission of the effect of an increase in incomes at a rate of six cycles per year. A fairly moderate increase in the total velocity of circulation of all means of payment, in response to the pressure created by the situation resulting from increased public spending, could easily take care of the requirements of the increased volume of business resulting. Thus it appears permissible to take provisionally a 2-month period to represent the time required for increased income to result in a secondary increase.

To avoid a misunderstanding which may result from comparisons between the figure of 6 cycles of secondary effects per year with 1.6 per year (the circuit velocity of money) it should be emphasized that the two are not quantities of the same order. The 6 cycles per year do not represent the velocity of circulation of anything, but rather the speed with which an increased velocity is transmitted through the economic system. To illustrate by a physical analogy, suppose the production of a commodity divided into 15 stages, each requiring 3 days, while 12 days' reserve supply of materials or intermediate products is on hand at each stage in addition to goods in process. Then there will be 7½ months' supply on reserve or in process in the whole system, and the average series velocity will be 1.6 per year. But it would take only 45 days for a unit of material to move through the series if it were not kept waiting in the reserve stocks. And, what is to the present purpose, if there were a sudden increase of demand for the final product (and if there were spare plant capacity at each stage) the speeding up of output could be transmitted back from stage to stage through the whole series, not in 7½ months but very possibly in 7½ days; indeed there is no physical impossibility in its happening in 7½ hours. This speed of transmission bears essentially the same relationship to the 7½-month period as does the 2-month cycle assumed in drawing chart 2.

Finally, as to the "leakages." One leakage consists of amounts spent for imported goods.[10] In Mr. Loucks' study with reference to the city of Philadelphia, all purchases from outside Philadelphia came in this class, and this represented a major part of all expenditures and constituted the dominant factor in his analysis, causing the secondary effects to shrink with extreme rapidity. For a country like the United States, 5 percent seems sufficient to deduct for this factor, under ordinary conditions of our foreign trade balance.

---

[9] See "Money, Prices and Production," Quar. Jour. of Econ., November 1933, p. 75, footnote. Prof. Alvin H. Hansen considers this figure too low for normal times, but possibly approximately correct for times of depression. The discrepancy between the two estimates may hinge on the inclusion or exclusion of savings deposits. Professor Pigou, in The Theory of Unemployment, has made an estimate of 3. Cf. A. H. Hansen, The Flow of Purchasing Power, in Economic Reconstruction, pp. 211–212, footnote.

[10] See discussions by Keynes, Kahn, and Loucks, already referred to.

Another leakage consists of savings which are not used to stimulate production other than what is already accounted for in the estimate now being made. In a time of depression, it may fairly be assumed that an addition to current savings would have no effect at all in stimulating actual expenditures for capital purposes, for the reason already given. Furthermore, for this purpose "savings" includes the repayment of debts by persons who have been living on credit resources of one sort or another. And when these resources have been heavily strained, the incentive to get back to a normal footing is so strong that it seems likely that an abnormally large percentage of increased income will go into savings of this sort. Twenty to 25 percent may be estimated as the leakage on this account, and even this may be too low in an extreme depression like the present. There may also be other deflationary uses of funds, such as liquidating standing inventories and replenishing weakened reserves. On the whole, a total leakage of about 33⅓ percent seems reasonable. There is, of course, the probability that the percentage of leakage will decrease as industrial conditions grow better, as individuals have less urgent need to get out of pressing debt, and as those with available savings find more opportunity to invest them in such ways that they will actually be spent for productive equipment. And it has already been noted that at the same time these same conditions that reduce the leakages also make it more difficult to raise money for public expenditures in genuinely inflationary ways. Thus, in a stage of early revival, instead of 75 cents out of every dollar spent representing actual inflation, only 50 cents may be of this character, while instead of a leakage of 33⅓ percent, the leakage may be reduced to 20 percent. The result would be to change the shape of the curve of secondary effects, reducing the first installment from 50 cents to 40 cents, but with less dwindling thereafter.

In treating savings as a leakage, under conditions of heavy depression, it is not necessarily implied that all of the savings made at such a time are completely idle. Some may be used in financing the increased production indicated, leakage being defined as a use of funds which does not increase production beyond what has already been accounted for in the formula. Underlying this is the idea that this amount of productive expansion will take place whether it utilizes these savings or not, but that the savings do not act as an originating cause of any further increase in activity. This question will be taken up more fully later.

Another factor which might be treated as a leakage, but may perhaps better be handled separately, is the amount of this added purchasing power which is absorbed in increasing prices rather than increasing the volume of production and real incomes. On this point it may suffice to say that, if a public-works program is so handled as to result in a material increase in prices, it will largely defeat its own purpose, expecially so far as it may increase the prices which go into costs of construction. The formulas and charts in this chapter refer to dollar volume of production.

Another conjectural factor is the effect of the program on private capital expenditures. Conceivably it might either increase them or diminish them. The increased demand for consumption goods might cause producers to make capital outlays which they would not otherwise make, though in a depression they would hardly expand their plants largely. On the other hand the very fact that the increase in consumers' expenditures is known to be due to public spending, on a basis which is certain to be temporary, may mean that private producers will not make capital outlays as readily as they would make them in response to the same amount of increased demand if it came from private sources. They are more likely to wait to see what happens when the Government spending falls off. Moreover, if the public-works program results in bidding up the costs of construction, it may actually prevent or retard private construction or private capital outlays which would otherwise have been made. If this happens on any considerable scale, it may completely neutralize the secondary effects of the public expenditures, or even more than neutralize them. Thus the secondary and tertiary effects may be extremely great or may be nothing at all, depending on conditions which cannot be reduced to a formula.

Another limit upon the secondary expansive effect of public spending may consist in the fact that the funds taken from the credit system by the governmental outlays, while they were not needed at the time by private industry, may come to be needed later when private industry expands. When this happens, the expansion may be limited by the previous drafts which the Government has made upon the reserve lending power of the credit system.

Another more general and intangible limiting factor consists in the fear of unchecked inflation, which may cause businessmen to be unduly timid about expansions which they might otherwise undertake. This may not be a logical reaction to the prospect of inflation, since business men might be able to secure expansion of productive facilities at a lower money cost if they carried it out before inflation rather than after. But logic probably has comparatively little to do with the actual reactions of businessmen when faced with a prospect of a generally disturbing character, and such a prospect is likely to have an actually retarding effect.

If these latter disturbing conditions are ignored and we go on the assumption of a 2-month cycle and a 33⅓ percent leakage, the secondary effects of increased Government expenditures can be calculated with exactness, as indicated in the accompanying charts. In chart I the series of rectangles of diminishing height represents the successive secondary expenditures resulting from an original expenditure by Government, which is represented by the first of these rectangles. The expenditure is assumed to be of a kind representing a true net expansion, or else only the expansionary portion should be considered. The total area of all these rectangles is finite and is equal to three times the area of the first rectangle, indicating that an original expenditure is followed by secondary effects totaling twice as much, and is thus ultimately multiplied by 3. This is the ratio of which Keynes speaks as the "multiplier", representing the expansive power of expenditures of this sort. It will be noted that the greater part of this multiplier is realized during the first year.

If public expenditures go on in this way indefinitely, then the ultimate total expansive effect realized during a given 2-month period would be represented by the original expenditure made during that period, plus the first installment of the secondary effect of the last previous original expenditure, plus the second installment of the secondary effect of the one before that, and so on. Thus it will be

the sum of a series of the same character as the series representing
the successive effects of a single public expenditure. If the factors
remained constant, the two series would be identical in amount, both
being equal to three times the original expenditure, and the same
multiplier appearing in two forms.   Thus the total effect of spending
a million dollars every 2 months would ultimately amount to an
increase in the national income of $3,000,000 every 2 months.   This
would happen only if the expenditures were continued at' a uniform
rate and maintained their expansionary character while the leakages
remained constant.   Actually, these factors would be certain to vary
and hence the ultimate effect would not be exactly the same as the

CHART I

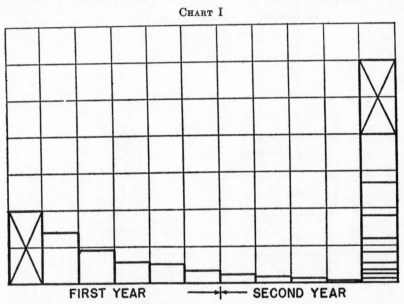

FIRST YEAR   ——+|—— SECOND YEAR

Assumption: Leakage=⅓, multiplier=3.
⊠ represents original expenditure; other areas represent secondary effects.
At left, successive effects of one expenditure.
At right, simultaneous effect of long-continued series of uniform expenditures, leakage remaining constant.
On this condition the two areas are equal, each three times the original expenditure.

total effect resulting from the first expenditure, but it would be built
up in the same way, consisting of one installment of original expenditure, plus the first installment of the secondary effect of a previous
installment of original expenditure, and so on.
The total effect is represented in chart II, which shows not merely
the dwindling successive effects of each original expenditure, but also
the building up of the total effect as these expenditures continue,
assuming the governing factors to remain constant.   On this basis
the effect of increased Government expenditures at the rate of
$1,000,000 a month would be, during the first year, $12,000,000 of
primary expenditures and approximately $13,000,000 of secondary
expenditures, after which the secondary expenditures would rapidly
approach $24,000,000 a year as a limit.   If the tendency to rising
prices were successfully combated, this would mean a very substantial
stimulus to industry.

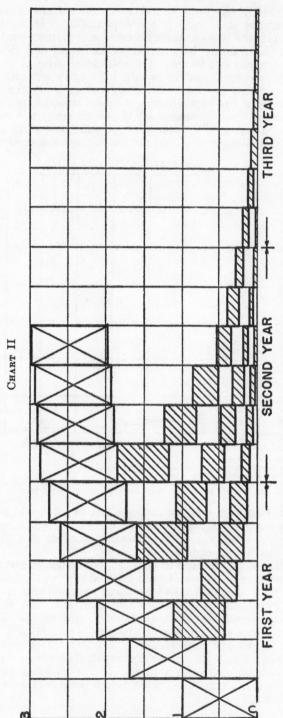

CHART II

Units of expenditure, at left; 1 represents $750,000, or $1,000,000 minus relief expenditure avoided.
☒ represents inflationary portion of Government outlays.
Other spaces represent effects of successive spendings (not separated beyond first period of second year).

Even the cases coming back to various governmental bodies from the increase in business would neutralize a material fraction of the original outlay—possibly as much as 25 cents out of the original dollar spent. Adding to this the amount of relief outlays avoided would bring the total reduction in the net cost to Government up to an amount whose general range of magnitude may be indicated by a figure of 40 to 50 percent (Kahn estimates 50 percent). This is under the most favorable conditions and hinges on a substantially complete avoidance of price inflation. This stimulus to business lasts only as long as the Government continues going into debt to make these inflationary expenditures. When these expenditures cease the effect tapers off very rapidly, if the original percentage of leakage continues to apply.

The assumption that conditions governing the leakages remain unchanged for this length of time, is as already noted, unrealistic. Actually, as incomes become more liberal, people will tend to spend more of the added incomes, thus reducing the amount of the leakage. Also if business begins to revive, the past leakages will come back into active use. At the same time, this creates a condition in which it will ultimately be harder for the Government to find, and acquire by borrowing, funds which would otherwise remain idle. These stimulative forms of expenditure would become more difficult to make without outright currency inflation.

It may be worth considering the reasons for thinking that the leakages would be greater in the early stages and less at later stages. As Keynes has suggested, when unemployed workers first get a job, they have incurred debts or have back taxes to pay, and all they can spare out of their increased income is likely to go into paying off such claims. Thus the leakage at first might well be over one-half of the increased income, instead of one-third, only decreasing when the most threatening debts are paid and some degree of confidence established. Thus the curve would rise more slowly at first and then more rapidly in the later stages. If the workers were keenly alive to what might happen if public works came to an end without establishing private recovery, they might continue to save much the same abnormal percentage of their increased income. Such an attitude is probably not typical. Nevertheless, a more conservative estimate of secondary effects up to the point where substantial private recovery becomes manifest, might be based on leakage of 50 percent, in which case $1,000,000 a month of increased Government spending would mean, in the first year, $12,000,000 of primary and slightly over $8,000,000 of secondary expenditures. Afterward, the percentage of leakage would presumably decrease. It is interesting to note that Keynes, with these considerations in mind, has estimated the leakage for the United States at one-third, in a paper delivered after the present writer had independently made the same estimate.

The particular constants assumed in drawing this chart are, of course, only estimates and it will be worth while to note how much difference it makes if different constants are used. Chart III shows a number of different curves which might result if the period of circulation of the increased income were shorter or longer than 2 months, and if the leakages were more or less than one-third. In this chart, curve A represents the conditions assumed in chart II, while the other curves represent other conceivable conditions. The shaded area covers what appears to be the most probable range within which the results are likely to fall during the first year. It is drawn on the assumption that the leakage will be greater at first and then will decrease.

As for the other governing factors arising from the state of increasing or decreasing confidence which have already been discussed, they naturally cannot be reduced to quantitative terms. In terms of these factors almost anything might happen after the first year, and therefore the uncertainty of the results becomes much greater. Therefore this shaded area is not carried beyond the end of that year.

CHART III

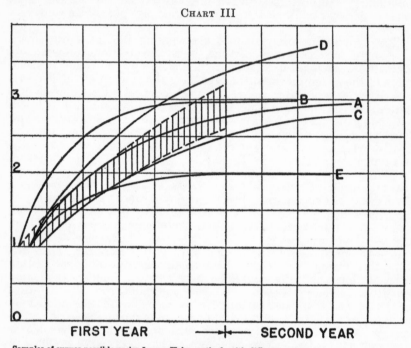

FIRST YEAR ————+|+——— SECOND YEAR

Samples of curves possible under Joynes-Kahn method, with different constants.
Line OA shows secondary effects, 2-month cycle, leakage ⅓, multiplier, 3.
Line OB shows secondary effects, 1-month cycle, leakage ⅓, multiplier, 3.
Line OC shows secondary effects, 3-month cycle, leakage ⅓, multiplier, 3.
Line OD shows secondary effects, 2-month cycle, leakage ¼, multiplier, 4.
Line OE shows secondary effects, 2-month cycle, leakage ½, multiplier, 2.
Shaded area, most probable range for first year; governing factors no longer assumed constant.

In general, the indicated probability is that, if the Government spends $12,000,000 during the year, the total secondary effects during that same time are likely to amount to approximately another $12,000,000.

The assumption that the leakages decrease has some interesting effects on the character of the curves. It means that the total effect of government spending is no longer limited to a given finite multiple of the original amount, but may increase indefinitely until brought to an end by some of the less tangible conditions of credit and confidence which have already been noted. It also has an effect on the promptness with which the stimulation of business activity falls off after the public expenditures giving rise to it have come to an end. In chart II, these effects were shown to fall off with extreme rapidity.

Under conditions of decreasing leakages, together with a possible return to circulation of the idle funds representing past leakages, this falling off in the effect would be much slower, and the stimulation would last longer after the public expenditures ceased to be made. In fact, under favorable conditions, it might continue more or less indefinitely. In short, if business were caught in a vicious circle of paralysis, and public expenditures lifted it out of this condition, normal activity might then continue without further public stimulus, though this outcome is far from certain.

The question of what happens to the funds which have been designated as leakages is a somewhat subtle one. The obvious assumption is that they lie idle, but this assumption is not necessarily involved in the processes and results shown in the charts. If it were, it would imply a rather inconceivable condition, since there would be a progressively increasing accumulation of idle funds, which would soon be going on at a rate which could not be supposed to continue. What is really involved in the theory underlying these diagrams is, not that the funds representing the leakages lie idle, but that they are not used in ways which increase the total volume of business by more than has been already accounted for in the diagrams.

In assuming that one increase of income brings about another increase of income in a period as short as 2 months, whereas the average circuit velocity of money, reckoned at 1.6 per year, implies a period of 7½ months, we are assuming that the volume of business increases faster than could be accounted for by the existing volume of purchasing media and their existing circuit velocity. In order to finance this rate of increase, either the circuit velocity must increase or business must acquire more circulating media, or both. Thus a certain amount of the savings which we have reckoned as leakage (or, for that matter, all of it during the early stages) may take effect in increased credit used by business in financing this expansion without bringing about any increase in the volume of business beyond what the formula already calls for. During approximately the first year and a half (see chart VI) the total amount of otherwise idle funds resulting from the leakages would not be sufficient to finance the indicated expansion of business at the existing rate of circuit velocity of funds, and an increase in the circuit velocity will be called for, even if all of the so-called "leakages" are taken and used by business. Subsequently, if the leakages continued at a substantial rate, this condition would be reversed, but by the time this happened, the total volume of business expansion would have passed under the control of factors not accounted for in these mathematical formulas. Thus the formula, if not carried beyond its proper limits of time, which would seem to be not more than about 12 months, does not call for an impossible progressive piling up of idle funds.

It may be worth reiterating that these diagrams and calculations have to do with the monetary volume of business solely. They make no attempt to show how much of this monetary volume is absorbed by increased prices. Professor Mitchell's studies have shown that in the very first stage of a revival, production is likely to increase somewhat before prices rise. In any case, at such a time, supply of goods is likely to be very elastic, making possible a relatively large increase in physical output with a relatively small increase in prices. This, of course, may be modified to some extent by governmental policy, especially in the field of prices of construction materials, for which the Government becomes one of the principal purchasers when it undertakes a large public works program during a depression.

D. Secondary Effects: the Approach via Volume and Velocity of Circulating Medium [11]

Those who are studying problems of business fluctuations from the monetary angle tend to be distrustful of the results of the type of theorizing followed by Keynes in dealing with this problem, and prefer, naturally, to treat the problem in terms of the volume of circulating media (including bank deposits) and the average rapidity with which these circulating media go through the entire series of exchanges which lie between one spending of the funds by an ultimate consumer and the next spending by an ultimate consumer. The circuit can be otherwise described and broken into at other points to define the cycle, but the essential fact is the ratio between the total amount of circulating media in the country and the total net volume of production, or the total national income, which those media of exchange serve to finance. This will be called in this study the "circuit velocity of money", understanding by "money" for this purpose all forms of media of exchange. This has been estimated by Professor Angell as varying from 1.5 to 1.68 per year, for the years 1919–28, inclusive, per year, and 1.6 is taken to represent the value in these circulations, giving an average cycle of 7½ months.

If this velocity remains uniform, then stimulation of business requires an increase in the volume of money, and the government expenditures, in order to produce a stimulative effect, must be inflationary in the literal sense of increasing the volume of the circulating media. In Keynes' treatment, there is no such necessity— indeed there is no such necessity even by this second method except as it is assumed that velocity remains constant. And the evidence indicates that velocity varies greatly, decreasing with business depressions and increasing with revivals.

However, if the velocity is taken as constant, then the effect of a given public expenditure involving an increase in the volume of money is expressed in chart IV. This may be compared with chart I, representing the same sort of sequence as analyzed under the other method. In this second case there is no dwindling of the effects with time. A given volume of money poured into the circulation continues to circulate and to maintain the increase it has brought about in the total financial volume of the national dividend at the rate of 1.6 times its own amount every year, or an amount equal to itself every 7½ months. Thus the "multiplier", in Keynes' terms, would be infinity limited only by time. The only essential feature which this very much simplified chart does not show is the distributed lag by which the successive effects follow the original impulse.

If government spending of the same sort continues, the cumulative effects are very roughly shown in chart V, which may be compared with chart II showing the effects as analyzed by the other method. In chart V it is assumed that a given expenditure goes on for 7½

---

[11] The only published example of this approach which the writer has encountered is by Vernon A. Mund: Prosperity Reserves of Public Works, Annals, May 1930, part II, pp. 15–19. Dr. Mund seems to use a mixture of the two approaches. He deals with wages alone, assumes a circuit velocity of 5 per year and a leakage of 50 percent, not compounded, thus deducing secondary effects in 1 year equal to twice the original expenditure.

months, after which its full aftereffects begin and go on indefinitely, while another installment of original expenditures also begins.   Thus, the total effect is shown as climbing upward by steps like a flight of stairs.   Actually, of course, these steps would be smoothed out as in the line AA .   One essential point in this method of approach is that there is no finite limit to the total amount of the ultimate effect,

CHART IV

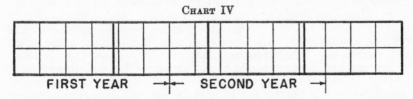

FIRST YEAR   →┼←   SECOND YEAR   →┤

either of one expenditure, or of the series of expenditures.   The effects go on indefinitely.   Production goes on increasing until something outside the formula stops it.   A given amount of added media of exchange injected into the economic system goes on circulating at the rate of 1.6 per year, so long as it remains in circulation at all.

CHART V

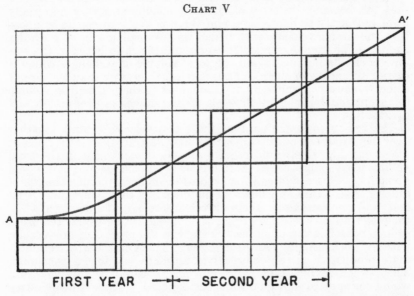

FIRST YEAR   →┼←   SECOND YEAR   →┤

In utilizing this first approximation—for none of these formulae are more than first approximations—as an approach to the problem of the actual effects of public expenditures, one of the crucial points is obviously what is likely to happen to the velocity of circulation. On this point the only real doubt is as to the short-time movements of circuit velocity during the shorter and milder business cycles, because the statistical estimates of national income which are necessary to a calculation of circuit velocity are available only by years. As far as they go, they seem to indicate some movement in harmony with the business cycle, but with a possible lag.   As to the longer and larger movement involved in the current depression, a cursory inspection of the figures for total bank deposits and volumes of money in circulation, as given in the Federal Reserve Bulletin, compared with the figures for national income (National Income, pp. 929–32, Bureau of Foreign and Domestic Commerce) makes it perfectly clear that from 1929–32 there was a decline in circuit velocity of approximately 33⅓ percent. Thus, if the circuit velocity was 1.6 in 1929, it was almost certainly less than 1.1 in 1932. This decline in circuit velocity corresponded to a decline of more than 45 percent in the total national income. On this basis one is justified in assuming that any stimulation which produces, let us say, a 15-percent increase in the national income would be accompanied by something like a 10-percent increase in the circuit velocity of money. Or a return of circuit velocity to normal would provide adequate means of handling a 50-percent increase in the national income from its 1932 level, without any increase in volume of media of exchange. Such an increase in production would call into existence a larger volume of bank deposits, whether government expenditures directly accomplished this or not.

As for the shorter cyclical movements, statistical estimates indicate that the exchange velocity of circulation fluctuates very materially from prosperity to depression, and there is every reason to suppose that the circuit velocity with which we are dealing follows a similar course. The exchange velocity represents the ratio between the volume of circulating media and the total volume of exchanges which is carried by means of them. Thus it is much greater than the circuit velocity, since it requires money exchanges to finance a given volume of the national dividend through all the stages of production and distribution.

The reason for thinking that these two velocities move together over the period of a business cycle is chiefly the fact that, if they do not move together, this would require a cyclical movement in the total volume of exchanges called for in financing a given amount of national dividend. This would call for cyclical changes in the movements of industrial structure and business methods of a sort which there is no reason to suppose exists. If circuit velocity remained unchanged while exchange velocity shrank during a depression, this would require a sudden consolidation of successive steps in the process of production, whereby goods would pass through fewer hands on the way from ultimate production of raw' material to ultimate sale to the consumer. Then, when revival came, this movement would be reversed, and would continue to shift backward and forward. There is no evidence that any such continual shift takes place.[12]

If it is true, as indicated by the above considerations, that business revival carries with it a large increase in the circuit velocity of money, then we should expect Government expenditures to produce a more rapid rise in production than is shown in the line of chart 5A and if, as business activity increased in response to this effect, subsequent Government expenditures were to a smaller and smaller extent financed by actual increases in the circulating medium, then we should expect this

---

[12] Prof. James W. Angell has discussed the relationship between these 2 types of velocity in his article, Money, Prices and Production, Quarterly Journal of Economics, November 1933, pp. 43–46, 75. On the latter page he indicates that movements of the exchange velocity over short periods can be used to interpolate figures for the short-time movements of circuit velocity, on the assumption that the 2 move together.

line to show a decreasing upward slope. By taking account of these factors, the straight line increase, representing the first approximation by the second method, is modified in the general direction of the curve of decreasing slope which represented the first approximation by the first method. And since there were general considerations pointing toward a modification of this curve in the general direction of a straight line, it would seem that the results of the two approaches might come together if all the modifying factors were known and fully taken account of.

In chart VI the results of these two approaches are compared on the same scale. Here the area below the line 1 on the chart may be

CHART VI

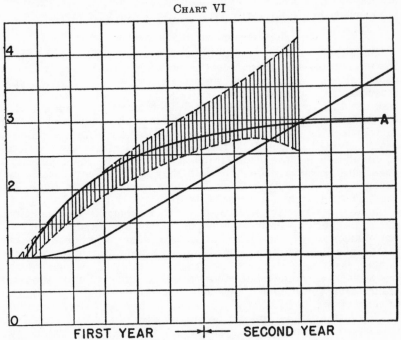

Line A, secondary effects, Keynes's formula, 2-month cycle, leakage ½, multiplier 3.
Line B, secondary effects, uniform income-velocity of money=1.6 per year.
Shaded area, most probable range, as in chart III, extended to indicate increased uncertainty after first year.

taken to represent a given volume of continuing public expenditures, and the sloping lines to represent the supplementary effects. Line A represents the results by the Keynes method, unmodified, and line B the results by the circuit velocity method, unmodified. By "unmodified" it is meant that the governing constants remain unchanged. The shaded area represents, as in chart III, the range within which it seemed most probable that the actual results would fall, when considered from the standpoint of the Keynes approach. In this chart this area is continued 6 months further, showing an increasing margin of doubt as to the probable results. For instance, if the stimulus to business resulting from public expenditures caused private business to start making capital outlays, the curve might turn upward. Or if fear of inflation or increased construction costs had a paralysing effect on private business expenditures, the curve might turn downward.

In view of what has just been said about the likelihood of increased velocity of circulation resulting from revival, and of a possible subsequent decrease in the percentage of Government expenditures which involve actual additions to the circulating medium, it seems that the modifications which need to be made in line B might easily bring it within the shaded area which represents modifications originally made from line A. In any case, the difference between the lower portion of the shaded area and line B, as it stands, is not a very large one when one thinks in terms of the enormous uncertainties attendant upon any attempt to predict the further results of any economic policy whatever. The two unmodified lines intersect after approximately 1 year and 4 months, and beyond that, prediction is too uncertain to be worth putting into quantitative terms.

E. Differences and Attempted Reconciliation

While there may not be any logically necessary difference between the two approaches, there seems to be a very real difference of attitude between the theorists who follow them. This shows itself especially in the attitude toward velocity of circulation. Keynes assumes this to be a passive factor, automatically adjusting itself to whatever is necessary in order to finance the volume of transactions, which he conceives to be governed by the elements which he describes. Other monetary theorists tend to assume that velocity of circulation is, to a considerable extent at least, an independent governing or casual factor. While they do not deny that it may change, they do tend to look for very specific causes tending to produce such a change and acting directly on the circuit velocity of money, not merely affecting it via increasing the volume of production. The implication of this position is that circuit velocity will not change unless something happens to make people want to turn their funds over faster, aside from having more business to transact.[13] From this standpoint, in its more rigorous forms, the argument that Government spending might increase circuit velocity, simply as a result of increasing the volume of business to be done, would be thrown out of court; it would be dismissed as putting the cart before the horse.

This last attitude appears definitely wrong. Circuit velocity of money is not an independent entity like the velocity of sound: It is a ratio between total production (or total income) and volume of circulating media. Its long-run average value is governed by habit and convenience as to balances kept relative to volume of business done, and by the structure of the economy as to number of exchange transactions involved in a completed cycle of production. But fluctuations around this long-run average, or sudden departures from it (which are the present point at issue), are almost always produced by more or less independent changes in one or the other term of the ratio, either volume of business demanding to be transacted or volume of media, when these fail to respond proportionately to movements in volume of business. Therefore to explain an increase in circuit velocity by an increase in volume of business is not out of order and is not putting the cart before the horse. The only question that need be asked is whether the change in velocity, which these conditions call for, is within its probable limits of variation. And

---

[13] This assumes what has already been said as to the reasons why circuit velocity and exchange velocity tend to move in harmony.

even these limits are elastic under extraordinary conditions. The war drove the circuit velocity of money up to 1.8 in 1918, and the present depression has reduced it to the neighborhood of 1, though its ordinary range of short-time fluctuations covers only one-tenth of this extreme range, so far as indicated by yearly estimates.[14]

On this basis the conditions described by Keynes and Kahn furnish a sufficient cause of increased circuit velocity of money, simply because they cause an increased volume of business without a proportionate increase in volume of means of payment. But without relying on this reasoning alone, still it seems that the nature of the process can be seen to tend toward increased circuit velocity.

Assuming that incomes are spent within the time limits already suggested, business finds itself faced with an effective demand for goods beyond what it is producing. If it has goods on hand it will fill the orders and immediately undertake to produce on an increased scale in order to replenish its stocks and keep production level with sales. This means an immediate increase in orders for materials and intermediate products, resulting in an immediate attempt by the producers of these products to speed up in the same way. While it may take a year or more for goods to pass through all the stages of production from ultimate raw material to final product, it may not take more than a week for the increased activity to work its way back along the same chain of processes and producers and to stimulate the production of the most ultimate raw materials. Agricultural products, governed by the crop seasons, would, of course, constitute an exception. Here the results of increased demand would simply be an immediate drawing down of the very considerable stocks which are always on hand.

All of these activities call for payments. If business has sufficient funds to make these payments, it will joyfully make them. In a depression, the ratio of cash balances to volume of business becomes larger than normal (another way of saying that exchange velocity is low, and with it circuit velocity also). These balances are kept, not employed to normal capacity, because nothing better offers. When something does offer, they will be promptly used, and an increase in rapidity of circulation will naturally result. If a particular business does not have sufficient funds, it will try to borrow them, and in that case will call into active use some of the otherwise idle funds which have been designated as leakages in the Keynes approach to the problem. Or if a business has sufficient funds to make the payments, but not sufficient to make them without drawing down its balances lower than seems desirable, then, again, it will try to borrow, but even if it fails it will not cease to do the increased volume of business. And there is nothing in this process to indicate a serious drawing down or exhausting of the total volume of balances possessed by business as a whole, even though that might happen at certain points, and there might be some net shifting of balances from business to personal accounts. Most of the funds will circulate within the business community; using them faster will not exhaust them, and business as a whole will always have funds available to make payments. These considerations seem to furnish ample cause for an increase in the velocity of circulation.

---

[14] In Angell's estimates, already cited, the largest short fluctuation aside from the World War, or the current economic crisis, was from 1.50 in 1922 to 1.58 in 1923.

By the time revival is well established, the proportion between business balances and volume of sales will presumably be restored to normal by a process in which increased volume of business is handled partly by increased velocity and partly by increased business borrowings which increase the volume of "money" in the form of bank deposits. This tends to an interesting conclusion—interesting as setting aside the key assumption with which this approach to the problem started. This conclusion is that there is no absolute necessity at any stage of the process for government outlays to take the form of an increase in the supply of purchasing media. If the attitude here taken toward changes in velocity is correct—and of that the writer has no doubt—this necessity disappears. No initial increase in purchasing media is necessary; and any increase which may ultimately be necessary can be furnished by the borrowings of private business. The original stimulus from government can equally well take the shape of setting in motion idle funds, and so increasing the flow of incomes. In short, we come back to the position taken by Keynes, that it makes no essential difference to the stimulative effects produced whether the initial expenditure by government is inflationary in the sense of increasing the volume of media of payment, or only expansionary in the sense of increasing the total flow of incomes. The increased flow of incomes is the essential thing.

If this difference between the two approaches to the problem is disposed of, another remains, namely, that under this second approach, the aftereffects of public spending have no inherent tendency to dwindle away but rather tend to continue indefinitely, so long as money times normal circuit velocity is sufficient to sustain it.[15] But we have seen that something very like this may happen under the Keynes-Kahn approach, if the "leakages" become very small before public spendings come to an end. The most favorable possible outcome is a revival of private capital construction which will itself support an increase in the volume of business without further aid from Government spending. If this happens, the problem solves itself, and the question of what brings the movement to an end turns into the question of what sets a limit on an ordinary private business revival. Presumably one of the chief factors in the building up of private productive capacity to a point at which further additions are not justified by the demand.

A less favorable outcome would be the engendering in business of a fear of inflation, the effects of which would neutralize the benefits from public spending. In this case, the attempt to lift business until it could carry itself along, would have failed. It would be necessary then to follow a deflationary policy, balancing budgets as nearly as possible, and waiting for business itself to revive under the stimulus of a need for capital to replace obsolescent units, and a prospect of profits at reduced cost levels. Between these two outcomes lie a number of intermediate possibilities. Rising costs of construction might retard private revival. Or if private revival began to occur, it might require sufficient funds to make it impossible for government to borrow without thereby taking funds away from private uses. Either of these conditions might put an end to the secondary stimulative effects of public spending. Whatever the

---

[15] By this is meant, for example, that if a given amount of expansionary public spending has taken place and has come to an end, leaving more means of payment in circulation, and increasing the national income, the national income will tend to hold this gain indefinitely, remaining constant at the increased rate.

outcome might be, and whatever different factors might bring the stimulus to an end, it seems clear that these factors will lie outside the range of either of the formulas which have here been used as first approximations. These formulas appear useful as approaches to an understanding of the earlier stages of the process, and of these earlier stages only.

F. Recent Experience in the United States

Any attempt to trace statistically the effect of the present public-works policy in the United States is extremely difficult, on account of the many other policies affecting business and employment which have been going on at the same time. Enthusiasts for the National Recovery Administration are inclined to claim credit for the major part of the increase in employment as due to the provisions of that part of the National Industrial Recovery Act. In trying to untangle the two groups of effects, it will be necessary to distinguish between stimulation of the total amount of production and of incomes, on the one hand, and changes in the distribution of incomes, accompanied by a policy of work sharing, on the other.

The main effect of the National Recovery Administration codes has been to spread a given volume of work among a larger number of workers, and to call for a larger volume of money payment for this work, at the expense, in the first instance, of profits and, to some extent, in the second instance, of consumers who have had to pay higher prices. While it may have had some effect in stimulating the total volume of business, by shifting income from profits, which are spent relatively slowly, to wages, which are spent quickly, that has not been its main effect, and even that may have been neutralized by other elements in its incidence. Expenditures on public works, on the other hand, have definitely carried an increase in the total volume of production.

In point of time, it is useless to try to estimate inductively the effects of increased public works spending prior to the end of the recession in business which came in the fall of 1933. This recession was not due directly to either the public works policy or the codes, but mainly to the fact that the boom which lasted from March to July was of a speculative, exaggerated, and temporary character which could not have any other outcome than a prompt recession. Furthermore, a considerable part of the increased employment directly due to the codes took effect while this recession was going on. Thus observations beginning with the end of this autumn recession may be considered to record, in the main, the results of public spending rather than the results of the introduction of the codes.

The effect of the codes upon hours is difficult to trace precisely, because it is combined with the effect of increasing and diminishing business activity. The index of weekly hours increased from about 98 in March to 113 in June and July of 1933, and then declined to approximately 90 at the end of the year, rising again to 96 in March 1934.[16] Thus the effect of the codes has largely been to prevent weekly hours from rising with increasing volume of business as they would otherwise have done. There was already much part-time distributed somewhat unevenly among different industries, due to the depression itself, and the more evenly distributed shortening of hours resulting from the codes has largely been substituted for this previous part-time.

---

[16] Monthly Labor Review, May 1934, p. 1020.

Professor Keynes's calculations of stimulative loan expenditures by the Federal Government (other sources being unimportant) since the 1933 autumn recession, are as follows, in millions of dollars, the general average through September being estimated at approximately one hundred millions per month: [17]

	Per month
3-month moving average centering on August 1933	$102
3-month moving average centering on September 1933	123
3-month moving average centering on October 1933	158
3-month moving average centering on November 1933	231
3-month moving average centering on December 1933	369
3-month moving average centering on January 1934	422
3-month moving average centering on February 1934	435
3-month moving average centering on March 1934	348
3-month moving average centering on April 1934	311

These figures represent a typical outlay of something like 11 percent of the total national income, after the program had gotten well under way. As the deficit expenditures at the beginning of the period represented something like 3 percent of the national income, the net increase was assumed by Mr. Keynes to be approximately 8 percent of the national income. His statements of the corresponding increases in industrial production, employment and pay rolls, department store sales, car loadings, and other significant items, run from 15 to 17 percent, indicating an expansion approximately double the amount of the public expenditures of an inflationary sort. This lies within the range of what might be accounted for according to his own method of computation, during this period of time, if leakages ran between one-half and one-third. In chart 3, for example, the lowest line rises to approximately double the amount of the original expenditure within a period of 8 months. This increase in the total financial volume of business has, in the main, represented an increase in physical volume also. During the time covered by Mr. Keynes's figures the amount chargeable to increased prices was 3 percent.

These figures are not conclusive, and may be modified by current figures at any moment. They do not prove that the whole of the existing revival is due to governmental expenditures alone. What they do indicate is that if the stimulative effect of public spending is as large as has been estimated in this discussion, then there is little or no evidence of any revival in business at present beyond what the public expenditures themselves would account for. Even on the basis of the unmodified velocity-of-circulation approach, which gives the lowest answer of any for the 8-month period, something like seven-tenths of the total revival would be accounted for by the effects of public expenditures. If there is a conclusion to be drawn from this, it would seem to be that we have no proof at present of an independent business revival of any magnitude. Inasmuch as support of business by public expenditures cannot go on forever, it appears that the most vital consideration in the present stage of affairs is, not so much to continue or to increase these public expenditures, although that may be necessary in the absence of private revival, but to see to it that conditions favorable to an independent private revival are cultivated and that any obstacles which may exist are removed.

---

[17] The figure of $100,000,000 is not published. The 3-month moving averages were published on the editorial page, New York Times, July 7, 1934, being there designated by the last month of each 3-month period instead of the central month as in the above table.

A. Contraction of Expenditures in the General Budget While Public Works Are Expanding

One outstanding illustration of the contradictions involved in our present policy is the fact that, because the Nation is producing less wealth than usual, it is now building more warships, while for the same reason it is cutting down its work of education. We may need more warships, but we also need more and better school teachers. And there is nothing in our present state of national impoverishment to make us need warships more, or education less. The treatment of these two branches of expenditure is not the result of a unified policy, but of different policies followed by different units of government. But these policies take effect on the economic life of one nation, and constitute a distribution of its efforts, the incongruity of which needs no argument. The reasons lie in the fact that one branch of government has larger credit resources and stands ready to use them, and warships happen to fall in its field and not education. Also durable assets are conventionally accepted as a more appropriate basis for borrowing than intangible current services, though they may offer no better security for repayment of the debt. Neither consideration is pertinent to the problem of distributing the country's efforts and resources in such a way as to do the greatest possible good to the Nation as a whole. Expansion and retrenchment need to be coordinated on a national basis.

As has already been pointed out, governments may retrench by cutting rates of pay of public employees, by reducing their hours, or by reducing the number employed. The economies made may take the form of consolidations of departmental work or other adjustments which do not reduce or impair services rendered, or they may mean a reduction of service.

If salaries are cut only to the extent that costs of living have fallen, there is little to be said; the real purchasing power distributed by government has not been reduced. If cuts go further than this, there is a reduction of purchasing power distributed which serves to nullify to just that extent the effects of any increase in distribution of purchasing power which may take place in special sections of the Budget, such as public works. The direct effect may not be nullified as to actual numbers directly employed, but the secondary effects on employment in general are nullified. The most obvious nullifying effect takes place when the number of employees engaged in regular current services is reduced.

This amounts to laying off one set of workers in order to hire another set, and decreasing the distribution of purchasing power to one group in order to increase the distribution to another. It obviously neutralizes the effects of increases in public works and is, in general, not a defensible economic policy. The main justification for expanded public works begins after the necessary current services of government have been provided for.

1. It has already been pointed out that the early proposals for the use of public works as an antidote to business fluctuations, presup-

posed maintenance of the regular governmental services. It was precisely because these latter are the things which cannot usefully be made to fluctuate with business conditions, that public works were picked out as the element best suited to take the fluctuations. There is, in general, more damage resulting from cutting down necessary current services than from postponing the least urgent part of a public-works program.

2. Some may regard such an emergency as an opportunity to apply pressure to squeeze down unduly swollen governmental budgets of current services. But while there are wastes, those who think that government in general renders too many services are wrong. Desirable pruning requires much discrimination, and not such a blanket cutting of departmental appropriations as takes place under conditions like the present.

3. What has actually happened is rather chaotic. Some services were cut from departmental budgets and put back through the Civil Works Administration. This included special forms of education, together with a considerable amount of regular school teaching, and numerous services of investigation and research. This served to mitigate, but not to eliminate, the serious effect of the depression in cutting down the funds available for these services. Some very useful bits of work were done for which there would ordinarily not have been room in governmental budgets, but this hardly balances the damage done to educational and health budgets and other vitally necessary services. There is a natural reason for not using Federal funds to support State and local deficits on current services. This, however, is a matter of fiscal expediency rather than of sound national economy. If States are to be aided at all, it seems that the arguments for aiding them in capital outlays and not in current services are not conclusive. This question will be taken up at greater length in the chapter on the financial aspects of a public-works policy.

4. The cutting of current budgets fits in with the principle that at least the regular budget should be balanced, and deficits be confined to works of enduring value (hence properly chargeable to capital account) or to outlays occasioned by a depression emergency and hence (presumably) temporary. The validity of this principle will be more fully discussed in the chapter on fiscal problems. It undoubtedly served its purpose in overcoming some of the resistance to enlarged spending, at a time when the unbalanced budget was creating considerable anxiety and there was a strong movement toward attempting to balance it. However, once this critical step was taken, people very quickly showed a tendency to ignore this somewhat arbitrary division of the budget, and talked in terms of total deficits. On the whole, this principle seems not to be a proper basis for an enduring fiscal policy.

5. Another criterion for determining whether particular activities should be curtailed or not, and one which is more pertinent from the standpoint of national efficiency, is the criterion of the service value of the works or services in question. In general, this argues for maintaining the regular current services of government before expanding public works, and certainly before expanding them beyond the limits of grade A projects. As has already been pointed out, losses sustained through curtailing such essential services as those of health and education are more hopelessly irretrievable than losses

sustained through postponement of public works, even those of grade A. Thus, if it were a choice between curtailing public works and curtailing such services as education, this criterion would argue for curtailing public works first, assuming that fiscal conditions were such that some curtailing was an absolute necessity.

If the fiscal canons and expediencies which underlie the principle of the divided budget cannot be superseded by some more pertinent principle, but continue to have ruling force, then the lesser evil in the case consists of minimizing the bad effects of this principle by extending the concept of public works as far as practicable into the field of intangible services. Under such conditions there is a great deal to be said for actual evasion of the principle of the divided budget by carrying out with public works or relief funds current services which have been omitted or reduced in the attempts to balance the regular current budgets of the various communities.

6. Another criterion is the effectiveness of the purchasing power distributed as a means, either of stimulating general business or of avoiding a repressive effect due to curtailment of expenditures. From this standpoint one of the first considerations is: Do the funds go to persons whose reserve resources are exhausted and who cannot otherwise go on spending at all, or do they go to persons who still have some reserves to sustain spending? In general, white collar workers may be assumed to have on the average (if averages are relevant to this problem) more reserve resources than common labor. In a mild depression, both groups are able to go on spending, though the white-collar class as a whole is undoubtedly able to come nearer to maintaining its previous rate of expenditures. As depression continues the reserves of common labor are used up first, but if it continues as long as the current depression has done, the unemployed of both classes exhaust their reserves and are on very much the same footing. Thus there is a certain stage in a continued depression, which may be roughly represented by conditions during 1931–32 in the present case, in which current private expenditures of incomes by the recipients would actually be increased by laying off white-collar workers, and spending the same amount of money to hire common labor. This, so far as it goes, is an argument in favor of curtailing current public services which are rendered by public employees of the white-collar class and expanding construction activities which would employ common labor. But to follow out this policy would vary quickly reduce these white-collar workers to a condition in which their reserves also would be exhausted, and then the advantage of this policy, even from this special standpoint, would cease.

There is even something to be said, from this special standpoint, for laying off workers who have continued to hold their jobs, simply because they have continued to hold them, and spending the money to hire workers who have hitherto been unemployed. However, this principle could easily be carried to a reductio ad absurdum, because it would mean hiring the less efficient, who have been out of work because they are less efficient, and discharging the more efficient, because they have held their jobs for that reason. However, so far as this kind of result might be obtained by curtailing services rendered by white collar workers and spending the money to hire construction workers, it might not be open to this particular criticism on a large scale, since unemployment in the construction field is so very general that it includes efficient as well as inefficient workers. On the same ground, if the distinction were practicable, a case might be made for laying off those provident workers who have accumulated savings and taking on the less provident—discharging the ant of the fable and hiring the grasshopper, but that, like deliberately discharging the efficient and hiring the inefficient, is hardly a policy which the country would deliberately follow with its eyes open. Any such considerations as these presuppose a condition in which attempts to stabilize employment have signally failed, and in which systems for the maintenance of income for the unemployed, such as the system of unemployment insurance, have not been put into effect. Since some system of unemployment insurance is a virtual necessity for the future, these considerations have only a very limited validity, if any at all, with reference to an enduring future policy.

Another consideration of this sort is the question of whether the outlays go wholly or mainly into wages and salaries which will be spent promptly, or to a considerable extent into business net earnings, which will be spent less promptly, or possibly saved and thus more or less indefinitely sterilized. Any shift of income from wages and salaries to business net earnings means a temporary reduction in the flow of purchasing power, which may be prolonged in its effect by the ensuing vicious circle of reduced spendings, reduced production, and reduced earnings. On this score, increased public works are inferior to the maintenance of current services of government, since money spent on current services of government goes almost entirely into wages and salaries, while money spent on public works goes to a much larger extent into business net earnings.

There is one condition on which this conclusion would need to be modified, namely, if the amounts which go into business net earnings resulted in inducing or enabling businesses to make capital outlays which otherwise would not or could not be made. In that case, the result might be an expanding, not merely of all the earnings in question, but of an additional amount drawn from the reserves of credit or of savings which would not otherwise be spent for some time in the future. In general, as we have already seen, business during a serious and prolonged depression is not likely to make large expenditures of this sort, even if conditions may be such as to make such expenditures financially possible. Here the chief thing to be done is to see to it that conditions are such that, when obsolescence of existing capital and postponed maintenance have reached a point where business will naturally make such expenditures, no positive obstacles are placed in the way.

7. Another criterion is that of stimulating those industries whose stimulation is most strategic and important from the standpoint of business revival. These may be the ones which are casually most important in bringing about a depression, or those which have suffered the greatest shrinkage; but the most important consideration is the stimulation of those industries which are most likely to expand their capital outlays as a result of a given stimulation. The construction industries are undoubtedly among those most important in bringing a condition of general depression, but this is largely because they are among the ones which suffered the greatest shrinkage, and it is not self-evident that they are necessarily the ones in which a given stim-

ulus will result in the greatest amount of increased capital outlays. In fact, precisely because they have suffered such a large shrinkage, they may be among the industries which will continue to use existing productive facilities rather than to undertake the construction of new ones. The chief ground for selecting for special stimulus those industries which have suffered most heavily would seem to be the possibility that bankruptcies and the wiping out of capital values in those industries may produce more serious disturbances to the values of collateral on which credit is based. And so far as that is concerned, the securities of construction enterprises are not widely used by large investment savings institutions, being inherently unsuitable to this kind of use by reason of their highly speculative character. Thus, from this standpoint the argument in favor of special treatment of the construction industries does not appear to be extremely strong.

On the whole, the argument for special stimulus in these fields seems to come down mainly to the comparatively simple fact that industries and workers in these fields have suffered most heavily and are in the greatest need of relief. This is rather a principle of relief than of business stimulation. It may, nevertheless, be entitled to serious consideration on this score.

B. Methods of Raising Funds Which May Counteract the Effect of Spending Them So Far as Concerns Stimulus to Business of the Sustaining of Purchasing Power

It has already been pointed out that public expenditures can be regarded as having a stimulative effect on business only to the extent that they involve a net addition to the volume of expenditures. On this score expenditures financed by increased taxation have only a limited effect, and in some cases may have no effect at all, or even a repressive effect rather than a stimulative one. This is, of course, peculiarly true of taxes on consumption. Here the principle is that such taxes completely neutralize the effect of the spending of the funds, so far as they result in restricting consumers' purchases. And in the main, they would seem to have this effect. To some slight extent they may cause consumers to spend a larger total amount, in the attempt to maintain their customary standard of living, and to save less than they otherwise would. To this light extent, even taxes on consumption may not completely neutralize the stimulative effects of the spending of the money so raised.

To a less extent the same is true of income taxes. So far as they go to reduce consumers' expenditures, they serve to neutralize the stimulative effect of the spending of the funds by government. But so far as they result in reduced savings rather than reduced spendings, and so far as these savings would otherwise have lain idle, public spending financed by income taxes will have some stimulative effect. This effect will naturally be larger in proportion as the income taxes come out of the high-income brackets, and smaller as they come out of the lower, moderate-income brackets.

The most clearly stimulative form of financing consists of public borrowing, but even here there is a distinction between borrowing which comes out of the expansive power of the credit system and borrowing which comes out of the ultimate savings of individuals. The former clearly means a net increase in the amount which would otherwise be spent. The latter operates in this way only to the extent that the savings which are taken by the Government represents funds which would otherwise not be used.   Even funds which come out of expanded credit may conceivably, to some extent, merely take the place of funds which private business would otherwise have secured from the same source, in case the expansion of credit is carried to a point which approaches the limits of what is possible in this direction.

In a severe depression, this question does not arise except in the form of a possible deferred effect.   Business will not use the funds at the moment, but there remains some possibility that, when revival has become a fact, business may come into the market for funds and find that the reserve funds, which ordinarily would be plentiful at such a time, have been drawn down by the public expenditures to such an extent that it cannot get all the funds that it would like to use.   This may, under certain circumstances, constitute a real danger, but there is no way of estimating its actual extent in advance.   And, in general, if a credit system will stand a given amount of demand for expansion during a severe depression, there is every probability that it will be able to stand a further expansion when a revival takes place and business prospects are more promising.   Thus this danger is probably not a very serious one.

C. Public Expenditures Which Will Ultimately Reduce the Field for Private Investment

So far as public expenditures during a depression take the form of self-liquidating works, competing with private industry, or of other works furnishing services which act as a substitute for services rendered by private business, they may reduce the field available for private investment at a later date when business shall have revived. The expansion of facilities for power production comes in this class, and so also does housing construction so far as it operates to reduce the effective demand for the class of housing in which private enterprise engages.

This would hardly apply to really successful low-cost housing projects, because they operate in a field in which private enterprise does not enter effectively.   Here whatever neutralizing effect takes place is distinctly of a deferred character.   And the question may be raised whether it is really a neutralizing effect at all, from the standpoint of industrial stabilization, or whether it is instead a means of limiting the expansion of private business which would take effect only at the time when private expansion is in danger of going too far and when some limitation may be highly salutary in the interest of avoiding a future slump by preventing the boom from going to exaggerated lengths.

On the whole, so far as public works of this sort are limited to periods of depression, their effect in forestalling a subsequent private expansion may be regarded as a benefit rather than a detriment. On the other hand, if there is a permanent policy of expanding public works of this sort, it may permanently displace a certain amount of private expenditure on similar or substitute facilities and may to this extent be neutralized.

D. Reactions in the Field of International Trade and Exchange

Students of international trade frequently state that a single nation, following a policy of revival, is likely to experience difficulties in the field of international trade and exchange; and that such a policy needs to be followed simultaneously by the chief countries if it is to be fully successful. These students are frequently concerned with questions of the maintenance of price levels, which is only incidentally involved in a public works policy, and mainly as a byproduct of reviving general demand if the policy succeeds in its object. Aside from one country's prices being maintained above the trend of world prices, revival in itself has some tendency to increase imports more than exports, especially as the industries using imported raw materials become more active and increase their purchases along with increased sales.

If this argument is carried to the length of claiming that one country cannot have a revival unless other countries keep fairly even pace with it, it seems to prove too much. For revivals do occur at different times in different countries; and whatever shifting of trade balances they bring with them does not seem to be a fatal obstacle. It is probably true, however, that the obstructions to trade and exchange which have recently grown up have made an import surplus a more serious matter, since the usual processes of automatic compensation are no longer allowed to work freely. It would be an instructive paradox if the policies by which nations aim to protect their economies from the impact of conditions in other countries had actually had the effect of making it more difficult than before for business in one country to revive, unless other countries revived simultaneously. As a protection against the effects of the depression, such policies appear to have been, in the aggregate, self-defeating; and this particular paradox may be only one case in point.

A case which has been cited is that of Germany following the expansionist program of 1932. The public works involved were designed to use German materials, but the increased volume of general activity (whether traceable to the public works policy or not) called for more imported materials. And inasmuch as the possibility of increasing exports to pay for these raw materials was rigidly restricted, the result was, according to one observer, an inability to maintain the balance of international payments.[1] Under normal conditions of trade and exchange, this would not be serious, and might be allowed to bring about its own correctives. Under the special conditions of Germany, with reparations payments to be made and with an artificially stabilized currency hovering on the brink of a break-down, such conditions might be little short of disastrous. One might conclude, not that Germany could not afford the costs of a public works policy as a means of stimulating business, but rather that, under the circumstances, she could not have a revival of business ahead of other countries, from whatever source it might come, so long as her foreign trade and exchanges were under such highly abnormal conditions.

The full effects of a program of stimulation in any country certainly include the effects upon foreign trade and exchanges, and this may be material enough to deserve consideration. That is perhaps the chief moral of this German instance. The particular effect which Germany seems to have experienced depends upon conditions which have no parallel in the case of the United States. And a more or less simultaneous revival in the 3 or 4 chief industrial countries is not impossible, even if it is not synchronized with absolute perfection.

---

[1] This situation is analyzed by Dr. Carl Landauer in a paper read before the Econometric Society in Berkeley, Calif., June 1934. This is, of course, only one possible interpretation. As this is being revised, a report comes of Dr. Schacht's plan for rationing raw materials to combat the shortage due to inability to secure sufficient imports.

E. Conclusion

It is evident that the stimulative effect of a public-works program is not assured merely by expanding public works. The effect depends upon how they are financed, on what is happening to the entire budget of public expenditures, and on the effect which these public expenditures produce upon the field for private capital investment and upon the supply of funds available for private capital expenditures. Thus, the public-works policy does not stand by itself. In one aspect, it is an integral part of the whole problem of public fiscal policy, and in another aspect it is an integral part of the whole problem of capital expenditures and the field for capital expenditures in the national economy as a whole. In general, the findings of this chapter are favorable to the policy of loan financing, though it should not be carried to such a point as to create wide-spread fear of unchecked inflation or such fear of the soundness of the credit system as may result in making it impossible for private business to secure funds when it actually wants them for increased capital outlays.

The most crucial consideration is the need of establishing a condition in which it will be possible for private expansion to come about and, when it does come about, to take over the load which public expenditures have temporarily assumed. If public expenditures are so handled as to tend to bring about a condition in which the volume of production and employment will become dependent on a perpetual continuation of such expenditures, then it will defeat the end of revival as that is commonly conceived, and will tend to bring us that much nearer the point at which the task of producing goods and maintaining the livelihood of the population could not be successfully handled by private business as now constituted. Instead of a compensator for disturbances, making the system of business enterprise more efficient in handling its great national responsibilities, the public works policy would be an undermining influence, tending to make business unable to sustain itself. This would be contrary to the character of the experimental policy the Government is now following. It would fit in only with a policy looking not to workable modifications of the economy of private business but to an early substitution of an outright collective economy.

A. General Need of Fiscal Overhauling

Regardless of what is done or is not done in the matter of a public works policy, there is need of a general overhauling of American fiscal systems in a number of respects. Some are matters of urgent need, which virtually insures that something will be done—for example, the clearing up of irregular accumulations of local debt and of the situation arising from abnormal percentages of uncollected taxes. Others are matters in which there is a general need for reform, systematization, and improvement, on which the need for action is somewhat less obvious and pressing, but on which action of some sort in the near future is nevertheless extremely necessary. This overhauling which is necessary on general grounds reaches into substantially all of the fields of fiscal problems in which a system of planned public works calls for changes in the fiscal mechanism in order to provide for raising the necessary resources at the time when they are needed. Thus the fiscal requirements of a planned public works policy stand in a favorable position for securing necessary action, to the extent that the existing systems are in any case due to be thrown open for investigation and possible change. As a result, while necessary changes are being considered, there is an unusually good opportunity for including consideration of such changes as a public works policy calls for. But this, of course, requires that there be a clearly formulated idea of what the fiscal requirements of the public works policy are.

The general overhauling for which the situation seems to call covers the following fields or problems: (1) The depression has resulted in weakening financial structures, increasing the burdensomeness of normal taxes, bringing tax delinquencies on a large scale, increasing the resort to short-term borrowing, straining the credit of local units, and reducing debt limits as assessments have been reduced. Real estate taxation has shown unexpected weaknesses and may have to be less relied on in the future. A general rehabilitation is necessary. (2) Study is being given to the problem of organizing State and local fiscal systems so as to make possible a more stable rate of spending in the face of business fluctuations which create instability in the revenues. This movement looks in two directions; first, toward increasing stability of revenues; and, second, toward mechanisms making it possible for expenses to be more stable than revenues are, by regular methods which will be recognized as sound finance and will not carry the suspicion of unsoundness which is created by irregular intermittent deficits. These proposed systems involve some development and modification of the prevailing concept as to what constitutes a balanced budget. (3) In connection with this program, there is need of modifiying the methods and machinery of borrowing and repayment, including amortization, in order to make them serve more effectively the needs of a system looking toward more stable public spending power. (4) The kinds of taxes on which we mainly rely for our revenues need to be reexamined, with some possible change

[1] T ese problems are more fully gone into in the appendix.

in the relative importance of different kinds of taxes.   (5) The relation of Federal, State and local finances is in need of reexamination, both with respect to sources of revenue and with respect to possible transfers of funds from one unit to another.   For example, Federal grants in aid of education are already being strongly urged.

All of these phases of financial overhauling have a bearing upon a policy of planned public works.   They may be so handled as to facilitate such a program, or to place obstacles in the way of it and to neutralize any good effects it may have in stimulating general business activity.   It is clearly desirable that they should be so handled as to recognize and provide for the necessary instruments and conditions of a successful public-works policy.

B. The General Financial Stringency

The financial situation in the various States and localities is sufficiently disquieting in more than one respect.   Tax delinquencies have shown a very heavy increase during the past 3 years.   Figures of tax delinquencies, collected by the Bureau of the Census, indicate very wide variations from State to State and from county to county within a given State.   Some of these variations are due to an unavoidable lack of comparability in the figures; for example, variations in the date of the observation range from the date when taxes become delinquent to 14 months after the second of two delinquencies dates. Other variations appear to be due to differences in the severity of the penalties for delinquency.   The percentages of delinquency which are reported range from 4.2 percent for Massachusetts to approximately 41 percent for two States, while the unweighted mean of the 17 States reported is 20 percent.   The most serious aspects of the situation is found in those regions where the percentage is very much above the general average.

As to the seriousness of this situation in relation to the future, there is naturally some uncertainty and difference of opinion.   In the general past experience, delinquent taxes for the bulk of the properties affected have ultimately been paid, though the time of payment remains uncertain.   The ultimate remedy of the Government, in the power to take the property for taxes, has usually proved sufficient in the case of properties possessing substantial value.   In some cases it is found that the necessity of paying back taxes before a clear title can be given in a sale of the property results in the clearing up of the delinquencies when the markets begin to become more active and transfers become more frequent.   Thus a revival of the market for real-estate sales may be expected to bring in a very considerable part of the taxes which are now delinquent.

On the other hand, the reluctance of courts and officials to take homes from their owners has, in the view of some observers, taught the owners that the payment of taxes is not necessary, with the result that there will be much greater irregularity in such payments in the future.   Whether this becomes a serious matter or not will depend upon the action of local officials and courts.   It seems probable that they will not allow this condition to go on indefinitely, after a revival of business restores the underlying power of the people to pay taxes.   Under such conditions, the ultimate prospect of a sale for taxes, coupled with the piling up of interest charges on the delinquency at a penalty rate, frequently 9 percent, should act as a strong stimulus to the repayment of the delinquencies as soon as such repayment becomes possible.

In the meantime, the situation has put the localities in a position in which there is a doubt as to their ability to control their revenues, even by increasing tax rates. The question is raised whether an increased tax rate will increase the amount of collections, or merely increase the amount of delinquencies. Thus, local financial officials, fearing the effects of an increased tax rate, have frequently resorted to borrowing as a substitute.

The result has been an extension of the policy of tax anticipation borrowing until it has in many cases reached the point where it no longer deserves that name, having gone so far that the next install- ment of taxes, when collected, will not fully pay the loans, and re- newals become necessary for an indefinite period. This is, of course, an unsound financial situation. It can be rectified only by funding the debt, where sufficient borrowing power remains within the statu- tory debt limits, or by either reducing expenses or increasing tax revenues.

Thus, in the next few years there will be increasing pressure on localities to reverse the procedure of the last few years, and to spend less than their receipts, in place of spending more. For a time, public works financed by borrowing will find little place in local budgets. If this movement is accompanied by a general revival of business, it may not bring about any drastic shrinkage of public expenditures and may not be out of harmony with the requirements of a long run public- works policy, viewed with respect to its effects upon industrial stabi- lization. For such a program calls for precisely this kind of action during periods when business is expanding, and when the need is for tempering expansion rather than stimulating it. In this respect the next year may prove critical, a great deal hinging on whether we can avoid the repressive effects of heavy taxes and curtailed public ex- penditures before business reaches a state in which it has established some power of self-expansion.

C. The Stabilization of Public Spending Power

We have seen that the stabilization of public spending power is a prerequisite to a desirable public works policy. We have also seen that such stabilization presents few difficulties during minor cyclical fluctuations of business, and that the same kind of machinery used for this purpose could, with little strain, go somewhat further and provide for moderate expansion of public works expenditures during minor cyclical depressions. During such periods, there is comparatively little shrinkage of State and local revenues, since sources of revenue which respond promptly to business conditions are to a considerable extent offset by others which lag heavily, such as income taxes based on the income of a previous year. This is especially true under the system now being tried in Wisconsin of basing the income tax on an average of several years' income, with the result that fluctuations should be much reduced and the lag in the response of this tax to business conditions should be very much increased. We have also seen that in a major crisis the mere demands of stabilization of public expenses become a very serious matter, likely to exceed the power of

State and local revenues to adjust themselves, even without adding the burden of a program of expanded public works. Thus reforms of this sort, while they may accomplish a great deal, cannot be expected to solve the whole problem or to forestall entirely the need for falling back upon the resources of Federal credit in times of serious emergency, as was done during the crisis of 1933–34.

There are two main methods proposed for closing the gap between fluctuating revenues and the need for stabilized expenses. One is the accumulation of reserves out of the revenues of prosperous years, and the other is the use of borrowing in years of depression.[2]

It is proposed, for example, that in years when the personal income tax exceeds the average annual yield over the past 3 or 5 years, contributions should be made to a reserve fund based upon a formula which could be automatically applied; and that in years when the yield falls short of the average for the past 3 to 5 years, withdrawals should be made from the reserve fund, also on the basis of an automatic formula. The proposed formula (on the basis of proposed tax rates not very different from those of 1933) would have resulted in the accumulation, during the years 1925–30, of nearly $246,000,000, and the withdrawal during the years 1931–34 of $198,000,000. This system would not have eliminated all fluctuations in revenue available from this tax, but would clearly have reduced them very considerably.

Such a system faces a number of practical problems of administration, as well as problems bearing on its economic effects. Like all systems involving cycle-stabilizing reserves, it calls for the accumulation of assets during good times which must be realized on during bad times, with likelihood of loss on the assets, and danger of adding to the demoralized condition of the investment markets when the assets are realized upon. If one State alone followed such a policy, this reaction upon the markets might be negligible, but if all of them followed it, it would be a matter for serious consideration.

And the further question would remain whether the existence of these reserves would not invite more liberal spending, despite the intent of the framers of the plan to the contrary. It has become almost proverbial in State and local finance that reserves are likely to be raided. This is one aspect of the political pressure toward increased spending when revenues are ample, which has already been noted as one of the obstacles to a policy of postponing public works during prosperous times. This question whether such a system of reserves could be successfully handled must remain to be answered by the test of experience. It may be that the stabilization of expenses must fall back in the main upon the simpler and more obvious device of temporary borrowing. In any case, since available revenue funds cannot be wholly stabilized, some temporary borrowing will be necessary.

The conception of a balanced budget is one of the things which such a plan aims to modify. It is coming to be fairly generally accepted among students of finance that the fiscal year, as a period for the balancing of the budget, is arbitrary; and that there is at least equally

---

[2] For a detailed elaboration of these proposals, see the Report of the New York State Commission for the Revision of the Tax Laws, 1933. Proposals for stabilizing the yield of certain of the variable taxes are elaborated in memorandum no. 11 of this report. Cf. also Shere, "A Statistical Approach to Certain New York State Tax Problems."

good reason for attempting to balance the budget, not during every single fiscal year, but over a longer period, covering a cycle of prosperity and depression. The greatest difficulty with this concept of budget balancing arises from the irregularity in the movements of business, both as to the length of the cycles and as to the relative magnitude of the rise and fall in any given case. Thus any system of budget balancing which aims at a balance over a period of years is necessarily somewhat uncertain as to the length of the period which needs to be covered and as to the possibility of bringing about a perfect balance at the end of the period.

In this latter respect, at least, the problem is not different in kind from that of yearly budget balancing but rather different in degree. Budget estimates are, after all, prophecies, and like all prophecies are fallible. A rational system of budget balancing does not insist that, if emergencies such as storm and flood create additional expenses which could not have been foreseen, other expenses must be rigidly cut during the last months or weeks of the fiscal year in order to bring the expenses precisely within the estimates. There is always a place for deficiency appropriations and emergency financing. What is called for in a rational system is that, if such contingencies bring about a deficit in a given year, the budget for the succeeding year shall include this deficit and shall take measures rationally calculated to extinguish it within the succeeding year.

In the case of balancing a budget over a term of years this same problem would arise in a much exaggerated form, and the results of unexpected contingencies might be decidedly more serious. In the present case, for example, such a depression as we have experienced would be bound to leave large deficits, which would have to be cleared up, if possible, during the next revival, in the face of the fact that this next revival starts from a much lower level than previous revivals and will presumably not reach anything like such great heights. Thus there will still remain the necessity of balancing revenues and expenses during a period which, compared to the period from 1924–29, is bound to be one of relative poverty. This concept of budget balancing over a term of years, then, while it expresses a valid principle, would not be so used as to delude the public mind into thinking that it will make possible a balance of the same degree of approximate precision as can be brought about over a single year. Nevertheless, it has its usefulness if too great reliance is not placed upon it.

Another modified concept of Budget balancing is the one embodied in the present Federal fiscal policy, namely, that of dividing the Budget into two parts, one representing ordinary current expenses and the other representing extraordinary outlays on permanent assets or on the meeting of emergency needs caused by the depression itself, which are therefore considered to be temporary. The present aim of Federal financing is to balance the ordinary Budget while permitting a large deficit on the extraordinary items.

With regard to this concept, it must be remembered that it was adopted at a time when there was growing fear of a deficit and a growing movement toward the balancing of the Budget. In the face of this attitude it appeared necessary to make large emergency outlays both to provide for relief and to stimulate business revival. The concept constituted a means of meeting this situation and of enlarging the emergency expenses while at the same time allaying fears that these expenses would lead to an indefinitely continued deficit and ultimate bankruptcy. But in some respects the logic of this divided Budget will not stand searching examination.

In fact, this logic comes near to a reductio ad absurdum when it justifies the cutting down of expenses for these services which are so important that they find a place in the regular schedules of the budget, while at the same time increasing expenditures for services which are, in themselves, so much less important that they are undertaken only as a means of providing relief work. These relief-work expenditures are regarded as due to the emergency, but if one is to view this matter rationally, one must remember that the special need which the emergency creates is not the need for these special services on which relief workers are employed, but rather the need for the employment itself and the disbursement of funds which it brings about. And so far as the amount of funds disbursed it concerned, that would be equally provided for if the services financed by the regular budget were maintained, and services of inferior grade were not substituted.

In short, there is no sufficient ground for classifying the regular current services as not due to the emergency and the relief work services of inferior grade as due to the emergency. The more logical principle underlying this device rests upon the question, not whether particular services are due to an emergency need, but whether the whole deficit is of a temporary character due to the emergency and destined to disappear when the depression vanishes. It is surely strange arithmetic which would regard a deficit of 40 millions on regular current services and 40 millions on extraordinary public works as a dangerous condition, but would treat as thoroughly sound finance a deficit of 100 millions on extraordinary public works, provided there were no accompanying deficit on regular current services. Such manipulation of fiscal categories should not be allowed to obscure the fact that in the one case the deficit is $80,000,000 and in the other case $100,000,000, and that $80,000,000 is less than $100,000,000. Or if the total deficit by either method were $100,-000,000, then one condition is no more serious than the other. What is needed seems to be a rational judgment as to the total deficit which can properly be undertaken, and a free hand for the Government to spend the money in those ways which will do the most good without being required to spend it under particular fiscal categories which, from this standpoint, are irrelevant.

D. Borrowing and Repayment

As we have already seen, if the fiscal policy of the Government is to serve the needs of industrial stabilization, it must borrow during depressions in ways which take and put into use funds which would not otherwise be used. Its borrowings must be in that sense inflationary. And its repayments must, if possible, be deflationary in a corresponding sense. As we have also seen, there is probably no need of taking special measures to see to it that the funds the Government borrows during a depression are funds which would otherwise lie idle. That result is almost certain to come about automatically. If there is any doubt in the matter, the marketing of loans through the banks, with privileges to the ultimate purchaser of borrowing upon them, can easily be made to bring about the desired results.

The problems of repayment, while much less obvious, are in some ways more difficult. Repayment does not automatically work in precisely the reverse way from the original borrowings, because it takes place at a different phase of the business cycle, and one in which the condition of the capital market is different. Borrowing may not reduce the volume of funds which would actually find effective forms of private investment, but repayment of loans during a prosperous period may increase the volume of funds seeking investment in such a way as to stimulate a boom, just at the time when repression, rather than stimulation, is the thing to be sought. If the demand for industrial equipment is not sufficient to absorb such funds, they are likely to flow into the securities markets fostering an unhealthy stock-market boom. It may be that reduction of the public debt during a period of prosperity needs to be accompanied by definite deflationary measures carried out by the Federal Reserve System, in order to neutralize this effect.

Methods of amortization present a further problem. Presumably loans made to finance an emergency program should be paid off before the next emergency in order that the next emergency may find the credit resources of the government in as strong a condition as possible and not weakened by the effects of the measures taken to meet the former emergency. This calls for very rapid repayment. The question remains whether this rapid repayment should be put in the form of a rigid requirement, such as a 5- or 10-year amortization period, or whether it should be left more to the discretion of the financial officials to determine when repayments can best be afforded.

Ideally, the latter method is the better one, since a rigid 10-year amortization period may be extremely burdensome during some of those 10 years when conditions are decidedly unfavorable, while it may be possible to repay more than 10 percent of the loan during the most prosperous years of the decade. On the other hand, it is not safe to count upon always having financial officers of ideal wisdom and discretion. On the whole, rather short amortization periods seem to be called for. However, an exception would most certainly need to be made in the case of housing, or possibly of other kinds of works which are to be self-liquidating, and which cannot reach the market they are designed to serve unless costs are reduced as far as humanly possible. Rapid amortization of housing bonds would impose a prohibitive charge, and make genuine low-cost housing impossible on a self-sustaining basis.

Rapid expansion of borrowing in an emergency calls for special preparatory measures, as has already been pointed out. Something must be done to overcome the obstacle afforded by the fixed debt limits under which local governments operate. Elastic debt limits can be devised and made workable without too much complication of the credit machinery. It is simple enough to provide an increase in the debt limit automatically by the same machinery which is used to determine the existence of a depression calling for expanded public works.[3] The only question calling for any ingenuity is the question of how the debt limit, when once expanded in this way, is to be brought back to normal.

---

[3] Suggestions with regard to administrative machinery for this purpose are made in the concluding chapter of this study.

If nothing is done to meet this problem, except to reduce the debt limit when the emergency is over, a community would be likely to find itself suddenly in a condition where its borrowings were in excess of its debt limit, and it would suddenly lose all its borrowing capacity until the excess should be repaid.   For this reason, the supplementary debt limit, and the loans contracted under it, should probably be kept separate from the regular debt limit and the regular borrowings, with provision for the rapid amortization of the supplementary borrowings, so that the next emergency will find them wiped off the books.   Then the regular debt limit could be allowed to remain, and only the regular borrowings charged against it.   Thus if a sudden need arose after the depression emergency was declared at an end, and before the supplementary borrowings had been completely amortized, the community would still be in a position to borrow, if necessary, to meet the need. This problem of elastic debt limits, then, is one which requires some serious thought but is not by any means a matter of extreme difficulty.

Another device which has already been suggested is advance authorization for borrowing, the amount being reserved out of the normal debt limit.   If this method were followed on a large enough scale, it might make it unnecessary to provide supplementary debt limits.   It could, of course, not be instantly put into effect by communities which are already close to their existing limit of borrowing power.

The emphasis on borrowing during the emergency should not be allowed to obscure the fact that a properly managed public-works policy need not mean an indefinite increase in debt.   If the policy of rapid repayment during prosperous times is followed with as much zeal and determination as are devoted to the expansion of public works during depressions, there need be no permanent increase of public debt.   In fact, there is every reason for approaching nearer to the pay-as-you-go policy, because the closer any community is to this condition in ordinary times, the better position it is in to meet an emergency.   In fact, an indefinite progressive increase in the public debt is precisely the thing which must be avoided if we are to be prepared to meet difficulties of this sort in the future.   If there is any temptation toward borrowing during emergencies and then neglecting to pay off the loans during subsequent periods of prosperity, then the program must be so drawn up as to call attention to that danger and provide against it, as, for instance, by requiring amortization of the emergency loans over an unusually short term of years.   The proper ideal of a policy of this kind is the ideal of pay as you go, applied over a term of years and not over a single year.

E. Kinds of Taxes To Be Used

The choice of types of taxation presents something of a dilemma, from the standpoint of industrial stabilization.   From the purely fiscal standpoint, it is desirable to have in the tax system considerable sources of revenue which are not sensitive to industrial fluctuations. From this standpoint, a sales tax is less sensitive than an income tax, and there is a strong impulse to use it.   On the other hand, from the standpoint of economic policy, it is important to use taxes which will not reduce consumption more than is absolutely unavoidable.   From this standpoint, the sales tax is definitely to be avoided and a highly progressive income tax is one of the best forms of taxation.

Thus the attempt to stabilize public revenues calls for one thing while the attempt to stabilize business by stabilizing private spendings calls for something different. This is one more reason for thinking that it is not wise to try too hard to stabilize public revenues, and that the wiser course is to rely upon revenue reserves or borrowing to stabilize public spendings in the face of unstable tax revenues. Then it will be possible to continue to use forms of taxation which seem socially desirable, in spite of the fact that they are more sensitive to business fluctuations than, for instance, the sales tax.

One of the taxes which has been considered highly stable and not sensitive to business fluctuations, namely, the general property tax, has been showing unexpected sensitiveness during the last few years. This tax has become substantially a real-estate tax, and constitutes a burden on this form of investment far heavier than the State attempts to lay on other forms. For a time, this seemed to have a certain rough practical justification in that the property could not escape, the taxes were paid, and people continued to farm the land and to live in houses on it, in the face of the discriminatory burdens.

But at present there are growing indications that real estate has reached the limit of its capacity to bear this burden without undesirable social consequences. Municipalities have found it necessary to grant exemptions from taxation for a limited time to new housing enterprises, in order to stimulate desired developments in this direction. And the movement toward subsistence farming serves to emphasize the fact that the tax system forces the farmer into just that specialization on cash crops which is responsible for some of the unsound features of the agricultural situation. It acts as a barrier against any who wish to take refuge from the difficulties of the cash crop in a subsistence type of farming. Even if all other needs were met without the use of money derived from the sale of cash staples, there would still be a large tax bill calling for money and compelling the farmer to find a cash market for a considerable amount of produce.

It would not be proper in this study to attempt to determine just what is the correct distribution of tax burdens between different classes of taxes. But enough has been said to indicate that the present emergency has thrown some new light on this problem and brought to bear new considerations which may lead to a reopening of the question and some readjustment of tax burdens. In such a readjustment, the needs of industrial stabilization should be sufficiently in evidence, even with due allowance for the limitation of our present knowledge, to justify giving them an important place in the readjustment of tax systems.

F. The Relation of Federal, State and Local Finances

In overhauling the fiscal system from the standpoint of relations between the different States and between Federal, State, and local jurisdictions, the more obvious fiscal problems are concerned with such things as double taxation and conflicting jurisdictions. But while these questions are being dealt with, there is also the need of providing machinery such as this study has shown will be needed in the handling of future emergencies. Perhaps the most fundamental need from this standpoint is the need arising out of the fact that, in a major crisis, adequate and unified action in the field of public spending can come only through Federal authority and Federal credit. Some localities have sufficient resources and some have not. Of those which have such resources, some would use them and some would not. Attempts to induce the local authorities to commit themselves to an extended program through voluntary planning face the basic difficulty that no current administration can be bound by the plans entered into by previous administrations. Therefore a prompt and coherent national policy for the meeting of future emergencies will depend on Federal action, including the use of Federal funds by way of grants and loans to induce States and localities to carry their share of the burden.

This being the case, it becomes vitally important to plan for such action in advance, so that the baffling delays inherent in such a situation can be reduced to a minimum. In other words, if we are going to make Federal loans and grants to States and localities in future emergencies, we may as well have the machinery ready to do it promptly, and to see that the States and localities are in a position to take prompt advantage of the opportunities thus afforded. This requires not only that the Federal Government should be prepared to grant funds promptly but that the States and localities should be prepared to submit projects well enough developed and maturely enough considered to justify the Federal Government in making grants or loans, and, as nearly as may be, ready for starting actual work as soon as the funds are made available. This calls for advance planning by the States and localities, with the further proviso that the Federal Government has a sufficient interest in the matter to justify it in making subsidies not only to the actual carrying out of the projects but to the advance work of planning and preparation to whatever extent may be necessary in order to induce the States and localities to make their advance planning really effective.

The making of Federal grants and loans to States and localities raises a host of questions in which customary canons of sound finance may stand in the way of meeting the needs of an emergency situation. By ordinary standards the Federal Government should not subsidize the regular current services of State and local governments, and any expenditures which it permits by a combined policy of grants and loans should be of a sort such as furnishes proper security for loans; in short, they should be limited to works of enduring value.

However, as we have seen, the Government action has already gone beyond these limits in carrying out relief work. Here it has not limited itself to permanent works, "properly chargeable to capital account." It has rather gone on the principle that relief work itself is an emergency need, justifying emergency outlays such as would not be justified in ordinary times. And in spending, for example, considerable amounts for education, it has undertaken support of ordinary current services of the State and local governments. Thus the attempt to limit the use of Federal funds to those which might be called capital outlays in the ordinary sense, appears to have broken down in practice.

As to whether this represents unsound finance and therefore something to be avoided so far as possible, it seems that there is strong reason to question the idea that durable works of a material sort afford any better security for loans than any other kind of emergency expenditure. It would seem, rather, that there are two lines to be drawn—one between works which are genuinely self-liquidating and those which are not, and the other marking off the limit of the total amount of outlays which the Public Treasury can stand, and still remain in a basically sound condition. Other distinctions might also be made, but they appear to be of minor importance, and extremely difficult to apply in practice. Aside from those works which are literally self-liquidating other works are to be justified on the ground that they tend to promote the general health and productiveness of the economic system. And in this respect, it is difficult to draw a line between durable works which tend to increase the economic productivity of society by their continued existence, and other outlays which tend to rescue the community from the economic paralysis into which it has fallen.

The important criterion of the soundness of loans granted to States and localities as stated in section 203A of the National Industrial Recovery Act is as follows:

"The President may consider whether action is in process or in good faith assured therein (i. e., in the locality) reasonably designed to bring the ordinary current expenditures thereof within the prudently estimated revenues thereof." In other words, the question is, not whether the particular expense yields a self-sustaining asset but whether the whole fiscal system of the community is in a sound condition. Even this principle may be too narrow if it is construed as meaning that local budgets must be balanced at any cost during the current emergency. If the agencies granting Federal aid require, as a condition of such aid, that localities shall levy increased taxes at a time when only sales taxes are available, the result may be to neutralize any good that might be accomplished through the Federal aid. The principle in question needs to be extended and liberalized by construing it in the light of the conception of balancing budgets over a period including both depression and prosperity, rather than insisting upon a strict balance each year. What may reasonably be required is action "reasonably designed to bring the ordinary current expenditures * * * within the prudently estimated revenues" not immediately but when something like normal conditions shall have returned.

As to the principle that ordinary local expenditures should not be shifted over to the Federal Budget, subsidies to public works may prove to be not so well justified from this standpoint as emergency subsidies to support ordinary current services, so long as these subsidies are limited to the period of the emergency itself. A community may use Federal funds in 1934 to build works which would ordinarily have come out of the local budget in, let us say, 1936; but it can hardly finance its budget of regular school instruction in this way. This aid to local current services is more certain to be confined to the needs of the emergency than is the construction of durable public works.

One fact which needs to be taken account of in any system under which one governmental unit bears a part of the cost of given services or improvements, while another unit takes the initiative in determining whether these services are to be carried on or these improvements are to be made, is the fact that under such a system the initiating body receives more than it spends, with the result that there is a definite stimulus to the kinds of services and works which are subsidized in this way. If this kind of subsidy is limited to a particular class of works, there is a tendency toward overbuilding of this class, as compared to other classes. State grants in aid of local road construction are a case in point. The result is that the subsidizing authority has a responsibility for keeping such expenditures within bounds. In other words, such a system sets up one more scheme of checks and balances which tends to complicate the work involved and to introduce elements of delay. This cannot be avoided, but the effect needs to be counteracted by other measures whereby the preparatory work of determining what projects are justified is carried on, so far as possible, in advance.

G. Limits on a Public Works Program Imposed by Financial Considerations

The underlying limits on a public works policy arise from the possible exhaustion of the ultimate financial power of the Government. As there is hardly any question of a grade A program exhausting the available fiscal resources, these limits become a live issue with respect to more ambitious programs involving a considerable increase in the total amount expended. The first limit arises from the possibility of increasing public borrowing to a point which exhausts the public faith in the soundness of the credit. This, however, does not stand wholly by itself, but is related to a still more basic limit; namely, the possibility of laying taxes sufficient to support proper charges for interest and amortization of the loans, without reaching the point where the taxes cripple business or interfere with it sufficiently to cause the whole process of raising and spending money to do more harm than good, from the standpoint of its effects on the volume of business activity. This, needless to say, is a very indefinite limit. At present, we have no tangible standpoints by which to judge it, even on the side of the hampering effects of taxation taken by itself.

Those who deal with this problem are commonly divided into two groups—those who look at the need for expanding public services and expenditures without intimate contact with the effects of the necessary fiscal burdens, and those who look at the size of the tax burden and argue that it has become intolerably large without direct reference to the importance to the community of the services which this tax burden serves to support. The weight of the tax burden, taken by itself, is at present a truly serious matter, though some factors of the situation are undoubtedly temporary. The total burden has been variously estimated, the largest figures running as high as one-third of our diminished national income. This estimate, however, refers to the total cost of government and not to the amount currently raised out of taxes, which is smaller. The amount of the tax burden is probably not more than one-fourth or less than one-fifth of the present national income. This is well over twice the proportion to which we were accustomed in the years preceding the World War and represents a burden which is not easy to bear. This burden consists in part of debt charges, veterans' relief and other minor burdens carried over from the World War, in part of a net increase in the extent of public functions, and in part of burdens of relief and similar outlays occasioned by the depression. The weight of it has been enormously increased as a result of the great fall in the price level which accompanied the present depression, resulting in an increase in the real weight represented by fixed interest charges and salaries and veterans' benefits, which did not decrease as the purchasing power of the dollar rose. But the largest responsibility for the increase in the proportion of the national income absorbed by government has been the decrease in the real national income resulting from general industrial stagnation. As to the prospect for the future, veterans' benefits and salaries have already been adjusted to a considerable extent, but the more important adjustments must wait until the burdens of depression relief are lightened and the volume of industrial activity rises to something like a normal level. When this happens, the cost of government will presumably settle down at a level somewhere between the pre-war level and the present abnormally high percentage of the national dividend. The precise level will naturally depend on the speed of recovery, which no one can predict with confidence.

Looking over a longer perspective, to possible future emergencies, the main question is whether we can carry a sufficient burden of taxation through the years which are to follow the present depression to wipe out the increased debt charges which this depression has brought with it, before the next considerable emergency arrives, and so avoid a cumulative piling up of these charges. This does not seem impossible. If it can be done, there is no need to fear that our ultimate power to finance an expanding public works policy in future crises will vanish.

As between those who look only at tax burdens and those who look at the necessity and importance of governmental services, there is frequently no common measure by which the importance of the plus-and-minus quantities can be determined. When this question is looked at from the standpoint of the use of public works to relieve depressions, it appears that something like a common measure is at least possible, because the question at issue concerns the effect of such expenditures on the total volume of productive activity without any necessary preference for one kind of activity as against another kind. But the difficulty remains that the total effects of such a policy on productive activity at large have not yet been sufficiently analyzed. The process consists of the securing of funds from certain sources and the spending of them for certain works. Each side of the process has both immediate effects and after effects. And it must be followed by another process of securing funds from tax sources and transferring them in repayment of loans. And the effects of this latter process are also two-sided, consisting of the subtraction of purchasing power through taxes and the addition of purchasing power to the funds of other persons or groups through the repayment of the loans. All of these phases of the process are equally important and any attempt to assess its effects must not neglect any one of them.

The more immediate effects of the process of public works expansion have already been stated, on the assumption that public loans during a depression take funds which would otherwise, at least for the time being, remain unused, while the public works expenditures put these funds into active circulation. There is a possible after effect, which has also been mentioned, when conditions become such that there is an active private demand for these loan funds, and when this demand may be limited by the fact that the loan funds have already been taken by the Government. The ultimate effects of taxation and revenues of the loans remain to be considered. This second shifting of funds will, in all probability, result in a net reduction of consumers' expenditures and a corresponding increase in the volume of funds seeking investment in the private markets. Thus, if it is true that the fundamental evil of our economic system is one of under-consumption and over-investment, the effect of expanding public works during a depression, on a credit basis, is largely to postpone the difficulty, rather than to avoid it. This represents a question upon which no final answer can at present be given. It is one of those matters on which agencies for economic planning must carry out systematic researches.

Among the more immediate limits on a public-works policy are those arising from the system of divided governmental powers and the general inertia of governmental fiscal machinery. Regular budgetary procedure is loaded with checks and balances, including requirements of legislative action or of popular referenda on proposals for borrowing. These have the admirable purpose of making necessary properly matured deliberation before public funds are spent; but they also have the effect of making prompt action virtually impossible. Moreover, the great number of local authorities concerned makes it virtually impossible to carry out any concerted policy over the whole country so long as matters are left entirely in the hands of these local agencies.

The overcoming of these limitations depends, first, on going through the process of mature deliberation in advance; and secondly, on allowing some central body to take the initiative toward concerted action, to give the signal for such action, and, if necessary, apply a fiscal stimulus. The carrying out of preparatory measures in advance needs, not merely to save time, but to save enough time to more than counterbalance the time which will necessarily be consumed in the process of submitting local projects to the central agency for final ratification and the securing of grants from such an agency when the projects are approved. The Federal Government probably needs to give some continuing moderate subsidy to the work of planning and preparedness carried on by State and local bodies, as well as to make it worth their while to accept and use Federal funds when the major emergency arises.

For the purposes of this study it is not necessary to discuss all phases of labor policy, only some special problems of public works policy. Here there is a natural distinction between regular public works and relief work, and within the field of relief work a distinction between the Civilian Conservation Corps and general relief work.

A. Selection of Workers

In the matter of the selection of workers, Public Works Administration Circular No. 1, page 4, laid down a number of principles, to the following effect:

1. Jobs are to be "equitably distributed among the qualified workers who are unemployed, not among those who merely wish to change one good job for another."

2. Jobs are to be geographically distributed as widely as practicable.

3. Qualified workers who are legally entitled to preference should receive it.

4. Excessive increase of labor in the vicinity of works projects should be avoided.

5. Local labor which is required and which may appropriately be secured through employment services should so far as practicable be selected from lists of qualified workers submitted by local employment agencies designated by the United States Employment Service.

6. Convict labor and materials produced by it should be excluded.

There seems to be no reason to quarrel with the general purport of these propositions. Foremen and supervisory staff would naturally be exempt from proposition no. 1, and it would probably be advisable to exempt a certain proportion of keymen also. The general principle of this proposition no. 1 seems to apply also to relief work, with the qualification already noted in a previous chapter, that in application there will be more emphasis on need and less possibility of choosing men specifically fitted for the jobs available. Regular public works will naturally have the first selection from the available labor force, and so be able to choose their working force more definitely on a basis of the workers' qualifications for the particular jobs in hand.

It would also seem that, so far as practicable, within the field of relief work, workers chosen more definitely with reference to efficiency should be put on separate projects, to avoid mixing them with unemployables or with employable workers who are not qualified for the particular kind of work available. The extent to which this can be done depends partly on the size of the relief works program, and on whether it is the main reliance for relief or only part of a more comprehensive program. In proportion as there are other adequate ways of caring for workers who may not be well qualified for types of work available, relief work may be more narrowly limited to qualified workers, though subject always to the tendency of local administrators to assign jobs on the basis of need, for reasons already noted.

The same considerations bear on the problem of discharge for inefficiency. From the standpoint of efficiency, such discharge should be possible, and the job should not be regarded as an absolute right of the worker, regardless of his performance. This implies that there should be provision for relief on which the discharged worker may fall back, which should be sufficient for the absolute necessities, but less liberal than the wages on relief work, which in turn should be less liberal than wages on regular public works or in private employment.

For the unemployables, or for those who may need to qualify for new kinds of jobs if they are ultimately to be placed in private business, special treatment looking to reeducation or rehabilitation is highly important.

B. The Avoidance of the Use of Machinery

In 1934 it was the policy of the Public Works Administration to avoid the use of machinery so far as that could be done without raising costs. The difficulty of determining precisely the effect of such a policy on costs in advance of trying the experiment is obvious. The net outcome of such a policy would be to give the benefit of the doubt— possibly of a fairly wide margin of doubt—to the policy of reduced use of machinery. The figures of direct employment on Public Works Administration projects, in proportion to total amount of money spent, seem to indicate that this policy has actually had a material effect, but these figures afford only very general indications. For the benefit of those in charge of future projects, it would be desirable to carry out a study of the results of this policy of reduced use of machinery, with respect to its effects on (a) direct primary employment, (b) indirect primary employment, and (c) costs.

C. Wages and Hours

For regular public works, the wage policy should be a consistent part of a comprehensive wage policy for occupations in general. Here there is need for as much study as possible as to what such a comprehensive policy should be. Provisionally, it seems that there is ground for distinguishing the field of construction and the production of capital goods from the field of production of consumers' goods in general, and adopting somewhat different policies in the two fields. The reason is that, in the field of consumers' goods, increased wages not merely increase costs but also come back to the industries in the form of increased demand for their products rather quickly, while in the field of construction and capital equipment, increased wages during a depression may merely increase costs without any corresponding effect, for the time being at least, in increasing demand for these types of products. Thus, if effective demand in these special fields is to be increased, or prevented from declining, some deflation of costs seems necessary, in which wages may need to bear a share of the burden. Specifically, if a low-cost housing program, for instance, is to have a chance of success, it appears necessary that construction costs should be deflated.

Thus the double principle may be laid down: (1) That wages and hours in regular public works should correspond with those in the general market for labor of this type, i. e., labor in the special field of durable capital goods; (2) that this general market rate should show at least some relative decline as compared to rates in consumers' goods industries and should not be bid up as a result of the governmental demand or of National Recovery Administration codes. Costs, including wages, should be moderate enough to offer an incentive to revival of private demand and not act as an obstacle to it. Judged by this standard, costs in 1934 in these fields seemed too high, and the governmental demand seemed responsible in part for the maintenance of wages and prices of materials at levels which actually discouraged private construction.

The principle that wages should correspond with those in the general market requires much adjustment to local differences. Blanket rates, determined from Washington, are virtually certain to be made too high for many localities in order to avoid being too low in localities—commonly large centers of population—where rates are above the average. There are indications that Civil Works Administration wage scales were high enough to bring about serious demoralization of the private employment market in regions where private wage scales were well below the average for the country as a whole, making it impossible for private employers to compete at wage rates which they could afford to pay. It has even been charged that in some localities workers were able to make savings on Civil Works Administration wage scales which would serve to carry them through the warm season and put them in a position to refuse normal agricultural employment. The experience of the current depression in this matter should be thoroughly investigated and the results should be made available to guide future policy and avoid such possible mistakes, both for the rest of the present emergency and for future depressions. The importance of this can hardly be overestimated.

As already indicated, wages on relief work should be lower than on regular public works, in order to afford a positive incentive to workers to remain in private employment or to get back to it as quickly as possible. The great difficulty here is that many private occupations pay such extremely low wages that it is impossible to maintain this principle and still pay enough to meet a reasonable standard of bare need. Even if the more extremely low wage rates in private industry were raised, actual earnings of the workers would still in many cases fall inordinately low on account of part time during depressions. A further difficulty arises where private employment carries board and lodging, with very low money wages. This makes a fair comparison difficult; and the public official must consider not only his own judgment of the relative advantages offered, but the workers' feelings about them, which may be different from the official's. Farm and ranch employment may be cited as an illustration. Here the workers receive board and lodging, but money wages are frequently so low as to make the relief-work wage scales appear vastly higher, however deceptive this appearance may be. It is not easy to prescribe a simple remedy for this difficulty, though a separate cash allowance for board and lodging might conceivably have some psychological effect. The general dilemma cannot be fully avoided until not only wages but regularity of employment in private industry are on a more satisfactory basis; in short, until we reach a state where relief work will not be seriously needed.

In the meantime, so long as we are not prepared to go over promptly to a thoroughgoing socialistic program, the dominant consideration would seem to be not to put excessive obstacles in the way of the re-absorption of labor by private industry. This means being content with a standard of pay on relief work which is bound to appear inadequate from the standpoint of humane administrators. This would further mean that it would be impossible to maintain any very large differential between relief work wages and levels of outright relief.

The policy announced by the Relief Adminsitration for relief work following the ending of the Civil Works Administration represents a compromise in which wage rates are maintained while total earnings are limited by an extremely short working week. Such a policy does not appear fully to meet the difficulty, because workers are likely to prefer the higher wage rate and the short hours to the same total earnings in private industry at lower rates and longer hours.

In short, while the policy of real work at real wages, as followed by the Civil Works Administration, probably made a valuable contribution as a temporary expedient, it seems certain that it was not a policy that could be usefully maintained from the standpoint of encouraging ultimate absorption of the workers in private industry, quite apart from the question whether the Government could stand the financial outlay. One local administrator has told the writer that his locality had been employing high-grade and low-grade workers at a uniform rate of pay, the high-grade workers being glad of the chance to do high-grade work on this basis, but that when rates were raised and higher scales set for the higher grade work, the cost became prohibitive and the higher grade workers merely lost the chance to do the kind of work which from their standpoint was more desirable, while the community lost the value of the resulting product.

D. Employment Exchanges

Any reasonably satisfactory policy for meeting these difficulties requires some improvement in the general organization of the labor market throughout the country. To this end, one thing which is vitally necessary is a really effective Nation-wide system of employment exchanges, with which both public works authorities and relief work authorities can cooperate in the securing of qualified labor. Even if employment insurance is destined to take the place of relief work to a large extent, such exchanges will be no less necessary for the effective administration of an unemployment insurance system. For this purpose such exchanges are indispensable, both for determining the actual state of the labor market in respect to wages, and for seeing to it that all possible opportunities for private employment are exhausted before workers are given either relief work or unemployment benefits. Employment exchanges will not solve all of the difficulties of labor policy, which have been mentioned—some of them are inescapable. But such a system affords the only hope of grappling with these difficulties in the most systematic and effective way.

XIII. THE CONSTRUCTION INDUSTRIES IN RELATION
TO A PUBLIC WORKS PROGRAM

Inasmuch as a public works program, while aiming at general benefit to business, is of immediate and direct benefit to the construction industries, the relation of the latter to the program is of particular importance. If there are abuses in these industries, and if a housecleaning is needed, it would be peculiarly unfortunate if the result of a public works program were to perpetuate the abuses and protect the industries against a salutary and needed housecleaning. Before a public works policy takes final shape, a thorough canvass of these industries should be made in the light of this problem. Industries of sufficient public importance to receive such aid would seem to be affected with a public interest of a special sort, justifying a requirement that they should do their part so far as possible toward a smoothly working economic system using the productive powers for the benefit of the people at large. If from this standpoint reforms appear to be needed, they may fairly be asked for in return for benefits afforded. If the Government is, in part, to support the idle overhead of these industries, it may fairly ask that the industries do all they can to keep that idle overhead down. The Government may also be able to help the various groups in these industries to cooperate to this end and to accomplish more in this direction than they could do separately.

A full program of this sort probably calls for action on a wider front than that of the construction industries alone. It calls for deflation of costs and prices by these industries in order to furnish an incentive to industry in general to make use of the construction industries in dull times, but as things are, this incentive by itself would probably not be sufficient The end in view seems to require also action by the construction—using industries and interests, to stabilize their demand for construction in return for concessions in costs during dull times. On this basis they might offer the construction industries a sufficient prospect of benefit to make the concessions worth while to both groups. In any such arrangement, Government as a purchaser of construction, with an elastic public-works progress as an inducement, might be able to take a leading part. Such a proposal is admittedly extremely difficult and success is highly problematical with the industries organized as at present.

As a measure of approach to such a program, there should evidently be cooperation between public-works authorities and code authorities in the construction industries, if code authorities or something like them persist in the future. Furthermore, the executive discretion resting with the public-works authorities might be made to include, not only the authority to initiate an expanded public-works program when an emergency is shown to exist, but the authority to decline to initiate it, or possibly to suspend it, if costs in the industry appear to be so high as to afford a positive obstacle to resumption of private construction.

As we have seen, this represents one of the greatest dangers of an unsafeguarded public works program, tending to defeat rather than promote the end of a revival of private business. For the construc-

131

tion industries themselves, a policy which results in stiffening the level of costs of construction so as to enable it to resist all deflation, might be a very doubtful benefit. The result might be that the revival of private construction would be postponed indefinitely—postponed until the Government program should have gone as far as public opinion was willing to carry it, or as far as the resources of public credit were able to carry it and should then have come to an end, after which costs of construction, no longer supported by public spending, would surely decline and private demand would then be able to come into the market without the consciousness that it was being asked to pay for construction at an inflated level of costs such as the general state of demand did not warrant. Thus the result might be merely that the evil day of deflation would be postponed, and that business troubles might thereby be prolonged rather than curtailed.

The question has often been raised whether Government could get its public works cheaper by doing more of them in dull times. Conclusive evidence on this point is almost impossible to obtain. Indices of construction costs show a slight reduction during cyclical depressions, but only a slight one. On the other hand, these indices are made up on the basis of wage rates rather than of wage costs per unit of product, and so do not take account of any increase in output per man-hour which may take place during depressions. Furthermore, the wage rates used are either union scales or are likely to be influenced by union scales to an extent preventing them from taking sufficient account of deflations in average rates actually paid to workers of all classes. And they take no account of the willingness of contractors to bid on a closer margin of profit during dull times. Thus, one private employer who has followed a policy of making enlargements more extensively in dull times than in prosperous times, has expressed confidence that he saved a great deal more money than the indices would show.

There are opportunities for economy. On the other hand, if all employers follow the same policy they would almost certainly not all get the same economies, because their sustained demand would tend to prevent deflation of costs. The same is true in much greater degree of a governmental policy, especially as ordinarily handled, with legislative authority determining that a given amount is to be spent without any conditions as to costs or prices, with the result that the industry knows that at least this much of the demand for its services is completely inelastic. And in a severe depression this would constitute a very large part of the total demand. Thus it seems that the Government cannot count on any economies through expanding its public works in dull times, as a result of purely automatic deflation of costs at such times. Unless it is in a position to bargain for such economies, it will not get them. A systematic canvass of construction costs at the present time has, of course, not been possible in the making of this report. Fragmentary evidence indicated that, in 1934, many of these costs were surprisingly near the 1929 level, and constituted a real obstacle to recovery.[1]

[1] Since this was written a reduction has taken place in lumber prices; but apparently other items of construction costs have not followed this lead.

A. Public Utilities as Adjuncts to a Public Works Program

In President Hoover's first effort to combat the depression by attempting to persuade industrialists to maintain capital expenditures, the one major group which responded to the extent of making an actual increase in these expenditures was that of public utilities. This suggests the possibility that they may afford the most promising starting point for an attempt to extend this policy beyond the scope of strictly governmental works.

It must be admitted that this experiment was not an unqualified success. The net increase in capital outlays was very small, and it is probable that many of the companies which responded to this appeal had cause to regret it afterwards. The attempt was made under the most difficult and unfortunate conditions possible. It came at the beginning of an unprecedentedly long and severe depression when the companies making increased capital outlays not only had to wait an indefinite number of years for a revival of demand to justify any increases in capacity which they might install, but had to live through a period of the most critical kind of financial strain, taxing their resources to the utmost. In some cases this was complicated by other conditions which may prove to have made a permanent change for the worse in the situation of these companies, curtailing their spheres of operation as compared to other agencies. And the experiment was tried without the benefit of any previous postponement of capital outlays such as might have served to accumulate in good times a reserve of work to be done when dull times came. Altogether, the conditions for this experiment could hardly have been worse.

This experience indicates that, whatever public utilities may be able to do in this direction in the future, it will probably be subject to rather narrow limitations. Some of the difficulties encountered in the present case may be reduced by planning, and some may be less serious in future cases than they were in this crisis, which stands unique in its combination of length, magnitude, and complicating and disturbing factors. Nevertheless, even if on a smaller scale, the same kinds of difficulty will remain.

On the other hand, if industry is to meet these emergencies by planning, as is generally proposed, the public service industries have certain definite advantages over ordinary private industry, fitting them to do pioneer work, at least to a greater extent than private industry in general. In general, the demand for their services is more predictable than that of private industry, and they are accustomed to providing considerable reserves of capacity in advance of current need and are sometimes ordered to render service calling for some additional investment which may not by itself yield profitable returns on the specific additional amounts expended. The telephone utilities afford a well-known example of long-run prediction of demand and adoption of long-range programs of capital investment in the light of these predictions. With such long-range programs in effect, and with the habit of carrying a certain amount of reserve capacity

133

beyond immediate demands in normal times, it would seem to be a practicable step to proceed more slowly with advance construction during prosperous times, letting the reserve of spare capacity get a little lower than is customarily done, and then to catch up with the long-run program when general business is depressed, or even to run a little ahead of it.

The limitations of such a scheme are easy to perceive. If the reserve of spare capacity is allowed to diminish very much, there will be an increased risk that the current prosperity will bring an unexpected increase in demand which will overtax the facilities already installed. And the increase of plant capacity when business is contracting will always involve a financial burden at just the time when such burdens are harder to meet. One device which might help this situation would be to allow the companies to set aside a certain amount of earnings as a reserve for plant extensions, under safeguards which would prevent the scheme from being used, in effect, to charge the public higher rates in order to build up capital investment on which the company would have the right to a future return. This safeguarding could be done in various ways, which are outside the scope of a study like the present one.

Even with the benefits of such a system, expanded capital outlays could not possibly be carried through the more extreme and prolonged depressions. And inasmuch as these most serious depressions are never labeled as such when they begin, a company could never tell in advance with any certainty whether it was embarking on a timely policy of capital expansion which would result in installing added capacity which would very soon be justified by reviving business or whether it was wasting money by expanding capacity several years before there would be any demand for it, and embarking on a rate of construction which it could not maintain later, when the depression became more severe and business needed the stimulus even more.

Such uncertainties are inevitable. Even more serious uncertainties are illustrated by the crisis through which street railways passed following the war, which resulted in a permanent shrinkage in street railway transport and the permanent abandonment of many lines. The railroads are at present facing a crisis which may result in a permanent shrinkage of the scope of their business, though not so severe as the one through which the street railways have passed. Major crises are quite likely to be accompanied by such possibilities of permanent change.

In the face of such difficulties, public utilities cannot be expected voluntarily to risk very large expenditures—not large enough to play a major part in sustaining general business, even in a moderate depression. And, so long as public utilities are in their present quasi private status, any such program must be, in the last analysis, based on voluntary consent. Public authorities may suggest, persuade, or even offer financial inducements. But they cannot dictate absolutely. This would involve, in the last analysis, substituting official judgment for that of the companies as to the technical problems of their business and the kind and extent of equipment needed for economic and efficient service. And this cannot be done under the present system.

One class of work where these objections do not apply, and which can absorb a very large amount of expenditure, consists of grade crossing separations. Here the Government may not only use increased pressure, but may offer to carry a larger percentage of the cost where the work is done in dull times in accordance with a public works program. For other classes of work the Government has the resource of offering to loan funds on easy terms, or even to make grants of funds on terms which would preclude the companies from adding these amounts to the valuations on which they have a right to a return. Thus it appears possible that something might be accomplished, even though the possibilities are limited.

The conclusion is that, under favorable conditions and with proper advance planning, a moderate amount of increased capital outlays may be brought about during the shorter and milder depressions, stopping short of an amount which would impose a dangerous financial burden on the companies if the depression should turn out to be unusually long and serious. In the latter case, the companies could not be called on for any further contribution. What they might be asked to do would constitute a part only of the first line of defense only. Along with moderate expenditures by public agencies, it might reduce the severity of the lesser depressions to a point at which the disturbance to general business would not be serious. If the depression went farther than this, public utilities and private industry must be expected to drop their part of the burden of sustaining capital expenditures, leaving it to be taken up by Government.

B. Transportation Coordination

The problem of transportation coordination is a large and many-sided one. It involves incidentally some questions of public works, but these are naturally secondary to the more important transportation aspects of the problem. These general aspects are in the hands of the Federal Coordinator of Transportation, so far as concerns general Federal policy. The problem is, however, so broad that there is hardly any important local or regional agency which does not encounter it in some phase of its work. The Mississippi Valley Committee was concerned with it, and made studies of the costs of different types of transport. State and local planning boards must inevitably deal with it in framing comprehensive plans—even in the limited field of public works. Intimately concerned in the problem are the Interstate Commerce Commission, State Railroad and Public Utility Commissions, State departments regulating motor vehicles and motor traffic, and all authorities concerned with highway construction, maintenance, and operation; all bodies dealing with aviation, tax authorities as governing the charges which different types of transportation have to bear, and all authorities concerned with waterway improvement and facilities, Federal, State, and local. This list includes the improvement of channels, the furnishing of public terminals, and any services which may be rendered in the actual conduct of transportation, such as the Federal barge lines. Last, but not not least, come the private interests which are engaged in transportation service and whose policies and developments cannot be simply disposed of by regarding them as under the control of the Government commissions and other agencies.

The system of transportation, which stands much in need of better coordination than it now has, includes railroads, street railways, and local rapid-transit lines, street and highway traffic, water transport of various sorts and grades, pipe lines, and air transport. In the railway field there are heavy-traffic main lines, subsidiary lines with light traffic, branch lines, and feeders. The traffic moved includes passengers and freight, long-haul and short-haul business, heavy goods moving in solid train loads, and miscellaneous merchandise moving in less-than-carload lots, and railroads which specialize heavily in particular types of business and other roads whose business is general in character. It also includes business originating and terminating on the rail lines, business requiring local collection and delivery, and business involving interchange with water lines or highway transport. Water-borne traffic and highway traffic are somewhat more specialized in the kinds of goods carried and the general nature of the business but still afford wide variety. Every commodity the consumer buys embodies an almost infinite variety of transportation services.

The relationships between these different means of transportation are governed not merely by costs, but by a wide range of questions of service as to speed and reliability, safety, convenience and comfort, and requirements as to packing and shipping and liability for damage. This whole system is such an organic unity—or it should be—that no one part of it can be organized without regard to the conditions and requirements of the other parts. A simple illustration is the virtual necessity for a standard gage on all railway lines, despite the fact that traffic conditions on different parts of the network would make different gages economical if each of these parts of the network stood by itself. A branch line might most economically be constructed and operated as a narrow-gage line were it not that this would involve so much waste in the interchange of traffic with main lines as to more than outweight any economy that would be secured in this way. And it is quite possible that the lines with densest traffic might be most economically constructed and operated on a wider gage than the present standard if it were not that this would involve either a prohibitive cost of interchange with other lines or an equally prohibitive cost in bringing the other lines up to a uniform gage which would be totally unsuited to other traffic conditions.

The relations of different parts of the transportation network to each other are of double sort; competitive and complementary. Highway and water routes take traffic which the railways might handle, and these are competitive; but highways also act as indispensable feeders to the railways, while railways in turn act as feeders to the waterway system, although probably to a much smaller extent than they might do.

So far as different type of transport are competitive, there are two main methods of approach to the problem of a proper adjustment. One is to fix conditions governing costs by different methods of transport in such a way that the burdens borne by the shipper, are so far as possible, equalized with the true economic costs of all the services they represent, including the use of publicly furnished improvements and facilities. This being done, the question as to which method is most advantageous is left to the automatic test of competition, the conditions of the competition having been adjusted with a view to the survival of the method which is most efficient in terms of all its costs.

The other approach is to attempt to determine in advance which type of transport is most advantageous for a particular kind of service, and then to hand over that type of service to that type of transport. The first approach is appropriate to the policy of government, so far as government is concerned merely with regulating rates and fixing burdens of taxes or tolls for the use of public facilities. But any agency which is engaged in the actual furnishing of facilities or services for transportation must necessarily, at least to some extent approach the matter from the second and more difficult standpoint. If a private company decides to invest capital in facilities for engaging in a particular kind of service, it must satisfy itself that it has at least the usual competitive chance to make the investment pay. And if the Government invests funds in roads, waterway improvements or terminals, in the same way the Government should satisfy itself, before undertaking the outlay, that it is not promoting a socially wasteful method of transportation. And this is the form in which the problem presents itself as a problem in public works.

The main elements of this problem are basically simple, but the application is difficult and there are incidental considerations which complicate it. Basically, it is a question of reckoning the total cost of transportation, including the overhead cost of the whole investment involved, whether that investment is made by the Government or by a private company, and whether the rates charged for the service cover a financial return on the investment or not. The question of the worth-whileness of building a highway or improving a waterway must be figured in these terms, quite regardless of whether or not, after the work is done, the facilities are made available to users without tolls or other money charges.

The crucial factor in this calculation is the amount of use which will be made of the improvement, and since this must always be a matter of estimate, the whole calculation can never be an exact one. This is, of course, particularly true of methods of transportation which are growing or declining, or which are decidedly different from the ones in current use. Optimistic estimates of the volume of traffic which will use a given waterway, for instance, may result in reducing the estimated cost per ton-mile of traffic to a small fraction of the cost which is ultimately realized when the traffic fails to develop to anything like the volume originally estimated. And as to the probable volume of traffic, this is a matter not only of cost but of convenience and quality of service and not easily reduced to definite figures in advance.

The writer has seen estimates of the cost of traffic by a proposed water route, in which the cost of operating a fleet of barges was conscientiously reckoned, in a way that was above criticism, but the performance of the fleet in moving freight was estimated on a basis which made no allowance for idle time due to irregularities of traffic, or for more than a minimum delay of barges at terminals, with the results that the estimated performance was impossibly high and the estimated unit cost was only a fraction of what would result under actual traffic conditions. Furthermore, the total volume of traffic carried by the waterway was estimated as equal to the full capacity it would have had if completely utilized by fleets of barges, all operating at this same impossible rate of efficiency, with the result that the overestimate of performance was compounded. Actually, long before the number of barges moved reached this theoretical capacity, congestion at locks would have become so serious that costs would rise and the users would find that the capacity of the waterway was already over taxed. Since waterway traffic develops comparatively slowly, the average utilization over a period of years could hardly be much more than half of the maximum capacity, figured with due allowance for the element of delay and interference which must needs be encountered in practice. Thus, in figuring on a basis of theoretical capacity there were introduced three compounding elements all operating to reduce the estimated cost far below any figure which could possibly be achieved in practice. Actual costs would have been several times as large as the estimated costs, figured in this way, despite the fact that the basic figure of the annual cost of operating a fleet of barges was complete and unexceptionable.

Where costs are underestimated in this way, they have the further result of enormously increasing the estimates of the volume of traffic which can economically use such a waterway. It may even be made to appear that a large volume of traffic will be available, where in actual practice the traffic which could make sufficient savings to justify the private outlay involved would be quite negligible. A further complicating factor is the cost of getting traffic to the waterway. Certain exceptional waterways have the advantage of large volumes of suitable traffic, originating and terminating on the waterway or so near it as to make it possible to use the waterway without any more transfers than would be involved in handling the traffic by rail. An example of this is the Monongahela River, where large volumes of coal can be unloaded from mine cars at the private water terminals of the companies operating the mines, and can be hauled by fleets of barges owned by large coal or steel companies and operated at high efficiency, and unloaded at large steel plants, coke plants, or coal company terminals at the water's edge. Transportation of this sort can easily compete with railways. But to gather miscellaneous freight, hauled by trucks which could just as easily deliver it at rail terminals, to combine it in amounts sufficient to utilize the capacity of an efficient water haulage unit, which is comparable to a trainload of railroad freight, rather than to a carload, and then to distribute it at its destination on the same terms, is a very different matter. This is especially true since manufacturing concerns, not located at the water's edge, can easily secure a spur track connection with a railroad and get the advantage of carload rates, even though their shipments are not large enough to fill up the much larger capacity of a towboat, with its complement of barges. The additional terminal problem caused by the very large rise and fall of American rivers affords another difficulty which is well known to students of this problem. Thus, the estimating of costs and of volumes of available traffic is a serious matter, and one in which conscientious and apparently adequate estimates may sometimes go far wrong. This is far from meaning that all waterway traffic is necessarily uneconomical; but it does mean that the problem of estimating costs must be very cautiously and thoroughly approached.

One factor which might very considerably modify the results of such a calculation arises from the fact that the construction of transportation facilities may be one of the things which government undertakes in order to utilize labor and capital which otherwise would stand idle in times of depression. Figured in one way, the government thereby saves something in the way of relief expenditures which it would otherwise have to make, and also gains something in the way of taxes from a larger total volume of business activity than would otherwise be possible. Figured still more liberally, from the standpoint of the national economy as a whole, any such facilities which are produced with labor and capital which would otherwise be standing idle may be regarded as clear gain, costing the society as a whole virtually nothing. This method of figuring may be, in part, correct, and may justify the construction of facilities which cannot yield interest on the investment, figured in the ordinary way; but there remains the question whether one type of facilities is superior to another type, figured on the same basis. In other words, while it may be socially economical to build some kind of transportation facilities at such a time, more or less regardless of the possibility of earning interest on their cost, this does not affect the question whether this amount of capital investment can most usefully be put into waterway improvements, highway improvements, or improvements in railway facilities. If waterways or highways are chosen simply because they are a class of facilities which government customarily furnishes, while railways are customarily financed by private capital on governmental grants, the result is a begging of the question of the most economical use of the nation's resources. Comparisons between these different methods of transportation should be based on a reckoning of the capital cost on the same terms for one method as for another, if the result is to be the most economical transportation system for the country as a whole.

This brings us back to the proposition already mentioned, that we should not leave out of the reckoning the possibility of furnishing capital for use by quasi-private "public utilities" on the same terms on which it is available for public construction of highways and waterways, but without allowing the capital so furnished to be treated on the same terms as ordinary private capital in reckoning the valuation on which the companies have a right to a commercial return.

These are all problems affecting the issue of transportation coordination as it confronts the authorities responsible for public works. Many other phases of the question fall outside this field, such as the question whether the railways should abandon large volumes of short-haul freight to the highways and should furnish improved facilities and services which will take from the highways corresponding volumes of long-haul freight which railways may be able to handle more economically. There is also the question of the burdens which fall upon users of transportation facilities in the form of automobile license fees, gasoline taxes, and other forms of taxation. Ideally, so far as these facilities compete with each other, the total burdens in the form of license fees, gasoline taxes, etc., which are borne by highway traffic, should correspond in amount to the burden of taxes and interest on the permanent way which a railway has to charge to its shippers. However, it is hardly practicable to make this rule effective for all traffic which uses any kind of public thoroughfare, including the public streets which are open to the use of all freely. There is bound to be some discrimination somewhere, so long as some kinds of transportation have to pay full interest on the permanent way and others can use it without any charge. Roughly, burdens may be so arranged that, as between really competitive classes of traffic of large size, there is something approaching equality, but beyond that it is probably not practicable to attempt to go.

In the past, railways have been justified in the feeling that highway competition was subsidized against them in being given the use of expensive highways without having to pay charges corresponding in amount to the taxes and interest which the railways must collect from their users. The recent increase in gasoline taxes and in license fees has considerably reduced the ground for this complaint. Superficially, there may even be some ground for arguing that the shoe is now on the other foot, since in some States the receipts from gasoline taxes are used to support the general budget and not confined to highway construction. This, however, is not conclusive, since the annual budget of highway construction is by no means a precise equivalent for the annual charges in depreciation, maintenance, interest, and taxes on the permanent way of a railroad. To repeat, there is at present no reason to suppose that the system is very grossly discriminatory in these respects. More accurate studies of costs, on a comparable basis are, however, very much needed.

C. Watershed Authorities

In the Tennessee Valley Authority, the Government is trying a novel experiment in the possibility of controlling the economic development of a region, in which the basic controlling factor is the system of public works, centering in the development of the water power from the rivers of the region. This, of course, is not the only feature of this development which involves also land-use planning and other elements, but it is the most striking and outstanding factor. It is frankly an experiment, with many difficulties to be faced if it is to come to a successful outcome. The satisfactory disposal of the large volume of electric power, which is the central feature of the experiment, requires very considerable developments, both in the way of industrial and domestic use; and the success of these developments cannot be guaranteed beforehand. Needless to say, this experiment, once embarked upon, should be carried through in a sufficiently thorough going fashion to afford a real test of the possibilities of this kind of regional coordination development. It is unusual in that ordinarily public works of this class proceed hand in hand with spontaneous industrial development, rather than taking the lead and undertaking to bring the development about.

There are many other watersheds in which watershed authorities might very usefully be set up for the coordination and increased effectiveness of the works upon the waterways themselves, if for this reason only. But the more ambitious project of controlling the economic development of a whole region, now economically backward, using such public works developments as a leverage, is something into which it would be wise not to rush wholesale until the results of this rather daring pioneer experiment have had a chance to appear and to be appraised. In other words, other watershed authorities may very well be set up, but it would be the part of wisdom to limit the scope of their undertakings more narrowly to the development and use of the water resources themselves, rather than to attempt immediately to set up many duplicates of the present Tennessee Valley experiment.

The Mississippi Valley Committee is an organization of a different sort, being more nearly a planning organization than one equipped to try experiments on a large scale, on its own authority with its own resources. This experiment also deserves a most thorough trial, and is all the more valuable because it is different from the Tennessee Valley experiment. Other experiments of still different sorts may well be tried.

D. Land Utilization

It is becoming evident that a coherent program for the utilization of the country's land resources is a necessity. This is true for two main reasons. One is the fact that unregulated private development has proved unable successfully to adjust itself to the changes in market conditions, governed as they are by world-wide forces and subject to all of the world-wide disturbances of the post-war period. Very rapid readjustments of this sort need to be assisted, if they are to be made in an orderly way and are not to involve ruinous loss and distress to millions of individuals, who are faced with conditions for which they are not responsible.

A second and even more compelling reason for a coherent public policy is the fact that the country is already following a number of different policies, which have at times been definitely inconsistent with each other. With one hand the Government has engaged in irrigation and land reclamation projects, resulting in increasing the area under cultivation, while with the other hand it has been attempting to reduce the area under cultivation by bringing about the abandonment of the poorest lands. These two angles of the Government's policy have recently been brought together under the guiding principle of taking out of cultivation areas of equal yield to those brought into cultivation. But this does not dispose of the whole question, so long as efforts are still being made to reduce the cultivation on the land which remains in use. The substitution of better land for poorer land is a gain under normal circumstances, enabling the same crop to be raised with less labor, but it still does not answer the questions raised by a situation which seems to call for a reduction in the crop and a still further reduction in the labor employed in raising it.

Experiments looking toward a more constructive answer to this question include the so-called subsistence homestead movement, which is an attempt to place families on small areas of land on which they can raise produce for their own use, while getting a money income from various forms of decentralized industry, conducted near their homesteads. This, like the Tennessee Valley authority, represents an experiment of which the outcome can only be awaited. In the meantime, it affords one of the fields into which public works funds can be directed. And, so far as it proves successful, it opens up a field which has become promising in that the kind of economic development it tends to produce is a more nearly self-sufficing one than the present system, better adapted to standing the strains of depression, and one in which the natural demands for fresh developments is likely to coincide roughly with future burdens of industrial depression, so that it affords a field in which expansion of public works expenditures during depressions can most naturally be carried on.

There are other needs and opportunities for public works in connection with a system of land use planning and development. Soil surveys are needed for guiding the utilization of the land, work in preventing erosion is needed to protect our basic soil resources from being rapidly destroyed, and forestation and the development of public park areas, in regions which have proved unsuitable to agriculture, call for very considerable expenditures. All of this is in addition to the kind of land use planning which is involved in the proper development of large regions surrounding the great centers of population, which is destined for large developments in the future, if these regions are to realize their full possibilities as areas in which human beings are to live and work under the best possible conditions.

E. The Problem of Low-Cost Housing

The importance of this problem has already been indicated, together with some of the difficulties. No single type of program can be prescribed for all situations—for example, it is impossible to determine for all localities whether housing near the urban center is better than housing on cheaper outlying lands, or whether housing on outlying lands can be successfully accompanied by the moving of industry to the outlying sections, or whether the people living in these developments must bear the expense and time of going into the urban center to their work. The program must be experimental and elastic.

It also seems doubtful whether the gap between housing costs and the ability of the low-income groups to pay rent can be successfully bridged without a simultaneous solution of problems affecting all the various elements of cost, including construction wages, prices of materials, capital and financing charges, economies of large-scale housing production, taxation, land values, and possible revisions of minimum standards of housing accommodations as prescribed in the housing codes. A hasty and large-scale program can easily result in competition with existing types of housing rather than successful reaching of a market not now reached, and may interfere with legitimate private construction without obtaining the end desired by the public program. Thus caution is indicated, even though the field is one of great potential usefulness.

The present policy of the Federal Government is of a twofold character. On the one hand, it is engaged in conducting actual housing developments and financing others with public funds. As already pointed out, attempts to force developments of his sort on a large scale before solving the problem of cost would probably be premature, and might do more harm than good. On the other hand, the attempt is being made to stimulate the investment of private capital in home improvements and other developments, through the method of guaranteeing mortgages. This also is experimental, but it has the great advantage that it does not substitute public enterprise for private enterprise in such a way as to create the danger of obstructing more developments than it stimulates.

Would it prove practicable to secure the temporary use of idle private plant capacity on easy terms? Could such use be taken under an extension of the principle of eminent domain, for a payment based on its value when idle: In short, by paying little above actual wear and tear? Or would the Government, if it went into the experiment, have to furnish its own plant facilities?

F. Efforts at Self-Help or Self-Sufficing Production

In this field widespread experiments have sprung up spontaneously throughout the country, raising the problem of public policy and attitude toward these experiments. Their usefulness is obviously limited by their local character, making impossible the efficiency which can come only with division of labor on a large scale. Attempts at voluntary correlation have so far accomplished little. Should the Government become a coordinating agency making possible local specialization on particular products and interchange on a national scale, and possibly furnishing capital where necessary for this purpose? Or would such an attempt merely wipe out the peculiar value of these spontaneous experiments and change them into something different which might fail? Should a nucleus of this sort of activity be maintained in readiness for expansion in future emergencies? How would a more extended system of this sort react on the prospects of private business recovery? Could it be safeguarded from the danger of permanently separating some of the workers from the more efficient private system of production and attaching them to a less efficient system? The importance of the experiment justifies a thorough investigation of these questions with a view to formulating a constructive policy.

In the meantime, the Government is itself engaged in the very interesting experiment of putting otherwise unemployed workers to work in producing goods for the use of the unemployed themselves. As already noted, this opens up one of the most natural avenues of demand for labor at a time when workers are in need of goods for the reason that private industry cannot find means to employ them and thus to give them the incomes necessary to purchase the goods in the ordinary way. The economic results of this experiment remain to be determined. Already there have been protests from private producers who see in it a reduction of the demand for their own products. To this answer has been made that the goods thus produced are goods which the unemployed would not have been able to buy otherwise, for lack of income. Perhaps a more pertinent answer would be that, while some of these goods might otherwise have been purchased from private employers by the use of relief funds and distributed to the unemployed, or bought by the unemployed themselves with relief doles, these funds must come from somewhere, and if the doles are long continued, the funds must be raised by taxes which would burden industry and reduce private purchasing power. Another answer which has been made is in the form of the question: "Could private industry employ these same workers and so afford them normal purchasing power?" It appears that, so long as private industry cannot do this, it has no vested interest, either in the market represented by the purchasing power these workers would have if they were employed, or in the reserve of labor power represented by the unemployed workers, standing idle and waiting for someone to hire them.

Production on this basis is not likely to be efficient enough to compete seriously with private enterprise on anything like a fair and comparable basis. The chief danger, perhaps, is that it may be made to appear more efficient than it is, and to afford the publicly employed workers a better living than they are actually producing by their own efforts, being supported by what amounts to a Government subsidy. If this danger is avoided, there is probably little real reason to fear that the opportunity for private employment of these workers will be permanently interfered with.

To sum up, the experiment appears to be a justifiable one under present conditions, and one to be carried out cautiously and with a view to avoiding the inherent dangers which can be seen in advance.

A. An Organic Network of Problems

It has been sufficiently evident in the course of this study that public works do not stand alone. They are part of more comprehensive policies which they must be made to subserve, and in which public works are only one instrument or agency, not adequate by itself alone to produce the desired result, but needing to be coordinated with numerous other instruments and agencies. If they could be regarded as a part of some one larger policy, and wholly subordinated to that one, the case would be simpler than it is. But there are a considerable number of policies or fields of policy, each broader than public works, in which public works play a part. Even to carry out the purposes most directly associated with public works themselves, there is need of coordinated action in numerous other fields.

The classification of problems and fields of investigation and action can be carried out on a number of principles, some of them quite metaphysical. For the purposes of this study, classification will be governed by the kinds of considerations which have a direct bearing on the organization of the actual work of investigating problems and of carrying out policies. Here the dominant consideration is the fact that certain kinds of work can best be done by an agency, such as an executive department or bureau, whose organization is adapted to that kind of work and whose personnel is experienced in it, and if the performance of any given branch of work needs to be modified by the introduction of new purposes, this frequently becomes a practical problem of introducing into the scheme of organization persons or groups of persons who approach the problem from the standpoint of these new purposes, and whose background is such as to make them familiar with the conditions which are necessary to see that these new purposes are successfully carried out.

It is becoming increasingly true that the economic field does not present an area of separate problems, but a network of interrelated ones. This network is an organic unity. Nevertheless, in terms of the practical considerations governing actual organization, it is not one single problem, and cannot be treated as such except in the realm of rather empty words. We can give this network a name, and call it "the problem of economic control" or "the problem of promoting human welfare by economic means." But such a name would not prevent the "problem" from being in fact many problems, nor would it help toward practical ways of handling their interrelations. Control is of many sorts, directed to many ends; and human welfare, as we actually deal with it, becomes a matter of adjustment and compromise between different values for which there seems no possibility of developing a common yardstick of measurement.

Even in the hypothetical case of a centralized and supreme authority—say, a personal dictator—in a country as large and complex as the United States, he would still have to preserve the system of Government departments on some basis very similar to the present one, with the result that these departments would still represent different purposes, different approaches to economic problems, and different perspectives limiting the scope of their view and the emphasis of their policies. The dictator might specify some policies in each department, but it would be physically impossible for all questions to pass through his mind and for all decisions to be made there. In matters he did not himself decide, he might set up methods of interdepartmental coordination which are not now in effect, but he would still face the natural impatience of any body of executives, whose immediate problem seems to require all their efforts and attention, at being asked to spend time and divert their minds to a consideration of the problems of other executive bodies, more especially if they are asked to modify their governing purposes and policies for some reason which to them is incidental. Such modifications may be necessary to the successful achievement of the main purpose of some other executive body, and an appreciation of that fact may reduce the resistance, but will not automatically abolish it. For a country which does not live under a supreme dictatorship, the problem is mainly one of coordinating the different purposes and limiting perspectives, rather than overruling them by executive fiat.

The amount of this work of coordination is growing, and will continue to grow. This means that the executive authorities must spend an increasing amount of their time in this way. And it would be only natural if the head of a department came to feel, at times, that it was more important to concentrate more of his attention on developing an efficient department of the customary sort, rather than to develop a department better coordinated with other departments but less efficient in its own work because its high officials have been compelled to dissipate their attention and energies. If this result is to be avoided, the organization of the departments themselves must be adjusted to this new set of demands, which means that there must be increasing delegation of the more routine executive work, leaving certain strategic officials (who need not in every case be the heads of the departments) sufficiently free to be able to do this work of coordination without sacrificing the efficiency of their own departments in their specialized work.

As an illustration of the way in which fields are interrelated, we might start with the problem of unemployment. This includes not only relief or compensation but also attempts to prevent the condition or cure it. Unemployment, however, is due to many causes. Part of it is due to business fluctuations. And if there is—as there is apparently coming to be—a fairly well-marked field of business-cycle policy, that field overlaps part of the field of the unemployment problem, both as to relief and as to prevention. It also reaches out into various other fields. There is also a definite field of fiscal policy, which differs from the field of unemployment and the field of business-cycle policy in that there is a definite governmental department which has it in charge. Unemployment relief raises fiscal problems, policies of unemployment prevention are likely to raise them, and general business-cycle policies also have fiscal aspects. More or less closely related with the fiscal fields is the field of money and credit, overlapping in some respects and autonomous in other respects, and equally likely to be concerned with policies of unemployment relief, unemployment prevention, or business-cycle remedies. Overlapping portions of these fields is the more definite and limited field of public-works policy, with its fiscal aspects, its aspects of unemployment relief and prevention, and of business-cycle policy, as well as other aspects lying outside of all these fields. One might try to represent these relationships in a diagram with overlapping areas, but no such diagram could do justice to all the inter-relationships involved.

B. Interrelationships of the Public Works Problem

1. If we look for the most simple and direct purpose governing public works in and of themselves, we find a little difficulty to start with, in that public works have no single purpose, but represent facilities needed for the promoting of a great variety of purposes of public service. But from the standpoint of the persons engaged in constructing the works these many ultimate purposes may be taken for granted. Certain things are wanted. The purpose of a public-works authority is to furnish these things as effectively and economically as possible, in proper amounts and of proper kinds. Even this, however, calls for some judgment as between the conflicting values involved in more or less adequate supplies of different kinds of public works in general and of saving the public's money for other purposes. But even with such consideration as is ordinarily given to these broader questions, the perspective of those directly engaged in furnishing public works is ordinarily a limited one, concerned mainly with technical efficiency and economy.

The actual official is likely to have a still more limited perspective, in which he is looking at one kind of public works by itself—a post office or a road—and looking at it in terms of existing conditions only. Actual budgets are made up largely by adding together projects, each of which is viewed in this way, and without reducing the whole to a really organic program. But if this program is looked at with a view to genuinely coordinating these different parts, and if in addition it is looked at in a long-time perspective, then the result is different. The outcome is public-works planning; and when this is carried to its logical conclusion it is nothing short of the designing of a setting for the whole economic life of a community. It cannot be successfully done solely in terms of the physical features of the community, routes of traffic, location of different types of industry, etc., as they are at a given moment, but must undertake to forecast them and, to a considerable extent, to direct them into the most effective system which can be foreseen and devised.

When this point is reached there is no logical way of refusing to take a still further step; namely, to take account of the effect on the course of economic life of the process of constructing the works. Economic life is affected not merely by the services rendered by the completed works but also by the process of completing them. It is a question not merely of the kind of physical equipment with which the community will ultimately be furnished, but of the stability and prosperity of the community as they are influenced by the process of building the equipment. This process is endless, and it would be a complete mistake to look forward to a time when the community shall have reached a final and complete development, with a definitive equipment of public works in which there is to be no further change. If it ever reached that point and further construction of public works were limited to replacements only, that would in itself be one of the most catastrophic changes that could be imagined.   In short, the logical development of public-works planning, starting with the narrowest conception of it, leads inevitably to a kind of planning which includes the effect on business prosperity of the rate at which construction of public works goes on.   This becomes one of the integral purposes of a public-works policy, though it is one which has been almost completely ignored until very recent years.

The practical problem resulting is one of introducing this objective into the administration of public works.   This becomes a question of introducing persons who have the background and point of view necessary for dealing with this problem adequately, or who will develop it through being specifically charged with this function.   At present the typical construction engineer dealing with the construction of public works does not have this background or point of view.   Some few engineers have it; many economists have it; and other individuals in various pursuits are developing it in varying degrees.   Not only must such individuals be found, but they must be equipped with the necessary tools in the way of research and statistical information and so organized and placed in the scheme of governmental agencies that they may contribute their part in the determination of policy without interfering with the efficient handling of the technical parts of the work which call for a different personnel with a different background and point of view.

2. But if public works are, or should be, a means of industrial stabilization, they are only one means, not adequate in themselves to perform the whole task.   Thus if there is a body of persons so placed as to become a working part of the administration of public works and looking to industrial stabilization as their main purpose in the scheme, they must not merely be a part of the public works administration, but a part of a larger scheme of organization, comprehending all the necessary elements of a stabilization policy.   This includes policies in the fields of prices—both general price levels and particular prices or groups of prices relative to others—wages and the distribution of incomes, credit, speculation, taxation and fiscal policy, production of capital goods or durable goods in general, savings and spendings, unemployment relief or unemployment insurance, and other incidental matters.   A proper public works policy depends on what is done in these various fields, and vice versa.

As already remarked, public policy in respect to industrial stabilization is coming to be a definitely recognized field of policy.   But, unlike fiscal policy or policy towards corporations or labor, it is not at present embodied in any definite agency or department.   It appears to be an inevitable next step in the development of our governmental organization that there should be a definite governmental unit of some sort in which all the problems of this field of policy should be brought together and considered as a whole.   How to correlate such a body with the rest of the governmental agencies is one of the important and pressing questions which we face in adjusting our governmental structure to its present tasks.

3. In the fiscal field, public works are only a part of the policy of governmental spending and revenue raising or of providing funds by borrowing, with ultimate repayment.   Viewed from the conventional public works standpoint, they raise new problems very essentially

different from the ordinary problems of financing governmental outlays. But when viewed as a means of industrial stabilization the method of raising funds becomes a vital part of the scheme, determining whether it promotes the end in view or not. The policy of spending needs to be better coordinated than it is now, and the policy of raising funds needs to be coordinated with the spending policy, as we have already seen. From this standpoint, sales taxes cannot be viewed merely as means of raising revenues, but must be judged according to whether they do or do not neutralize the effect of the policy that is being followed in the field of public spending, by diminishing private consumption.

As we have also seen, the depression has disturbed the balance between different classes of public spending, in such a way as to do obvious violence to the principle of apportioning public funds so that more important services are not sacrificed while less important purposes are being carried out. Education is being seriously interfered with, while works of much less value are being pushed forward. We have seen that this results in part from the fact that some governmental units have exhausted their power of raising money, while others, especially the Federal Government, still have power to raise large sums on credit. We have seen that it further results from the traditional conception of a yearly balancing of budgets, and from conceptions of permanent assets as proper bases on which to issue loans, these conceptions being borrowed from private industry and needing very basic alteration before they can properly be applied in the field of public finance and to permanent assets which do not yield any money income. We have further seen that the situation is complicated by fiscal considerations concerned with loans and grants made by one governmental unit to another. All these considerations seem at present to stand in the way of the basic principle of apportioning the funds at the country's disposal in such a way as to produce the most effective result for the Nation's economy, viewing that economy as a whole. We have also seen that there is need, on ordinary fiscal grounds, of a fairly general overhauling of the fiscal system, and that these special considerations should find a place in such an overhauling and may do so if their claims are properly presented and supported. There is evidently need of coordinating treasury policy and fiscal policy in general with the kind of considerations which are likely to be worked out only by a body devoting itself to the general problem of industrial stabilization.

4. Public works policy is also a part of a general policy toward the capital-goods or durable-goods industries. The public demand for construction is a vital part of the demand in these industries, but it must never be forgotten that these industries are a part of an economic system, and that the Government is not their only customer. In the long run, private demand is more important than public, and support from the Public Treasury may be a doubtful benefit if it is so handled as to stand in the way of revival of private demand—as, for example, by bidding up costs unduly. Thus public works should be so handled as to permit a return to normal conditions, neither retarding normal recovery of private demand, nor accentuating any tendency to an unhealthy boom, as might be done if debt repayment resulted in pouring funds back into the capital markets at a time when business tends toward over expansion and when these additional funds may provide a stimulus to an undue increase of private investment.

5. Public works policy is also one part of the policy of unemployment relief, which is in turn part of the general problem of unemployment. Regular public works and relief work stand in a peculiar relationship to each other, since despite their obvious common feature they are governed by different principles and follow different policies as to wages and the selection of workers, as well as in the selection of work to be done. These policies need to be made consistent with each other on some rational plan, without doing away with the differences which are presumably essential to a rational correlation, since the functions of the two kinds of work are different. The available resources of the community must be spread over the various forms of activity making up a program of relief and stimulation in view of the fact that relief of some sort for all those who are destitute is a basic necessity, while the other forms of policy are more expensive and at the same time yield additional benefits of a different sort. It would be desirable to furnish something better than bare relief for everyone who needs it, but is does not seem possible at present.

While it would seem to be desirable, in view of these facts, to make sure that all the activities resulting in relief for the unemployed should be coordinated into a harmonious policy, the actual evils resulting from failure to coordinate perfectly seem less serious in this field than in some others. It may be that the effective limitations on relief work are found mainly in the field of relief work itself and that the same is true of regular public works, with the result that little is lost by lack of coordination, so long as the more expensive policies do not absorb so much of the available funds as to leave the relief funds too small to give the minimum necessary relief to those in absolute need of it. It also seems appropriate that relief work and regular public works should be handled by separate bodies, though with definite provision for coordinating their policies.

6. Public works are also a part of a general policy toward the creation and distribution of purchasing power. Viewed in the largest aspect, this has to do not merely with the total amount of purchasing power but with the whole question of policy toward the distribution of incomes and also of the disposition that is made of them. Thus it becomes a question of policy in the matter of consumption versus savings, so far as public action can affect this matter.

7. If we think in terms of the distribution of real incomes, of goods and services, instead of merely of money incomes, it is clear that public works affect this from another angle. They represent means by which services are rendered to the community and to its members, usually free of charge. An increase of public works almost inevitably means an increase in this volume of free services or free social income—free in the sense that the individual does not have to pay a price for it on receiving the service. Or, if the services are not free, they are likely to be rendered more cheaply than private enterprise would render them, on a basis which sometimes amounts to a public subsidy. It may be that the scope of public works will be broadened in the future as a result of a policy of increasing the amount of this free social income, in part at least in a deliberate attempt to alter the distribution of command over the necessaries of a safe and worthwhile existence, and causing these things to be more evenly distributed than they would be if they were all furnished on a private business basis. This is a matter of long-run development, and has comparatively little to do with the ironing out of cycles of prosperity and

depression; although the movement may receive a special stimulus in times of depression, both on account of the increased need for free public services which is felt at such a time and on account of the willingness to undertake new kinds of service in the process of finding ways to enlarge the budget of public works.

8. Overlapping this question is the question of policy toward the extension of public ownership, with or without public operation, to forms of productive wealth which are ordinarily handled privately. Every special extension enlarges the proportion of the total income of the Nation which flows through the channels of public works. Properly speaking, such an enlargement of the field of public works should be merely an incident to a wise decision as between public and private ownership and operation. This was probably the case with the Tennessee Valley experiment, although the need for increased public works expenditures in themselves may have played some part in reducing opposition to the acceptance of this program. At a time when the Government is ready to spend more than usual on public works, and to do it without asking quite as insistently as usual whether the results will be worth the expenditure, in ordinary money terms, a proposal for such an experiment as the Tennessee Valley Authority is carrying on has a better chance of favorable reception.

This illustrates a very baffling sort of interrelation between purposes, and one which there is very little hope of settling in an ideally rational way. But the fundamental reason is merely the fact that there does not exist any such thing as an ideally rational social mind. No one would deliberately embark on a public-ownership program, otherwise considered undesirable, merely because he is hunting for ways in which Government may spend public-works money. That would be quite irrational. What happens is that certain groups regard the public-ownership experiment as justifiable on its merits, while others regard it as unjustifiable on the same grounds, and still others are in doubt. The situation simply tends to strengthen the position of one group and to weaken the resistance of the other. As long as ultimate decisions in such matters are made by legislative bodies, this sort of confused relationship between issues cannot be wholly avoided. It will not be wholly avoided even by setting up a scientific and impartial planning board and charging it with the duty of weighing the issues in the light of impartial research.

9. Since public works are a part of the market for goods and for labor, the Government is embarked on activities which influence prices and wages. Traditionally, Government as a purchaser acts much like other purchasers, though often it is more liberal than private buyers who are under the pressure of competition. However, Government is coming more and more to have general policies toward prices and wages in the economic field as a whole; and this means that either its own activities as a buyer must be harmonious with these general policies, or else it is likely to be guilty of inconsistency.

Inconsistency between different Government policies affecting the same subject matter is no new thing. It is particularly likely to flourish in times of emergency when new policies are being rapidly struck out in various directions by various agencies which have not had time to compare notes and to work out the more far-reaching implications of what they are doing. The result, of course, is likely to be mutual defeat and waste motion. And there is a great need for somebody especially qualified to search for inconsistencies of this sort and either work out a consistent policy or bring together the departments whose policies are in conflict, in order that they may work out a consistent policy between them. The question of wage and price policies at the present time is undoubtedly a case in point.

10. Public works policy is, as we have seen, a part of the long-run planning of the physical conditions of life affecting the social and economic development of regional units. In other words, it is a part of the whole movement of local and regional planning, whose character and background have already been described and which is quite separate from the movement toward industrial stabilization, in terms of its background and associations. The fact that this movement is broader than a mere public works policy is illustrated by the studies now being carried on under the various State planning boards. These studies are very broad, covering substantially the whole field of the material conditions of economic life, the proper use of land and water resources, and similar matters, while public works represent only one group of studies. Coming back to the practical considerations of organization, this seems to mean that public works need to have the benefit of the kind of approach represented by the class of persons who have developed the concept and practice of regional planning as it now stands, while not making this approach supreme over all the other points of view and approaches which have already been dealt with.

11. The public works policy is also a part of what may be a rather far reaching change in the structure of political government. This change represents the necessary adaptation of government to the kind of procedure represented by the term "planning", or rather to the next steps which are destined to be taken in the development of that procedure. The result of this development is likely to be an increase in executive functions and a reduction in the extent to which legislative bodies participate in the detailed framing of policies.

If planning is to be effective, it requires that policies shall be put in force and allowed to remain in force over considerably periods of time. If every successive legislature of Congress completely reverses the policies of its predecessors, planning can never be effective. This raises a question which may appear somewhat like an insoluble dilemma, in view of the fact that no legislative body can bind its successors, and that the executive is, in theory, limited to carrying out the will of the legislature. There is little likelihood of any change in the structure of government which will remove the formal supremacy of the legislature or the formal freedom of every succeeding legislative body to alter the acts of its predecessors. What is likely to happen is something slower and less spectacular, but perhaps no less important.

As things stand, the legislative body and the chief executive constitute the two agencies through which inconsistencies of policy between different departments may be arbitrated and an integrated policy worked out. But if the whole trend of the foregoing discussion means anything it means that there are destined to develop organs of correlation within the general executive structure itself, whereby conflicts of objective or of policy may be worked out and unified policies developed. If adequate and workable policies are formulated in this way, within the structure of the executive departments, they are likely to acquire a vastly increased weight and to be much more likely to carry with them the sanction of the legislative body. This will not be because the legislative authority will have been formally curtailed in any way, but simply because the enormously difficult job of correlation will have been done in all probability better than the legislature could have done it and on a basis which would require rather weighty considerations to justify the legislature in upsetting the adjustment and proposing a new one. In other words, policies proceeding from the executive department of government may acquire added authority of the sort which automatically accrues to the proposals of those who are in closest and most comprehensive touch with the work which is actually to be done, and whose proposals represent the maturest balancing of all the interests involved. An increase in executive authority, so long as it is on this basis, presents no serious dangers, since the legislative body can always overrule the executive if its power is wrongly used, or if a great popular wish arises.   Thus we do not need to be afraid of entering upon changes which give the executive more power in the formation of policy than it has had in the past, so long as those changes are merely of the sort needed to enable the executive to frame a more effective and comprehensive policy, and rely on this alone for the power necessary to put the policy into effect. This same development would naturally carry with it a greater stability of policy over periods of time, to the extent that the problems facing the executive departments remain fundamentally the same, and a considerable part of their personnel does not come and go with changing administrations.

There is, then, no possibility of setting up a planning board which shall be in a position to adopt a program and preserve it inviolate against the power of succeeding legislatures to change it. But there is a possibility of setting up machinery for the working out of policies which shall have a great deal more stability than corresponding policies have had in the past, not by curtailing the formal power of the legislature but by virtue of meeting the needs of the underlying economic situation more comprehensively and providing means of meeting recurrent future emergencies more consistently and properly than could be done by legislatures working out fresh policies on their own responsibility.

C. Conclusions Bearing on Basic Governmental Organization

1. THE FEDERAL GOVERNMENT

We may take it for granted that in the future there will be some increase in general planning, at least in the sense of efforts to coordinate the many divisions of economic policy whose interrelations have been traced in the foregoing discussion. This is true, whatever may be the policies themselves which ultimately result from such attempts at coordination. Government is concerned with economic life more intimately than before, and in a larger number of interrelated ways. This change will be left as a sequel to the New Deal even if the Government should in the future retreat as far as possible from the position of increased control in economic affairs which it has taken under the present administration.

Furthermore, it seems to be a sound principle that, if a particular interest is to be promoted, it can best be done if there is a special body whose main function it is to promote that interest. In other words, there are powerful advantages about setting up some body which will be definitely concerned with the task of correlating policies and working out a unified policy. Different executive departments, each primarily interested in carrying out its own departmental work, will not have this same degree of interest in the task of correlation, which has been shown to be so vitally necessary. The natural conclusion is that there should be set up a body charged with this function of correlation and of working out a unified policy.

It seems clear also, from what has gone before, that this body should not be expected or permitted simply to take over the work of forming governmental policies and imposing them on the existing departments, who should be required to carry them out. If it attempted to do this, its policies would fail to have precisely that kind of weight which, as has already been shown, might cause them to be substantially accepted by the legislative bodies and successfully carried out by the departments concerned. Such a body must work with the existing departments and not attempt to impose its will upon them from without. It may initiate policies, but any assumption of arbitrary authority to force their adoption would be fatal. This type of body may be called, for lack of a better name, a general planning board, or perhaps, a general planning and coordinating board, with the definite understanding that its planning is of the sort already indicated and that it does not represent in any sense a committee of economic dictatorship.

Such a body would deal largely in research and fact finding, such as are necessary to the framing of coordinated policies. Even here it should not supersede or duplicate the work already done by many existing departments, but should rather establish itself as a clearing house for the results of such researches, with the further function of bringing to the attention of those bodies now engaged in research various needs for information or for modifications of the classification of data, which may be necessary in order to make the results shed the proper light on particular problems. It should, of course, be free to supplement this information by its own researches to any extent which might appear necessary. It should, then, have a department of research and fact finding, which might ultimately become fairly extensive.

Another important function would be to initiate and participate in conferences between various departments concerned with particular problems and whose policies may need to be harmonized. This much seems to be called for, whether the country does or does not enter upon a program such as is nowadays being advocated under the title of "a planned economy." It seems clear that we are not prepared at present to embark successfully upon the kind of policy which is commonly conveyed by this phrase. The kind of planning board here indicated would be a necessary first step toward preparing ourselves for such a planned economy, if it is to be ultimately developed; but such a board may be limited to the development of a general correlated governmental policy without such a radical extension of control in the economic field as would be represented by the term "planned economy." In either case the kind of planning board already indicated seems to be equally necessary.

One reason for dealing with this question of a general planning board in this study, which is specifically directed to the particular problem of public works, is the fact that there are many things to be done in carrying out a successful public works policy, which such a general planning board could best do. In fact, it seems virtually impossible to work out an adequate public works policy without such a general planning board to assist in correlating all the features of fiscal policy, credit policy, labor policies, and others which have already been indicated, as well as to perform some more specific functions which will be pointed out in the succeeding chapter.

In addition to the general planning board, there is need of another board dealing with the specific problems of public works as such. It might or might not ultimately engage in the actual construction of public works, now in the hands of a large number of separate administrative bodies. In either case, its most essential function is to bring about unified policies in the public-works field. The scope of its functions would, of course, be determined by the nature of the policy adopted.

To be more specific, the minimum functions of this board would be somewhat larger than those of the Federal Employment Stabilization Board. Its work would fall into engineering and financial sections, the financial being mainly concerned with loans and grants to States and localities in cases of major emergency. This board should have effective liaison with the departments carrying on Federal works, possibly with representation of those departments on the board in an advisory capacity but without power to dominate its decisions. The investigations and findings of this board should be given definite standing in the procedures of the Bureau of the Budget, under a standing program for stabilization of grade A outlays over a period of years—say 6—which would have the effect of making the findings of the board prima facie valid so long as they keep within the total amounts called for by the 6-year program. Ultimately, if the board commands confidence, its findings might become final as budgetary proposals within these limitations. In short, what is proposed is a reconstituted Federal Employment Stabilization Board with enlarged functions and better defined standing relative to the various departments and to the Bureau of the Budget, and with emergency functions corresponding to those now exercised by the Public Works Administration.

2. STATE, LOCAL, AND REGIONAL ORGANIZATIONS

Each State should have bodies performing the same general functions as these two bodies already indicated for the Federal Government, although not necessarily organized in the same way. The general planning body will be less concerned with framing a national policy of general economic stabilization, and more concerned with the kind of problems appropriate to the physical planning of regional developments. Both the general planning body and the public works planning body may have offshoots in smaller regions and localities, or may cooperate with bodies established in these regions and localities. The Federal Government has an interest in the setting up of these State and local bodies, which has already led it to furnish technical assistance and to set up certain standards tending to make these various bodies fit into a common scheme. This kind of Federal relationship is entirely proper. The Federal function should be limited to furnishing stimulus and incentive to the setting up of bodies which will serve the general purpose and fit into a coordinated scheme, without prescribing details of organization.

A. Essential Elements in a Consistent Policy

It is not the purpose of this study to deliver a final verdict as to precisely what policy must and should be followed. What can be done is to present the alternatives, and to indicate how the various factors to be dealt with are bound together, so that one can say: "If such a policy is to be followed with respect to this one part of the field, consistency requires such and such complementary policies in other parts of the field." And finally, it may be possible to present some fairly definite conclusions as to the relative importance of different features of a possible program, so that it may be possible to say: "A should be done before B. If A is not done, then it is inconsistent or unwise to attempt B." Some things may be decided as being practically necessary if any intelligent program is to be followed at all. On other matters there is room for wide difference of opinion and need of a great deal of further study before we shall be properly equipped to decide the issues involved with any large degree of confidence. In many of these doubtful cases, not merely study but actual experimentation will probably be necessary.

1. One of the most important elements of a consistent program is consistent treatment of expenditures as between durable public works and current services. The general rule would seem to be that current services should be maintained during a depression before we think of expanding public works. So far as the object of a public-works policy is to increase general purchasing power in order to offset the decrease due to industrial contraction, it is an inconsistency to contract expenditures on current services at the same time that expenditures on public works are being expanded.

So far as it is merely a question of preventing outright unemployment, or of modifying distribution of purchasing power with a view to placing it where it is most needed, this general rule is subject to a certain amount of elasticity. A case may be made for transferring a certain amount of purchasing power from the class of regular Government employees to the class of construction workers, if there is a limit to the total amount of purchasing power which Government can safely distribute through its own expenditures. If the Government is already distributing all it safely can, and if there appear to be sufficient grounds for diverting some of this amount to help the construction industries and their workers, then there may be a case for some economies in the field of the regular current governmental services. The forms which these economies can take have already been indicated. In general, they cannot consistently go to the point of actually laying off public employees and creating unemployment in this field, while relieving it in other fields. Another limit which can reasonably be set is that essential public services, such as those of health, police, and education, should not be curtailed at the same time that Government is being more than ordinarily liberal in other directions. This is a definite inconsistency of policy.

This general rule of policy carries with it financial implications. It requires that public expenditures should be more stable than public

155

revenues; and this implies that there will be deficits at certain times, which should properly be balanced by surpluses in more prosperous times. In other words, it calls for the principle of balancing budgets over a term of years, rather than insisting on a balance during each 12-month period. In the case of the Federal Government, this policy presents little difficulty during minor depressions, since the Government will, for many years to come, be in need of reducing its funded debt, and will be employing surplus revenues for this purpose, at least during times of prosperity.

During minor recessions a reduction in the rate of debt retirement will afford sufficient leeway to maintain a stable volume of current expenditures, without necessitating a deficit. Where a definite sinking fund has been already created through regular charges set up for retiring debts, these debt-retirement charges may create a technical deficit, even though there is a real surplus of revenues above current expenses. Such technical deficits are, in most cases, not a sufficient reason for curtailing current expenses during periods of moderate depression. This principle of stabilized current expenses carries with it the necessity for setting up certain kinds of fiscal machinery, such as elastic debt limits and possibly provisions for Federal aid to States and localities during serious emergencies.

2. With regard to the question of expanding public works during depressions, the principle may be laid down that it is more important to expand public works during serious emergencies than during minor depressions. Minor depressions create less serious economic and social evils; and furthermore, they appear to have the quality of curing themselves; while major crises may reach a point at which the automatic forces of recovery lose their power to act. If it were possible for the Government, by increasing public expenditures to the utmost extent possible, and stretching its resources of credit to the limit of safety, to bring about complete stabilization of minor fluctuations in business, this would not be a wise or consistent policy to follow, since it would leave the Government with its capacity to help industry exhausted at just the time when it would be most critically needed. Thus, if public works are to be increased during depressions, it is more important to be in a position to increase them during major crises than during minor recessions of business.

3. We have already seen that, as means to stimulate general business, expenditures financed by credit are vastly more effective than expenditures financed by increased taxes of such sorts as would be available at such times. Thus consistency requires that credit policy should be coordinated with public works policy. Furthermore, the policy of raising funds for public works by the use of credit needs to be fitted in with the general policy with regard to the credit structure as a whole, and special measures taken if necessary to counteract any undesirable effects. For example, it has been noted that an unduly rapid repayment of the public debt during boom times may need to be counteracted by deflationary measures in order to forestall a possible unhealthy speculative movement in the investment market.

4. Consistency also requires that, so far as public-works policy deals with wages and prices, it should be coordinated with a consistent general policy in these matters. This implies that there should be a consistent general policy in these fields—something

which has not as yet been fully worked out, but which is urgently called for if the present policies of the Government are to be organized into a consistent whole. Such a wage and price policy is an integral part of any policy looking toward industrial stabilization, and also a part of possible more far-reaching policies of economic development in general.

5. As already indicated, the kind of consistent policy toward public expenditures in general which has been laid down requires provisions for the use of Federal credit as a backing for State and local expenditures, in times of major emergencies. This is true, even if nothing more is attempted than the maintenance of the customary rates of expenditure at such times; and still more if expenditures on public works are to be increased.

6. If there is to be a policy of altering the timing of public works so as to increase the amount of such work when general business falls off, this will require machinery involving a very large increase in administrative control in this field. To a smaller extent, such an increase in administrative control will be required even if the objective is limited to the stabilizing of public-works expenditures. Even this will call for a program drawn up in advance for a term of years, and having sufficient standing to prevent it from being disregarded by every successive legislative body (Congress or State legislatures, as the case may be). The standing of such a program will, as already noted, depend largely on the character, soundness, and thoroughness of the work which the program embodies. However, since this procedure cannot be set up except through legislative acts, it will have at least the authority of past legislative bodies behind it, and they may be slow to stultify themselves by disregarding such programs, even though no legislature can be absolutely bound by the acts of its predecessors.

B. Optional Features of a Public-Works Program

There are many phases of the public-works question in which the proper policy may be in some doubt, even after a decision is made on the one or two basic underlying questions of policy. Here the first thing to do is to formulate the questions at issue as clearly as possible, even where one can go no farther at present toward a final answer.

1. Should public-works expenditures be expanded in time of minor depressions, or merely maintained at a uniform rate?

We have already seen that the more important thing is to preserve a margin of resources available for expanding works in the most serious emergencies, and that if the attempt to expand public works during minor depressions threatened to be a serious drain on these reserves, it would be an unwise policy. The decision of this question will depend, in the first place, on how large the reserve margin of spending power appears to be, and secondly, on whether a policy of expansion during minor depressions can be worked out which will not constitute a material drain on these reserves. Thirdly, it may depend on whether a policy of moderate expansion during minor depressions may actually serve to increase the prospect of success when it comes to expansion during major crises.

It is quite possible to develop a program which will result in expanding public works during minor depressions without putting any heavy strain on the governmental reserves of credit. So long as a program of this sort is properly laid out and conscientiously followed, increased public works expenditures in 1 year will be balanced by decreased expenditures in other years, and the financial resources of the Government will not be progressively weakened. And the experience of such a program might be a positive advantage in developing methods and techniques which would be of use in overcoming the many obstacles which always confront such an attempt, and thereby might pave the way for more prompt and successful expansion of public works in future cases of serious crisis. On the basis of these considerations the balance of the argument seems to lie in favor of a moderate expansion of public works during minor depressions, but with no attempt to drive through a heavy program at such times. This is the kind of program which has been called the grade A type— in which a schedule of works is laid out for possibly 6 years ahead and carried out at varying rates in different years, but without altering the total amount of the program.

2. If there is to be expansion in dull times, should there be preliminary contraction of public works below a normal long-term rate, during prosperous times?

While this question is put in the category of optional questions of policy, it is very likely to settle itself as things actually work out. When the present public works drive relaxes, there will automatically come a time when governments will be struggling to reduce their debts and rehabilitate their finances, while a considerable volume of public works will have been built earlier than would otherwise have been the case. In short, a part of the normal program for the 2 or 3 years lying just ahead, will have been anticipated. For both these reasons there will be a natural falling off in the rate of public works expenditure.

It seems further probable that the effect of straitened finances will last a good deal longer than the surplus of public works themselves, with the result that construction is likely to fall behind a normal long-run program during, let us say, the 5 years following 1934. Thus any program which may be adopted is likely to get under way in a period of comparative poverty when public works programs are likely to be something less than generous.

3. How far should expansion go, and just how should it be timed?

Here, again, is a question on which there is difference of opinion, but where a good deal of this difference is likely to vanish automatically when it comes to the test of action. Practically speaking, it is hardly possible to initiate a supplementary program of increased public works early enough to catch a depression in the first stages of declining business, and it is much more likely that such a program will not get under way until business is more than half-way down the slope of its decline. The question really becomes one of whether expansion should come as early as practicable, or whether it should be deliberately delayed with the idea of allowing business to reach bottom before beginning to attempt to stimulate recovery. As between these two policies, it seems clearly desirable to make the expansion as prompt as possible, consistent with waiting to be quite sure that the conditions are such as to require it. There is still a considerable margin of discretion in applying this principle, leaving much room for the personal equation.

4. Should there be permanent expansion of public works designed as an antidote to oversaving?

As bearing on this question we have seen that there is a fair prima facie case for the existence of oversaving, and a strong prima facie probability that this condition could not be corrected on any large scale by permanently increasing our public works expenditures and financing them in such ways as would be necessary. Both these prima facie probabilities remain subject to possible modification, and therefore this question must be put in the doubtful class.

5. Is relief work desirable, and if so, on what basis?

Should it be a permanent feature of policy or a regular feature of the emergency measures? Should it be limited to a comparatively small amount of work of high grade, compensated at regular wage rates with the attempt to limit it to the "elite of the unemployed"; or should it be more wide-spread? For example, should everyone who receives relief contribute some work in return for it? Should there be a combination of these policies or a compromise between them? If unemployment insurance is set up, what will be its effect on the desirability of relief work and on the need for it and what is the proper place of the Federal Government in a scheme of relief work?

On these questions the experience of the United States in the present depression should afford a considerable amount of fresh evidence, though it may not lead to any radically new truths which had not been revealed by the long experience of earlier efforts. At any rate, it seems to be a settled thing that the present experiments in relief work will go on. Certain features of them, such as the Civilian Conservation Corps, may prove to have a permanent value, although experience may lead to changes in the form of the organization. Certain kinds of relief work are undoubtedly wasteful and worse than useless, and should never be repeated. Thus the answer to this question is likely to be neither a sweeping yes, nor a sweeping no. As to the proper place of the Federal Government in relief work, the answer which naturally grows out of our current experience is that the proper place of the Federal Government is to stand ready to take up the burden of relief work, along with the burden of relief and of maintenance of current expenses—in short, all the necessary fiscal burdens which ultimately become too heavy for States and localities, if a depression continues and is extremely severe.

6. Should Federal aid be granted to localities to support their current services as distinguished from enduring public works?

Here there will be opinions on both sides, influenced by considerations of different sorts, which it is difficult or impossible to weigh against each other with any accuracy. There is some argument for Federal grants in aid of education in ordinary times; and in times of great depression the need is obviously very much more serious. On the other hand, there is a very genuine disadvantage in doing anything to undermine the fiscal self-sufficiency of the States and localities; and the fact that some undermining may have happened already does not diminish the danger involved in carrying the process further. In short, this question is not only highly controversial but likely to remain so, with firmly convinced partisans on both sides.

7. Should the concept of public works be extended into the field of current services or should public works be narrowly construed in traditional terms of durable material structures and improvements?

Of course, a mere question of nomenclature is not in itself worth quarreling about; but the real question underlying it is the question whether a particular kind of administrative body, which has had large funds at its disposal during the present crisis and may have large funds again during future crises, should extend the scope of its operations beyond the traditional concept of public works.

On the whole, the device of extending the range of these emergency organizations beyond their natural limits, simply because they have funds to spend and there are needs to be met which lie outside those limits, is essentially a temporary makeshift. In the case of the Public Works Administration, the bad effects of extending its functions to current services are minimized by the fact that it is not an operating organization, but rather an organization for the apportionment of funds to other organizations which will take technical charge of the actual work. In determining whether to allot funds to various purposes, it does not need to gain the same kind of expertness in these fields which would be needed to carry out the work at first hand. The budgetary authority which allots funds to road building, forestry, or education does not need to be a competent road builder, forester, or educational administrator. Nevertheless, it remains true that an organization is likely to be efficient in proportion as it stays within the bounds of its more or less specialized material. And if the principle is followed of maintaining the current budgets before attempting to expand public works there will be little or no need or demand for expanding the operations of a public works administration beyond the field ordinarily covered by the concept of public works.

If there is to be relief work, that offers a somewhat different question, since there is always a tremendous pressure to hunt high and low through all possible classes of useful service for forms of employment available for relief work. In fact, relief work is in a different kind of category and does not carry the same implied limitations as do regular public works. On the other hand, there are peculiar objections to using relief-work funds to finance anything which might properly be a regular current expense of government, particularly of a State or local government. This principle might easily degenerate into a policy of getting services at relief rate of pay rather than at regular market rates, not to speak of the drawbacks of allowing States and localities to throw part of their current expenses on the Federal Government by a sort of tacitly accepted subterfuge.

On the whole, the balance seems to lie in favor of keeping regular public works authorities within the natural bounds of the traditional conception of public works, so long as other functions are adequately supplied with funds. On the other hand, relief-work agencies can hardly function at all unless they are fairly free to search out useful forms of work without being hampered by narrow limitations.

8. Should there be large expansion in the field of self-liquidating works?

The chief cases in point at present are housing construction and the supplying of electric power. Success in both these fields is contingent on so many uncertain factors that it is impossible to predict with confidence whether the existing experiments, or others following them, will or will not be sufficiently successful to justify further investments of the same sort on a larger scale. Apart from the success or failure of particular kinds of projects, there seems to be no general principle by virtue of which the question could be decided a priori. It appears to be a question which must be left to be determined by such guidance as we can derive from experience.

9. What policy should be followed toward self-help organizations and in the related matter of directing relief work to the production of consumable goods for the workers themselves?

Here, again, we have a problem which cannot be answered by any a priori general principles, and which must be treated experimentally. The chief conclusion would seem to be that the attempt should be made to give self-help experiments a chance to show what they can do and should be made adequately and whole-heartedly, but without committing the country or the Government to any permanent policy. In all cases of this sort, there is need of avoiding the danger of interpreting the success or failure of the experiment without due regard to the amount of the Government subsidy which has been granted directly or indirectly.   This danger should naturally be avoided if the outcome of the experiment is to be correctly judged.

10. What should be the precise extent of administrative discretion in the handling of public works policies?

As already noted, a policy of public works planning involves an increase in the initiative and discretion accorded to administrative bodies, since the legislature must allow plans to be carried out, at least in general outlines, without intervening at each session to make them over completely; or else it is hardly proper to talk about planning at all, since the plans would be no more than pious wishes.   Precisely how far this increase in administrative functions should go is a question which will probably be answered, like some of the other questions, by the test of experience.   Certain powers must clearly be given to administrative bodies in order to carry out any planned program. On the other hand, the underlying power to make any change at any time cannot formally be taken away from the legislative body.   Only experience can tell precisely where the balance will ultimately be struck in the actual practice of government.

It is worth noting that these optional matters of policy include a considerable number of questions on which there is need of research and investigation, of the kind which the body which has been called the "National Planning Board" is peculiarly suited to carry out.

C. A Minimum Program

The most limited objective which could possibly be set up is that of stabilized governmental spending.   This must logically apply both to current services and to public works.   Such a program would not constitute a positive stabilizing force in business disturbances, but it would at least prevent public expenditures from being numbered among the forces which tend to aggravate the disturbance and propagate its cumulative effects with increasing violence.   This program of stabilized expenditures appears quite modest, but to carry it out in the face of major crises would be far from easy.   If such a minimum program is to be carried out, it will require certain machinery, procedures, and organizations.

1. In the first place, it calls for an advance program of public works which may be limited to works of grade A, and which needs to be scheduled in fairly uniform annual installments for possibly as

much as 6 years ahead. This program must be made by some administrative body, either in the Bureau of the Budget or standing between the Bureau of the Budget and the various executive departments whose requirements the program is designed to supply. As is often the case with new units of governmental organization, this public works planning unit could hardly be given supreme authority at the start, disregarding or overriding other bodies which have the final word at present. As over against these older bodies the new one would have chief authority, if it could, largely by virtue of the soundness of its work.

2. If this program is to be carried out during major crises, it will call for fairly far-reaching measures of fiscal preparedness, such as have already been discussed in other chapters of this study. At such times even this minimum program can hardly be carried out without Federal aid to State and local budgets.

At this point serious questions of wisdom and expediency will arise, and the outcome will presumably be a compromise rather than a complete and unqualified carrying out of a program of absolute stability. Since these major emergencies come at comparatively long and irregular intervals, each is likely to be treated as a new case by the Federal, State, and local administrations which are in office at the time. But so far as a general rule can be laid down in advance, it seems proper to grant Federal aid in serious major emergencies to localities whose fiscal systems meet appropriate tests of soundness as judged by whether they are adapted to bring the budget into balance within a reasonable time, but not necessarily to balance it while the emergency is in full force.

To such localities, aid should surely be granted to the amount that may be necessary for the maintenance of the more essential current services. Even this represents a compromise rather than a literal carrying out of the principle of stabilized expenditures. But the situation is one in which some compromise of this sort is almost inevitable. This program, then, of maintaining a stable rate of expenditures up to the point at which fiscal considerations are bound to force a compromise, may be considered as representing the smallest program which could consistently be advocated.

D. A Sample Program of a more Adequate Sort

Most serious students of the question would not be satisfied with a program which leaves public works in a neutral position, but would call for a program in which they would render some positive service toward industrial stabilization. The program which is outlined hereafter is a program of this sort. It involves some increase of public works during mild depressions—a thing which can be comparatively easily done—but it reserves the largest effort for the occasional major crises. So far as concerns these two main features of the program, they seem to be essential, if anything at all is to be done beyond the minimum program already suggested. As to the detailed mechanisms suggested for carrying the plan out, some of the chief features of these mechanisms appear to be almost equally essential, being dictated by the main tasks which must be done in order to carry out the program. Beyond this point, however, details of organization and procedure are nonessentials. What follows is a fairly specific outline of the program, the mechanisms, and the main procedures involved in carrying it out. Needless to say, these are not meant to be final, down to the last detail. In fact, they are presented chiefly because the question has reached the stage of incipient action, calling for the formulation of concrete proposals, to be criticized and modified.

This sample program presupposes the setting up of administrative organizations of the general types already indicated. It assumes the existence of a general planning and coordinating body, called for convenience the "National Planning Board", and of a Federal public works planning body; also bodies with similar general functions in the States, collaborating with regional and local bodies so far as these may be set up. The precise functions of these State and local bodies would be naturally somewhat different from those of the national bodies, insofar as Nation-wide policies would naturally originate with the Federal authorities, while many of the more specific matters concerned with carrying them out would necessarily be in the realm of the State and local bodies, rather than in that of the Federal Government.

This program starts with a long-range program of public works of grade A, precisely as in the case of the minimum program already suggested; but it adds the proposal to shift the timing of these works so far as practicable, postponing them when business is above normal and carrying them out when business is below normal. In addition it calls for additional works to be initiated, with the aid of Federal grants and loans to localities, on certification of the existence of a major emergency.

Assuming the carrying out of experiments initiated during the present emergency in housing, power production, regional development by watershed authority, relief work including production of commodities for consumption of workers on relief, policy toward self-help organizations, and other matters best regarded as experimental, the program includes a thorough assessment of results when these shall have become apparent, with a view to deciding on continuance, abandonment, or modification. The authorities engaged in these works will of course report on them; and the National Planning Board should probably be asked to make more impartial assessments and recommendations. The program also includes a number of other projects of research or investigation, to be carried out by the National Planning Board or under its sponsorship.

1. PREPARATION OF PUBLIC WORKS PROGRAM

The Federal, State, regional, and local Public Works Planning Boards should have charge of preparing basic schedules of works for 6 years or other suitable period ahead. These works should be such as could properly be carried out if conditions remained normal, with allocation of the work to each year of the period on as nearly uniform a basis as practicable.

For the projects named in the schedule for 2 or possibly 3 years in advance, designation should be made of those which could without material ill effects be postponed or advanced or both (the same projects might not be equally susceptible to shifting in both directions). Those not designated as capable of postponement would become the minimum program for each year. The others would then become primary supplementary projects for the year in question, and those available for the coming year or possibly 2 years should be listed as secondary supplementary projects for those years in addition to the basic schedule. The schedule would be revised each year, including minimum and supplementary items.

If, in any year, the minimum program only were carried out and the supplementary program postponed, the postponed items would naturally become parts of the supplementary program for the succeeding year, when the annual revision of the program was made. Some of these might become sufficiently urgent, after being postponed a year or two, to take a place among the products constituting the minimum program for these succeeding years. In this way the minimum program might grow larger in proportion as the supplementary program had been postponed, although it would probably not increase by the whole amount of the postponed items.

Supplementary projects for the current year should be so prepared for during the preceding year as to be so far as possible ready for immediate initiation.

If continued prosperity should result in the postponing of the supplementary part of the program for several years in succession, the total amount of postponed works would naturally increase cumulatively. It would be necessary, of course, to set a limit on this cumulative postponement. One natural way of doing this would be to provide that, when the volume of primary supplementary work which has been postponed comes to exceed half of the normal yearly program (minimum plus primary supplementary) the excess shall become part of the minimum program for the succeeding year. On this basis, a continued period of prosperity would result in the accumulation of a reserve of postponed works equal to half of the average yearly amount of the whole grade A program, but no more; and after this reserve should be accumulated, work would go on at the normal rate (minimum plus primary supplementary program) until a depression should call for an increase in the volume of works through putting into execution the reserve of postponed projects.

In the same way, if a continued period of mild depression should lead to a cumulative anticipation of the works scheduled as primary supplementary works for future years, a limit would need to be set on this cumulative anticipation in much the same way. It should probably not be allowed to become larger than half of a normal year's program, after which the work should go on at the normal rate until there is some change in business conditions. This condition is not likely to come about since mild depressions are usually short, and do not continue for years without ceasing to be mild depressions and becoming major crises.

From projects submitted but not accepted as part of the basic (grade A) schedule, a further schedule of grade B projects should be made up, but not necessarily assigned to particular years. When the initiation of supplementary grade A projects is determined upon, preparatory work should begin in the preferred list of grade B projects, possibly to a designated amount such as half a billion or a billion dollars. At the same time, State and local bodies should be invited to submit for examination projects in their schedules on which they may apply for grants or loans or both in case a major emergency is in future certified to exist. This procedure should not act as a bar to the submission and consideration of fresh projects, Federal, State or local, when the emergency arises. For this purpose, projects for emergency use should also be chosen from among grade A projects scheduled for a time too far ahead to place them in the list of suppletary grade A projects for the year in question.

Similar procedure should be encouraged on the part of States and localities, with the stimulus of some current Federal assistance to their work of planning, and the propsect of qualifying more promptly for Federal grants and loans in case of a major emergency.

2. FINANCIAL MEASURES

For the Federal Government, once the financial effects of recovery are sufficiently felt to establish some margin in the budget above current needs, the mechanics of financing the elastic public-works program should not present difficult problems. As already noted, there is a large amount which must go to ultimate reduction of the national debt; and variations in the amount so used from year to year would be sufficient to take care of discrepancies in the movements of revenues and expenses during most of the minor fluctuations, without much need of resorting to actual increases in debt to meet the costs of expanded public works under the grade A program. Professor Bowley has suggested for England a uniform budget of national debt repayment plus loans to local governments for public works, the one to decrease as the other increases. The proposals here made would automatically produce a somewhat similar effect as to the total of debt reductions and Federal public-works outlays.

For each year there should be available unconditional appropriations for the minimum public-works program for that year, plus contingent appropriations, to become effective on determination of conditions calling for the supplementary grade A program, equal to 1 year's normal program of public-works outlays. Or, as an alternative, the contingent appropriation might be enough to cover the supplementary part of the current year's program plus one half-year's normal program in addition. Borrowing sufficient to finance this program, if necessary, should also be authorized. On initiation of the supplementary grade A program, the President should transmit to Congress a request for additional contingent appropriations and contingent borrowing power, to become effective on determination of the existence of a major emergency and sufficient to finance the grade B program for 1 year. At the same time the President should request a grant of contingent authority to the Public Works Planning Board to make loans and grants to States and localities to finance their grade B projects.

State and local bodies should be stimulated to adopt financial measures of similar effect, including elastic debt limits for localities. No provision is included here for Federal aid to States and localities in minor depressions. Time should probably be allowed to see whether sufficient cooperation can be secured without this stimulus; and whether the results of efforts in the Federal field indicate that anticyclical timing can be successfully carried out to a sufficient extent to be of important benefit.

3. SYSTEM FOR DETERMINING EXISTENCE OF MINOR DEPRESSIONS AND MAJOR EMERGENCIES

Indexes of general business conditions and of conditions in the construction industries should be maintained, both for the Nation as a whole and for regions. The National Planning Board should be responsible for such indexes, being free to use material compiled by the Bureau of Labor Statistics, the Federal Reserve Board, or other bodies, or to compile indexes of its own.

A minor depression should be certified to exist when the general index falls definitely below normal, with due allowance for the uncertainty of a normal-trend line carried forward to the current moment; provided the construction industries are not at the same time definitely above normal.

A major emergency should be certified to exist when (a) unemployment becomes so large as to threaten to impose a burden of relief too heavy to be successfully borne by the regular local resources; or (b) when depression is so serious as to threaten a wide-spread credit collapse, or (c) when it threatens a period of unusually prolonged prostration with absence of normal power of private business recovery.

These provisions place great discretion on the planning Board, but seem preferable to a purely mechanical rule. However, such a rule, in terms of the percentage showing of specific indexes, is an alternative possibility.

The National Planning Board should also keep in touch with the Public Works Planning Board, keeping it informed of current movements of the indexes, and of any indications of what may be expected in the near future.

4. EXECUTION OF PROGRAM

One problem arising is that of possible exclusion from supplementary grade A program of works located in regions in which business conditions are normal or better at the same time that business in the country at large is below normal. Probably the National Planning Board should have authority to recommend such exclusion to the Public Works Planning Board, and the latter should have authority to put it into effect.

Another question is the use of three magnitudes of grade A program—minimum, normal, and normal plus supplementary—instead of two—minimum and normal plus supplementary. The National Planning Board would then have to define a zone of normal conditions. as well as conditions definitely above and below normal. This seems of doubtful expediency; and it might lead a conservative board to defining almost everything as normal. The problem of varying the amounts of work set in motion under the grade A program could probably be taken care of by the varying degrees of executive pressure exerted by the Public Works Planning Board, according to the seriousness of the situation. According to the system already suggested, the minimum program would automatically expand up to the amount of a normal or average grade A program, as soon as prosperity should have lasted long enough to bring about the postponement of a reserve of supplementary projects equal to more than half of 1 year's normal program. In the same way, after supplementary works have been anticipated for a certain length of time, the expanded program would come to an end and work would return to the normal rate. This would, in effect, bring about much the same result as if the original program were divided into 3 grades instead of 2.

The problem of wage and price policies may become serious. Here the Public Works Planning Board should keep in touch with the National Planning Board and through them with any other agencies dealing with these problems. A first line of defense might be to include in the discretion of the National Planning Board power to determine whether prices and costs in the construction industries are being maintained at so high a level as to constitute an obstacle to private recovery of demand in these fields, with the result that for the Government further to sustain these levels of prices and costs by an increased construction program would tend to defeat the end of private business recovery. If it is so found, it should withhold its certification that conditions call for expanded public works.

A second line of defense would be power on the part of the Public Works Planning Board to order the rejection of bids if they are too high by the same test—not all bids to be so scrutinized; merely after determination that costs in general are too high. This would interpose a serious element of possible delay in the program, where one of the great purposes of advance planning is to remove the baffling delays now holding back any such policy and reducing its usefulenss. It is only the conviction that the usefulness of the policy is in danger of being seriously undermined in a different way, by bidding up prices and costs against private buyers or by stiffening the resistance to needed deflation, that makes it seem advisable to include such checks as this.

5. PROGRAM OF RESEARCH AND INVESTIGATION

It is taken for granted that study will be given by the National Planning Board to unemployment insurance, health insurance, old-age pensions, and other questions only indirectly affecting public works policy.

The Public Works Planning Board should cause to be made such studies as may be pertinent, including studies of the extent to which the time of carrying out public works can be altered without serious results, the effects on costs of minimizing use of machinery, and other problems of importance.

The National Planning Board should, of course, have a free hand in conducting studies of any issues of importance, using investigations made by other bodies, supplementing them, making independent studies under its own direction, or sponsoring studies by research foundations or other bodies. Among the pertinent topics bearing on public-works policy are the following:

Wage and price policy.

Savings and capital formation and the field for productive investment, with a view to the possible effect of oversavings as a cause of economic dislocations.

Work relief: The results of experience and its place in a scheme, both with and without unemployment insurance.

State and local finance, their relations to Federal finance and to the problems of public works policy; e. g., the problem of Federal grants in aid of education, or to maintain local current services generally in major emergencies.

Self-help and the production of goods by the otherwise unemployed for their own and each other's consumption.

Possibilities of regularized capital outlays by public utilities, and of anticyclical timing of such outlays.

Coordination of transportation.

E. Program of Permanent Expansion of Public Works to Absorb Oversavings

It is not evident that such a permanent expansion of public works has sufficient prospect of practicability to be a wise thing to adopt at the present time. The program already suggested includes an investigation of the theoretical basis underlying the proposal for such a permanent expansion; and under existing conditions this is as far as it seems wise to go.

F. Conclusion

The writer has been reluctant to appear to make specific recommendations, especially in the administrative field. But it appeared that the requisites and implications of at least one program should be made fairly specific. In the writer's judgment, some program of the general character indicated in D above should be adopted. On the purely economic side, this conclusion seems reasonably clear. As to the precise character of administrative bodies, scope of administrative discretion, and precise points at which matters should be referred to the ultimate legislative authority, the suggestions above are to be taken as illustrative only.

Such a program in the public works field alone will not cure the evil of business instability. If successfully carried out, it should result in mitigating these disturbances, but it can hardly do more than this. The general character of this program is one of compensating for the fluctuations of private business by counter-fluctuations in the field of public expenditures. This can be done only to a limited extent, and leaves the basic causes of the private fluctuations still to be dealt with. More thorough-going remedies for these causes rest upon alterations in methods of conducting business and industry in general. The hope of a desirable outcome is intimately bound up with the question whether adequate changes of this sort can be brought about without too much delay, by evolutionary methods. On this question, confident prediction would be rash but the problem represents the greatest single task facing American industrial statesmanship at the present time.

APPENDIX

FISCAL ASPECTS OF PLANNED PUBLIC WORKS

By J. Wilner Sundelson

(These Preliminary Findings and Conclusions were prepared during June 1934, and were revised in August. The research on which this report is based, was being pursued in conjunction with a more-extended study planned for submission in the fall of 1934. However, the writer was compelled to devote the major portion of his efforts to other work and was unable to carry out the more-extended study. The appended report represents preliminary findings and conclusions which might have been amplified.)

In order to clarify the relationships between fiscal activities and the general economy, it is essential to bear in mind that these relationships have only recently been recognized as significant. The great mass of public finance literature does not concern itself with the problems that these interreactions raise. This is explained by the fact that in the past the size of Government expenditures, both in their relative position to the national economy and in their absolute amounts, have been considerably smaller than they are at present.

Fiscal scientists were aware of the steady growth of Government outlays and formulated these tendencies into laws. Wagner speaks of the "law of increasing State activities" while Adams arrives at a "general law of expenditure for progressive peoples." However, these authorities naturally did not concern themselves with conditions which would be expected to arise after the laws had continued in operation for some time. Furthermore, the laissez-faire body of economic theory with its emphasis on the individual did not encourage a study of the problem. Additional reasons are found i the fact that money was not the medium with which the political economists operated and was generally considered to be insignificant. The attributes of permanency, compulsion, and a nonprofit incentive were considered as distinguishing the public from the private economy. A theory of dichotomy between the two so-called separate economies arose.

The public finance theories which have been influential in molding fiscal legislation have protrayed the relationships of the individual to the state but have failed to analyze those existing between the state and the economy. We have studied taxes from the point of view of cost, benefit, minimum sacrifice, or ability to pay. It is seldom that a tax is criticized or defended because of the effects of such a tax policy on the general economy. Single tax advocates, led by Henry George, or Socialists, exemplified by Rignano, have tended to place an unorthodox stamp upon the more comprehensive concepts of fiscal problems. It is only recently that cycle sensitivity and national productivity have been used as taxation norms, the former in Germany and the latter in Italy.

The above-mentioned growth of Government finances may be attributed to social theories, wars, and economic factors such as the current depression. The expansion of governmental functions has been translated into activities and expenditures. The monetary, banking, and credit aspects of the expenditure and tax policies have become increasingly important as the bulk of the fiscal items represent transfers of money magnitudes. (Money outlays or transfers are not required for the execution of a number of important governmental functions. The economic regulatory acts of the Federal Trade Commission, Interstate Commerce Commission, and the National Recovery Administration are in this group. Nevertheless, a fairly constant relationship between the growth of Government functions and public expenditures may be assumed.) In extreme cases, exemplified by Russia, the Government is almost identical with the economy. The Soviet budget mirrors the entire economic picture; it is considered an economic program rather than a project for the public finances.

We can realize the influence of the fiscal system on our economy by recalling that our annual tax bill is at present approximately 10 billion dollars. The Federal debt of 27 billion or more is accompanied by a State and local debt of some 20 billion. At present (August 1934) some 6½ billion of authorized but unexpended Federal funds, still to be covered by borrowing, are recorded. Though these figures may be subjected to criticism as being related to an abnormally small national income, it is difficult to expect a decline in the trend of these magnitudes. Existing tax legislation will reap into the public treasuries a substantial part of any future increases in the national dividend. Social and economic programs now being planned will easily absorb these additional funds. We may expect no decrease in the share of the public finances in the national economy unless an entirely new economic orientation is pursued.

The budget is one of the greatest dynamic institutional instruments available in economic life. In countries possessing centralized forms of governmental machinery it would be possible to exert efforts toward furthering economic welfare through conscious and planned control of fiscal affairs. In federated governments, particularly in the United States, the set-up is such that it is difficult to expect unified action. The diversity of dominating ideas and practices in the many political subdivisions make it imperative that attempts be made to measure local fiscal problems in terms of broad economic needs. Centralized activity may assist in the solution of what now appear to be unavoidable local difficulties. It is unfortunate that all fiscal affairs are subordinated to administrative jurisdictions based on political boundaries. A national planning board, thinking and measuring problems in terms of national and regional economic aspects, is offered a major field of activity in relation to nonfederal finances. The scope of possible action in relation to economic stabilization in general, and planned public-works programs in particular, is here under discussion.

Part I

Economic fluctuations are one of the most pressing problems with which fiscal systems must cope. Denying for the present any casual relationship between the fiscal system and business cycles, it is evident that depressions disrupt governmental finances to such an extent that unbalanced budgets and disordered fiscal affairs eventually become directly associated with the further development of the cycle. In the interest of economic stabilization it is therefore imperative that steps be taken to eliminate any contribution of the fiscal systems toward the accentuation of a depression. This is in addition to the fact that unless the public finances are relieved of a greater part of their cycle sensitivity, their ability to carry out essential governmental functions is threatened. Political and social stability has been seriously disturbed as a result of the fiscal collapse in many communities. Furthermore, any use of the fiscal systems as an active agency in recovery efforts is predicated upon their ability to complete successfully their normal functions. With respect to problems raised by emergencies of a noncyclical character, economic and otherwise, it is important to note that the federal finances must take them into account and retain reasonable margins of taxing and borrowing power. The United States is subject, by virtue of its physical geographical characteristics, to natural catastrophes. Our willingness promptly to alleviate the incidence of disaster is illustrated in the current drought situation. We must anticipate the potential costs involved. The recent trends of expansion in public expenditures give to this emergency financing question a vital importance.

The fiscal systems have, by means of budgetary techniques and procedures, short-term borrowing, and other devices, been able to offset the effects of seasonal fluctuations. Their success in this field encourages belief that the fiscal systems may be equally fortunate in coping with cyclical problems. It is necessary at this point to note that severe limitations on efforts for cyclical adjustments are imposed by the inadequate body of knowledge and by the absence of uniformity of opinion concerning major cycles. This places an emphasis on planning for flexibility rather than for specific problems.

Minor depressions present no extraordinary reactions to, or burdens on, the fiscal systems.

1. Lags in the reaction of economic movements on the public finances prevent the minor depressions from being mirrored in most tax receipts until after the trouble has passed.

2. The mildness of such reactions which do take place makes it unnecessary to adjust the public finances to them.

3. Attempts to deal with minor depressions through the slow processes of fiscal machinery (through public works or otherwise) will result in accentuating the following booms rather than in assisting in recovery.

4. The limited territorial scope of the incidence of minor depressions gives rise to strictly local problems.

These conclusions point to the advisability of abandoning further consideration of minor depressions.

It will be necessary to discuss at greater length the questions raised by major depressions. These are characterized by long duration and extreme intensity. Because of the infrequency of their occurrence and the dynamic nature of the economic system, which is responsible for broad structural changes between major depressions, it is impossible to formulate any specific characteristics applicable for all declines. It will be necessary, therefore, to concentrate on this depression and its background.

The war affected the Federal finances in several ways; the most outstanding results being a new high level of expenditures, a heritage of public debt, additional war liquidation costs and a tax system containing several powerful new fiscal engines. Because of these factors which dwarfed the other fiscal items in the Federal Budget it may be truly said that predepression Federal finances were primarily war finances. Wars, past and future, are estimated to have motivated 87 percent of the expenditures during the 1920–30 decade.

It is important therefore to remember the basic reason for the expansion of the Federal finances and to judge the nature of the economic and social elements involved. The States and localities were not directly involved in the financing of the war nor in the liquidation of its costs. They underwent an expansion independent of direct war elements. Aside from veterans' relief and institutional care, only the price inflation and the general industrial expansion may be said to be war influences on State and local finances.

The general economic conditions were so favorable during the post-war decade that maintaining the new high level of Federal outlays became a relatively light burden. Our taxes returned handsome surpluses to the Treasury. It was not necessary, therefore, to introduce levies designed to search out the most elusive public dollar. Such a tax system might have shown a decreased sensitivity to an economic crisis. The rapid debt retirement did grant the Government a greater nominal borrowing capacity during the current depression and reduced debt service requirements. However, the economic effects of public debt redemption with revenues from taxes may be such that the redemption policy may act as a factor accentuating the boom. Particularly the concentration of Government securities in the hands of institutions and high-income recipients may mean that debt retirement accentuates "over-savings." The property tax underlay local finances to such an extent that the expansion in State and local budgets may be directly linked to the predepression real-estate inflation. It is fortunate that a few States dropped the property tax and that many others added income, inheritance, gasoline, and motor-vehicle levies. In the absence of the last two above-mentioned taxes there would undoubtedly have been an even more serious disruption and collapse of non-Federal finances. It is probable that those who supported the elimination of the property tax or advocated the adoption of the other levies did not think in terms of flexibility. In addition to the fact that local revenues were being collected with apparent ease, there was pressure for the abandonment of the property tax from the real-estate elements in the community. With perhaps the exception of the public utilities, these are the most powerfully organized group of militant taxpayers in the country. This particular phase has been singled out to illustrate the nature of the motivating forces in financial affairs.

The maintenance of the fiscal systems was therefore closely linked to a permanent high rate of activity in business. A superstructure of activities and expenditures built upon prosperity gave no recognition to the possibilities of a recession.

During the depression the major problem has been that of upholding (especially in non-Federal finances) the structure of education, roads, hospitals, and other social services. These represent a financing issue of major import. In the face of the collapse of the private economy, the Government was confronted with the further problem of adding growing relief expenditures, to the inherited burden. The resulting breakdown and the ultimate assumption of the strain by the Federal Government is not difficult to trace.

In general, the private economic structure has shown distinct deflationary trends since the initial crash. The public economy ma hed

these trends only after a lag of almost 2 years with a similar deflationary tenor. Attempts were then made to meet the decreasing
revenue yields with poorly maintained expenditure structures. By
the time the incidence of the depression added new demands on the
treasuries for work, unemployment and welfare relief, the first really
unfavorable reactions on tax receipts were making themselves felt.

It is necessary to differentiate between Federal finances and State
and local finances. No two individual States or counties with their
multitude of cities, towns, school districts, etc., have been faced with
the same conditions. Few, if any, have met their problems with the
same policies on borrowing, expenditures, and taxation. Occasional
similarities with respect to steps taken are the basis for such general-
izations as are made in this study.

Prior to 1932, political and other pressures made it difficult (assuming attempts were even considered) for the Federal administration
to recognize the depression and to take active steps regarding the
fiscal system. Lags in the falling off of receipts did not make any
action imperative; the political subdivisions absorbed the first relief
demands. However since 1931 revenue collections (measured against
estimates) have fallen sharply; the Federal income tax especially
showing itself to be extremely sensitive. The capital gain and loss
provisions have played a large role in the shrinkage of income-tax
receipts.

Increased Federal highway aid to the States and budgetary economy
measures went alongside of each other, while the public debt began its
big upswing. Deficit financing involving billions of dollars, carried
on at that time, has aided in giving subsequent borrowing an excessive
character. The Reconstruction Finance Corporation outlays, carried
directly to the public debt without appearing in the Budget, may be
considered to have opened the expenditure program and to have
anticipated the present status of affairs. We now have a multiple
budget policy allowing a nominal balancing of current outgo and
income while all expenditures not financed through current taxation
are linked to specific recovery borrowing.

The reaction of the depression on the finances of the States and
localities shows about the same time lag as it does in Federal experience. It is evident that biennial budgets in many States concealed
the situation in cases where annual budgeting might have called attention to matters at an earlier date. Furthermore, some States and
localities entered the depression with weakened or disordered finances
and it is difficult to differentiate cyclical from other causes. Arkansas,
Mississippi, and North and South Dakota among the States and
Chicago among the large cities, are outstanding examples. It is
interesting to note that the lags enabled some States (including
New York) to take active steps in the direction of make-work policies
in 1931. Others had been able to build up general fund surpluses
which enabled them to stave off the crisis in their finances until 1933.

Since the middle of 1932, State and local finances have been characterized by many different features. The stronger States took the
burden from the localities. Wisconsin, which has displayed a stable
revenue system; New York, which is one of the few remaining States
with an excellent credit standing in the fourth year of the depression,
and North Carolina are in this group. In Georgia, Iowa, Massachusetts, Michigan, and Pennsylvania, the burden rests in one form or

another on the localities. Such borrowing as was permitted by the States and localities either for deficit financing or, more recently, for relief, has not been of any great significance in terms of the magnitudes involved and, excepting Federal purchases of municipal obligations, borrowing at present is minimized. It is claimed that the long-term borrowing of States (R. F. C. and P. W. A. loans omitted) has not exceeded $248,000,000 in any one year since 1928 and was only $192,000,000 in 1933.

Only a few of the States, notably New York, Massachusetts, and Pennsylvania, have any real credit standing. There is, however, an artificial market for State and local securities existing by virtue of the fact that obstacles have been placed in the way of the flotation of nongovernmental issues. Large underwriting houses are eagerly scanning the horizon for public flotations in order to keep their distributing units occupied. It is not improbable that a boom in State and municipal bonds will take place. Such a boom may develop because of the inactivity in the private long-term investment market and may be unrelated to the fiscal condition of the localities. Furthermore, Federal spending to relieve property owners will react favorably on property tax yields and on legal borrowing capacities.

Expenditures present a particularly unfortunate history. It is questionable whether economy programs which mean curtailment of services are desirable. Nevertheless, our cumbersome machinery of State government and the jealously guarded powers of the executives and legislatures have made it almost impossible for States to formulate and to carry out sensible retrenchment policies. Budgetary systems in many States are highly inadequate and it has been difficult for States in any way to maintain activities within the scope of decreased money expenditures. Procedures and techniques built with regard to considerations of political safeguards and liberty have been notoriously inadequate in terms of administrative efficiency.

A major portion of the State expenditures are for goods and services. It would have been feasible, in view of falling price levels, to maintain activities with decreased funds. Instead, we find both money expenditure decreases and curtailed activities. There were cases where the government received goods and services and then did not pay for them. States are also known to have paid excessive prices for materials and foodstuffs at the same time that school teachers and other employees were unpaid. In general, inelastic budgetary procedures made it impossible for any national economy program to be carried out.

North Carolina, Ohio, and Virginia put economy programs in the hands of the executive and had much better results than those States which attempted to work through slow legislative machinery. An outstanding example of the breakdown of a State finance system is found in Georgia where a budgetary law, enacted during the depression, required that all expenditures be reduced pro rata with the falling off of revenue yields as compared with estimates. It is superfluous to point out that such steps as were taken in Georgia were bound to interrupt the proper functioning of government. State and local outlays vary in many cases 50 and 35 percent below 1931 figures. Vital services such as education, hospitals, and fire and police protection have been curtailed in addition to unemployment created by wholesale dismissals.

The States and localities have not been inactive with tax legislation, although, strangely, some of it, especially with regard to property taxes, has been of a restrictive nature and has further complicated matters. Outstanding has been the general sales tax, of which 17 examples are now in force. Eleven of these were put into effect in 1933 and 6 since then. Gasoline tax yields have decreased but slightly in some States and have usually borne additional burdens. (The widespread specific assignment of fuel-tax receipts has kept highway funds from collapsing and in more than one instance the highway fund has been made available for general purposes.) Now beer and liquor taxes have added to the march of consumption levies which are beginning to become a feature of State finances (and with the spreading of State-local sharing provisions, of local finances as well). A general ineffective and lax tax policy on the part of States, except for sales taxes, can be seen from the following quotation: [1]

In terms of taxes rather than States, it may be said that there has been a fairly widespread willingness on the part of legislators to pay the personal income tax, but virtually no inclination to increase the rates drastically above the levels prevailing in most States in 1929. Gasoline tax increases have been fairly common. Comparatively little has been done with selective sales taxes on tobacco, etc. Taxes on business have been revised upward (and not greatly so) in only a few States. Death taxes have been called upon for almost no additional revenue. Special-rate intangible taxes have been used but rarely. The property tax has been greatly reduced in many States and temporarily increased (for State purposes) in only a few. Automobile registration fees have in almost no instance been increased and in several States have been sharply cut.

With few and isolated exceptions, the tax systems have shown themselves to be extremely sensitive to the influence of the depression. The ability of some income taxes (Wisconsin) to remain stable while some sales taxes (West Virginia) show considerable decreases indicates that a portion of the sensitivity may be due to administrative factors, to structural features, and to minor loophole provisions not inherent in the tax itself. It is obvious, however, that unless a tax base includes within itself some balancing provision i. e. (averaging income over a period of years) the tax yield can, after the elimination of time lags, behave no better than the tax base.

This assumes that rates remain constant. The raising of rates, especially in the case of indirect taxes, is often insufficient by itself to prevent yields from falling. In the highest income brackets the rates were raised on nonexistent bases. The belief that direct taxes are inadequate during depressions may be partly due to the fact that insufficient attention was paid to the broadening of tax foundations. This is evident in comparing our Federal income and death taxes with those of Great Britain. Under the British system, minimum exemptions are very low. Many people in this country who were exempted from paying income taxes would merely have fallen into a lower bracket under the British schedule.

Benefit taxes or those levied on large masses of people regardless of equity notions, or on consumption, were considered reliable revenue sources. Of all the indexes, the sales volume and prices of nondurable consumption goods (retail) have fallen least during this recession, and the progress of events has seen frequent resort to this base for tax purposes.

---

[1] Haig and Shoup: The Sales Tax in the American States. p. 15, New York, 1934.

In the light of traditional concepts of justice, ability to pay, and progression in taxation, the choice becomes one between a good tax system and a tax system displaying a small degree of cycle-sensitivity.

Many of our States and localities are extremely unfortunate, since they have tax systems which are both bad and sensitive to fluctuating backgrounds. Efforts to improve the tax systems will result in lessened cycle-sensitivity, even though the cycle criterion is given only minor consideration. A well-rounded system comprising income, death, and business taxes, combined with a property-tax administration which does not tolerate needless delinquency, would prove to be of relatively low sensitivity.

In all events it is difficult to conceive of a government with a sound tax system which can rely on maintained revenue yields during all varying phases of business activity. Unless we discard all our theoretically ideal norms of taxation and abandon the taxes built upon them, reserves or some variation of borrowing must be employed to help maintain current services. Furthermore, the maintenance of a nonsensitive tax system may have undesirable economic reactions during booms which outweigh any advantages accruing during recessions.

Part II

The ideal goal of economic stabilization efforts in relation to the fiscal systems is primarily the elimination of fluctuating revenue yields, the maintenance of expenditures, and a balanced relationship between income and outlay.

Efforts at cycle-smoothing should take into consideration the expansion of governmental activities which is to be expected during recessions. The question of calling upon the fiscal systems for cycle preventative efforts as well as for the support of recovery measures must await a satisfactory solution of the problem of maintaining ordinary as well as reasonable emergency services.

The latter category includes the type of expenditure known as minimum relief. These social requirements take precedence over economic or other ideals.

The specific objectives of stabilization efforts may be summarized as follows:

With relation to booms, the control of expenditures volume is desirable:

(a) To discourage unsupportable structures impossible to maintain during depressions.

(b) To prevent governmental expenditures from accentuating private economic inflationary tendencies.

(c) To leave ample current revenues uncovered in order that the liquidation of depression policies may be assured. These are chiefly debt-service charges. It is necessary to abandon private-capital productivity and solvency notions for deficit financing. The use of general revenues for debt service rather than specific-income creating sources introduced through the initial expenditure of the capital outlay is implied.

(d) To encourage (as far as financing limitations permit) the retardation or postponement of capital expenditures in order to concentrate public works activities and expenditures during depressions.

The qualitative control of expenditures is desirable in order that:
    (a) Government outlays may be prevented from entering channels likely to accentuate booms.
    (b) Reasonable depression economy efforts may permit activities to be maintained even with decreased expenditures.
It is essential that tax policies be directed toward:
    (a) The maintenance of high levels of current revenues.
    (b) The prevention of economic reactions of tax policies which might accentuate inflationary tendencies.
The objectives with regard to debt policy during prosperity periods are contradictory though it is reasonable to assume that within our institutional framework it is more desirable to reduce public debt as rapidly as possible though it is necessary to avoid any over-investment tendencies which are assumed to accompany the retirement of public debt.

The objectives of boom tax policies are less concise. It is desirable to support all expenditures, but at a certain point it becomes necessary to consider the injurious economic reactions of tax policies. It is well nigh impossible to formulate the policy to be pursued with respect to the choice among tax types. In many instances we know very little of the economic effects of taxes.

A survey of the techniques for achieving the various objectives leads to the following results:

1. During booms it is possible to aid in cycle-smoothing efforts by the conscious use of the nonrevenue aspects of taxation. In addition to the fact that taxes aid in redistributing income, there are certain uses other than the collection of revenues, to which tax policies may be put. It is possible to prevent the building up of excessively large corporate surpluses, to divert consumption to specific channels, and to encourage or discourage savings. A change in our tax exemption arrangements might lessen the likelihood of undesirable borrowing by governments.

It is chiefly with income taxes, death duties and business levies that nonfiscal designs can be achieved. These levies rank high with respect to cycle sensitivity when their rate structure is aimed against the higher brackets, and we must take into consideration the fact that an extremely sensitive tax structure will be built up. Also if we may assume that borrowing to maintain expenditures during depressions can be justified, our tax concepts can be considerably revised.

Conclusions regarding expenditures are that political and social factors will make it impossible to achieve any qualitative or quantitative control of them during booms. Expenditures usually denote benefits to particular elements in the community and it is not a likely occurrence for the flow of funds to be turned on or off at will. Certainly the cutting of expenditures is most difficult when the motive is preventing some future danger.

Because of the accepted concepts regarding the fixity and constant expansion of expenditures it is likely that appreciable stabilization or cycle-smoothing demands of any appreciable size must look elsewhere for assistance. Theories using classifications of expenditures on the criteria of urgency or postponability, are not convincing.

2. During depressions efforts to increase tax yields are possible but undesirable. A nonsensitive base often implies a disregard for equity

considerations. Attempts to work with schemes of added tax structures during depressions appear economically objectionable in addition to offering severe practical tax administrative difficulties. It does not appear likely that we can eliminate the regressive sales taxes but we should avoid levying them only during depressions when they are most objectionable.

Expenditure programs offer no real leeway other than the possibility of the improvement of administrative efficiency. Budgeting procedures, coordination of functions, elimination of waste, graft and corruption, and the reduction of artificial rigidities maintained through assignment of revenues and specific use-fund policies, offer particularly favorable grounds for reforms in State and local finances. Even with expenditure policies calling for minimum outlays, inefficient administration defeats any desired purpose.

The coordination of boom and depression finances have been repeatedly offered as a means of achieving fiscal stabilization and cycle-smoothing goals. Those advocating reserve policies assume that it is possible to thesaurize the unneeded boom surplus to aid in depression financing. The general theory states that over the course of a complete cycle, it is possible to find sufficient good and bad effects to compensate each other.

Reserve plans which involve specific assets available for conversion during depressions have come into prominence because of the feeling that prosperity finances might have been "held over." Unless the reserve assets consist of cash, it will be necessary to dispose of them by sale. This would signify large governmental support to the undesirable liquidation movement, largely through the medium of the sale of securities.

Such action would be decidedly deflationary and antagonistic to recovery efforts. Losses to the fisc because of depreciation are possible in magnitudes large enough to destroy the validity of the plan. Furthermore, the political aspect leads one to assume that funds of any magnitude will hardly remain untouched during boom years. In general, asset reserves decrease the flexibility of the fiscal systems, pledge the State to a particular course of action, and offer few advantages not inherent in straight borrowing. Minor funds have a definite place in State and local finances but offer merely minor assistance toward the solution of basic problems. Rather than striving for the development of fund technics, localities should attempt to revise their borrowing capacities.

The problem of "hidden reserves" requires mention because of the fact that during the current depression they have played such a role in saving many fiscal systems. These aids are seldom planned or consciously related to cycle finances, but their existence during boom years is known and a policy not to disturb them implies some positive action. The English refer to these fiscal devices as "hen roosts." They are usually obscure funds which might otherwise be raided. A classic illustration is the French scheme of relating the revenue of 1 year to 15 months' expenditure. Subsequently, through a change of dates for fiscal period during the depression, 1 year's revenue was called on to cover only 9 months' expenditure.

Another type of hidden reserve is found in lax tax administration. Tightening collection procedures and plugging loopholes helps to increase the yield of taxes. It is needless to add that no policies along these lines need be suggested but they do show that the fiscal systems adjust themselves to some extent to the "hold-over" problems.

Cyclical budget balancing is a frequently advocated policy. It is clear that funds must be available and in the absence of tax and other revenue yields, cash funds or convertible assets, governments must engage in some form of credit operation. The particular techniques for calling forth increases in the long- or short-term debt are of minor significance alongside the basic problem of pay-as-you-go versus credit financing. Favorite borrowing devices are tax-anticipation warrants, intergovernmental transfers and unpaid bills. Even tax-delinquency toleration is often a credit operation since the communities will not be able to collect back taxes and penalties which they consider as assets. There is ample experience available in American and foreign fiscal histories, both national and local, to prove that tax-anticipation financing and balancing over a period of years are pure and simple deficit financing. Furthermore, none of these devices offers the advantages of conscious and planned borrowing policies, wherever these are possible.

In spite of the numerous plans, programs, reforms, or devices which may be instituted, the conclusion is reached that there can be no equalization of budgets over a period with current revenues. Although much can be expected in a planned economy which may reduce the amplitude of fluctuations, the maintenance of fiscal equilibrium will inevitably involve borrowing.

There is usually no attempt at coordinating taxing and borrowing policies; when the actual choice is made during depressions, the question is usually solved on the basis of negative reasoning. Borrowing is made when taxation is impossible and equally taxation is resorted to when borrowing is impossible. In terms of recovery objectives, a creation of new purchasing power generally, and the stimulation of heavy durable goods industries specifically, seems to be desirable. Taxation can at the best result only in a shifting around of available sums; it cannot exercise the same type of influence which borrowing, financed by credit expansion, can exert.

The Federal Government acknowledges no limitations on borrowing. In the States and localities the body of debt-limiting legislation, often embodied in constitutional provisions, may prevent these jurisdictions from following a rational deficit financing plan. The alternatives are therefore a change in local borrowing capacity (which appears highly inadvisable for the present because of their tax systems, their administrative machinery and their poor fiscal condition) or a shifting of the burden to the Federal Government. With respect to deficit-financing, and also in connection with the specific problem of financing public-works activities, it is interesting to note that there is a growing interest in a Federal corporation or financial institution to discount or otherwise facilitate State and local borrowing. A coordination of non-Federal with Federal borrowing would be highly desirable because of the regulatory elements involved and because of the deflationary effects of much of our State and local financing. It is difficult under our present arrangements to achieve financing by means of credit expansion for non-Federal activities.

Justification for deficit financing can be found only in a negation of the strict private capital solvency notions. Particular emphasis on money rentability of the Government loan expenditure, on material asset security, and on self-liquidity, will not justify deficit borrowing. Still, a valid case for this type of credit operation (for financing cycle deficits of sound fiscal systems) can be made by using a revised set of principles. These do not stress the financing aspect (relating borrowing to a specific expenditure) but seek limitations through the imposition of strict amortization rules. Safeguards to assure debt service can have no ulterior effects on the fiscal system.

The problem of the effects of borrowing on the financial system is discussed hereafter. In general however, the emphasis has been to disregard the economic effects of Government loan operations. The future incidence of a public debt-retirement program or the question of the total or per capita governmental debt burdens may have some bearing on the problem but greater attention should be given to the immediate effects of the loan flotation.

Quantitative analysis is not possible to the same extent that the old money productivity criterion allowed, but according to a recent study,[2] it is considered possible to maintain "sound" national finances as long as the borrowing is related to the maintenance of current and essential services. Apparently fiscal systems have no alternative if there be any attempts to preserve fiscal balance. Borrowing by the jurisdiction best suited to do so points to the conclusion that planned deficit financing by the Federal Government is desirable. (We are assuming throughout that no serious consideration need be granted to the possibility of a resort to fiat money operations as a means of expenditure financing.)

Part III

Keeping in mind the above-mentioned conclusions, the problem of financing a major planned public-works program may appear in a revised light. It is impossible to rely on the normal tax system for any support other than that which public-works expenditures and their effects contribute. This necessitates a careful approach to the financing problem which is essentially the basic problem of public-works programs in general. Assuming the desirable economic stabilization effects of having public-works expenditures, adjusted to cycles, it is a question of justifying the financing measures.

Portions of major public-works programs which replace essential current services or which take over reasonable relief requirements may be absorbed into the normal scope of fiscal stabilization efforts. The decision to maintain normal services and to assume necessary depression relief allows for the inclusion of a portion of the Public Works program. This means:

1. The assurance that no contraction will take place other than that caused by cost decreases. A minor group of normal public works will be accelerated if cost and profit items are taken into consideration while another group might be retarded because of poor profit outlook. Decreased labor and material costs might allow some projects to appear attractive while on the other hand, decreased consumer purchasing power may mean that rentability of some self-liquidating projects may be lessened.

2. To the extent that the public works programs support essential work-relief, they might be absorbed into a loan-financed budget. Conslusions based on expenditure per labor-hour, point to the fact

[2] Myrdal, G.: Finanspolittikens Ekonomiska Verkningar. Stockholm, 1934.

that only the "raking-leaves-back-and-forth" category of public works projects should be considered here. The purpose in limiting the projects to these work-relief categories is to assure that the major portion of the expenditure will accrue directly to the laborers employed and not to material and durable-goods costs.

This policy of maintaining predepression budgets and of financing minimum work-relief programs would enable our fiscal systems to absorb the 1920–30 level of public construction in addition to work-relief of the E. C. W., C. W. A., and F. E. R. A. type. Quantitatively, this will easily reach billion dollar levels annually. This would represent the amount of public works financing which may be expected from the security afforded by the maintenance of functioning fiscal systems. A decision to continue boom expenditure levels decidedly implies a "recovery" expenditure element. There is also the additional safeguard derived from the fact that our normal public works financing consists largely of current revenue financed projects. Funds for Federal construction and in many States for road building, were obtained from taxation. If a retardation scheme is adopted during a revival, while revenue yields are recovering, there is some assurance that current funds for debt retirement will be available. This is based on the presumption that we will overcome the tendency to use surpluses as an excuse for tax reductions. By decreasing expenditures actual cash is made available. Otherwise only a more nominal relief in the form of decreased needs for bond flotations is afforded. An available legal borrowing capacity is less valuable, under any circumstances, than current revenues.

It is evident that the public works financing problem, if the numerous objectives which the program calls for are considered, goes beyond this point. It is necessary to think in terms of a program involving several billions of dollars. It has frequently been claimed that the postponement or retardation of normal public works would enable a concentration of activity in depressions. It is extremely unlikely that it will be possible to count on this feature. Several reasons for this are given below.

1. The conclusion must be reached that physical needs, pressure on Government for expenditures, and the unlikelihood of getting individual or social sacrifices on a large scale for possible future depressions, will make actual postponements problematical. Particularly armaments, a large Federal construction item, seem unlikely to lend themselves to postponement schemes. Even booms following depressions in which public works were carried out on a large scale will probably not witness an appreciable falling off of construction because of "overbuilding." On the contrary, the usual maintenance of high levels reached in public finances lead to the conclusion that each boom will, because of the hangover of the program of the preceding depression, carry more public works than the depression period itself.

It is often stressed that "the regenerative characteristics" of public works projects will lead to further construction. It has usually been assured that this will be private construction although it is likely that further construction, if any, will likewise be public. Social activities, if any, tend usually to cease only when the financial system collapses; the opposite would be exceptional.

2. Assuming, however, that physical postponement is possible, failure to borrow will only assure a formal remainder of borrowing

capacity. Under our present local structure the falling off of real estate assessments may cut borrowing capacity independent of the size of the debt. There is no guarantee that the borrowing capacity will remain the same. Unless we assume new economic bases for governmental debt capacity, the failure to borrow during one period may not necessarily mean a hoarding of that capacity for a subsequent period. It is obvious that ability to levy and collect taxes and to float loans successfully is independent of any formal remainders, though this may determine the potential size of the tax or debt increase. The fact that taxing is effective only when there is a substantial tax base and borrowing is possible only when there is a market for obligations, definitely leads to the conclusion that physical postponement does not mean storing of a reserve of financing power. Specifically, during this depression, potential taxing and borrowing capacity has proven useless for many governments.

3. The use of reserve funds to finance public works projects is subject to much criticism when they are to be part of a postponement program. We plan to retard our normal works programs in order to benefit from the potential recovery elements in the financing and expenditure features of a timed public works policy. A reserve fund system, especially when adopted by many States and localities, would involve the accumulation of large reserves. It has already been stressed that the conversion of these reserves into cash would involve the deflationary influences of large-scale liquidation or the depressing influences of a dumping of a large amount of securities. It would not be possible to assure that under a disposal of fund assets a method of financing which is most effective as a recovery measure, namely, credit expansion, can be achieved.

The problem is not solved by assuming that the funds will have been invested in the Government's own securities. Debt retirement may not be a feature of the next depression. Conversion and refunding possibilities are hampered by reserves in one's own securities. The reserve fund is not supplied with any purchasing power to finance public works unless the Government obtains cash to retire its own securities. Cash for the payments of wages and the purchase of materials does not grow out of any intragovernmental fund bookkeeping maneuvers.

The conclusion may be reached that little or no support may be assured the financing of public works programs because of postponement. For limited time and in small amounts, retardation may be possible.

Undoubtedly there will actually be a cumulative expansion of public works with accelerations during depressions. A retardation tendency may result from over-building during depressions. It is easier, however, to imagine the continued development and improvement of a program once begun than to visualize any kind of slowing down. There are also some indications that financial exhaustion or collapse may necessitate a retardation before the boom period ever gets under way. Another probability is that public works will end after a depression only with respect to the changed methods of financing. After the transition from recovery efforts to prosperity phase activities, the use of taxation or borrowing from real savings should be favored for the financing of public works. Popular support for such a policy would be easier to obtain than for a physical discontinuation or retardation of public works projects.

Two minor problems remain to be discussed. One concerns the techniques and devices accompanying the financing arrangements. The utilization of semipublic corporations and authorities, the guaranteeing or matching of funds, or some system of Federal and local grants and loans, all have a basic bearing on the ultimate burden of the financing, and on the practical problems of carrying out programs. It is, however, evident that the problem of the source of the funds and the economic influence of the financing is not fundamentally altered by the existence of these techniques. A more comprehensive study of the problem will have to treat with these financing practices and the related benefit and cost allocations.

The second minor problem relates to the role of the fiscal system in encouraging private construction. Tax exemptions for new construction, although they may mean a nominal loss to the fiscal, indicate a substantial gain to the general economy. The usual procedure is to grant tax exemption for a few years after completion of new buildings. This enables profit possibilities necessary to encourage private construction activities, to appear more readily.

A new dwelling exemption which was in effect as an emergency housing measure in several New York State counties for 10 years, expired in 1932. Italy has incorporated a tax-exemption program, designed to encourage new construction, in its real property tax system and has coordinated this with its general public-works program.

Governments can, in general, through some medium, reduce construction costs and can call into existence a large amount of building activity which might otherwise not seem feasible. Numerous devices are possible to enhance profitability and to make projects appear closer to a self-liquidating basis. Legislative support for measures designed to accelerate private construction may be easier to obtain than funds for what some consider to be Government intervention in private business.

The theoretical plans concerning the most desirable financing methods are primarily influenced by considerations of the objectives of public-works programs. In each case the expenditure must be financed by a method consistent with its purposes and one unlikely to destroy or nullify its desired economic reactions. Keeping in mind general economic stabilization desiderata, it is doubtful whether taxes or reserves can be warranted in any case.

A primary objective of public-works programs is likely to be a direct increase of consumer purchasing power. Unless special taxes are devised which will act as confiscatory capital levies, it is extremely difficult to see how any other method except credit expansion will avoid a mere transfer of purchasing power in the community. It is commonly conceded that only inflationary borrowing can really create effective new demands. Furthermore, it is extremely doubtful whether sums large enough to materially affect new demand can be raised in a short period through taxation. Several authorities [3] have stated that increased taxation may become part of a comprehensive loan-expenditure program because of the enlargement in tax bases due to the effects of the governmental spending. It must be remembered that this does not detract from the necessity of financing the original spending program through credit expansion. The opportunities for increased or added taxation are offered to offset the infla-

[3] J. M. Keynes, "The Means to Prosperity", London 1933, and G. Myrdal, "Konjunktur och offentlig hushallning ", Stockholm 1933, have stressed this feature of public-works financing in their writings.

tionary tendencies created by excessive credit development. While there can be no doubt that tax yields will grow, the time lags connected with most types of direct taxation may seriously hinder the usefulness of the tax program as an expansion brake. Furthermore, the pouring-in of funds at one end of the funnel does not imply that yields at the other end will continue when the pouring-in ceases.

Other objectives are:

1. Stimulating capital goods industries.
2. Providing work relief.
3. Public ownership.
4. Carrying out elements in a more basic social and economic program.

With the exception of work relief, which is a welfare type of outlay to be guided primarily by social demands, it is probable that the conclusions about loan expenditures are applicable in these cases. It must be recalled that during depressions such a portion of the national income is taken over by taxation (and may still be insufficient to cover current and necessary relief services) that additional taxation may not only nullify the public-works objectives, but may threaten collapse of the fiscal system. Up to a certain point taxpayers will consciously pay taxes, but beyond that point indirect taxation methods become necessary. In addition to undesirable economic reactions, taxation becomes difficult from an administrative viewpoint. Subsequently pressure from the community for cessation of the expenditure giving rise to the revenue makes itself felt.

In terms of the objectives, therefore, it is reasonable to conclude that borrowing alone can successfully finance a major public-works program. The conclusion about deficit borrowing, namely, that it is not practicable for the State and local governments, is equally applicable here. The limitations on local indebtedness offer no basis for borrowing of this type. State debt limitations were largely formulated about 85 or 90 years ago and were aimed specifically against the repetition of wild-cat speculative construction activities. It is difficult to adjust these limitations to encourage construction activities against which these prohibitions were specifically aimed. The constitutions do not make the fine distinction between beneficial or cycle-adjusted public works and other construction projects sponsored by the State. Finally, the conclusion is evident that the States and localities cannot support the main burden of a public-works program because they are unable to borrow enough. Our problem thus far is primarily one of Federal borrowing. This is in addition to the burden of deficit financing already recommended for shifting to the Federal Government.

Before turning to financial limitations on public-works programs, other obstacles will be briefly considered.

There is no way of judging beforehand what the relation may prove to be between loan expenditures and returns based on the completed project. A large share of the types of public-works activities offer no direct or even indirect chances for money returns. They do not even represent an increase in Government shares in the ownership of productive enterprises. The make-work group fill this category. Others, such as armaments, call for a dilution of the productivity notion so that a perversion rather than an extension is reached.

Approaching closer to a direct return, we find road building (apart from the striking possibilities offered by tolls) definitely laying the ground for the elaboration of the property, gasoline, and motor-vehicle tax bases. It is conceivable, however, that new roads generate the need for additional expenditures which may absorb funds flowing in from the freshly created tax bases. It is also conceivable that there will be no funds growing out of the road taxes which will be available for debts retirement.

The most favorable kinds of projects insuring returns are those which are to be sold or those types for which adequate security, eventually convertible, is assured. It is theoretically possible, therefore, to conceive of a public-works program so constituted that, apart from price changes, no ultimate financial incidence will be borne by the fisc. To the extent that such a program is carried out, one type of limitation is absent.

The possibilities for such a policy are remote, and it is reasonable to suppose that there will be strong resistance in the community to programs of that type. Furthermore, much of the supposed self-liquidity of the projects would disappear with the further deflation following an excessive expansion. In this respect public-works projects are subject to the same chances and certainties which threaten all business enterprises. To the extent, therefore, that self-liquidity does not form a feature of an expenditure outlay, the loan expenditure must seek justification in its general economic and social desirability, related more to the financing of the spendings and their general effects than to the project itself.

The scope and size of public-works programs influence the problem of financing. It is primarily through the reaction of the financing methods on the economic structure that the size of the Government outlay makes itself felt and subsequently determines to what extent Government-loan expenditure is possible without harmfully diluting bank assets.

During future depressions, the debt burden for the maintenance of current services is likely to grow. In relation to public works an additional borrowing quota must be justified. We are assuming that in the future no more absurd economy programs will be tolerated. A deflation of the general budget in order to facilitate the financing of an extraordinary budget is hardly a sound recovery measure.

Closely linked to the size of the public-works program is its timing. The progress of the deflationary movement is such at the beginning of the depression that deficit financing has not yet made its appearance and the absorptive capacity of the community for Government bonds is still ample. A loan program may be more successfully launched during the first stages of the depression than any other period. However, it is doubtful whether the business community will approve of such a radical step. Furthermore, in the early stages of this depression the political elements would not encourage the defeatist attitude implied in such a program. It is possible that in a planned economy these resistances can be overcome. Unless, however, the initial impact of Government spending can stem the deflationary tides, it is reasonable to assume that the pouring-out of funds will be a continuous need until such time as the private economy may revive. Apart from the desirability of keeping up the outlay, it is extremely likely that various types of pressure will be exerted by the community on the Government to maintain its program. Legislators are notoriously prone to disburse funds which do not carry the onus of having taxed their constituents. There is continuity implied in any public-works program regardless of its timing. This will militate against early depression efforts.

There are two additional institutional factors which may determine financial policies. One of these is the benefit theory expressing itself in much of our fiscal and economic legislation.

This theory creates a sentiment calling for tangible advantages to be derived from each sacrifice. It is not difficult to see how this will make itself felt in public-works programs. For example the general community may resent the concentration of aid to the construction industry. Groups in the community who feel that they are adversely affected by the reactions of the borrowing program or who feel that they will bear the burden of future debt retirement without deriving immediate benefits, may create obstacles for public-works borrowing. Sectionalism thrives under incentives such as these. The current depression has adequately shown that these difficulties exist.

The greater the amount of self-liquidating projects, the more the ideal of benefit financing will be ultimately approached. In order to compensate for the lag in relating benefits and payments, pressure will make itself felt in demands for the localization of projects all over the country. This is another fact which will tend toward expanding and continuing the program once begun.

Every phase of the program will have to face administrative difficulties. In relation to financing borrowing authorizations, spending appropriations, and a myriad of other questions must be dealt with. In view of the fact that more basic questions of policy place definite limits on the scope of major public-works programs, much attention has not been given in this study to these limitations of an administrative character. A successful public-works program depends nevertheless on their satisfactory elimination.

The result of the discussion up to this point indicates that a policy of borrowing through credit expansion is implied in a major public-works program launched during a depression. The writer believes that the results of such an expansion policy may be inimical to recovery efforts because they result in an undue disturbance of the banking system. The course of events which lead to this conclusion are briefly stated, because on the basis of this reasoning the belief is reached that major public-works programs are severely limited by the possibility of undesirable effects caused by their financing.

Following the initial stages of a deflation of trade and production, there is a cessation of new investment. Idle funds lie unused in the banks. Natural incentives for new private investment being absent, long-term capital market activities are restricted almost exclusively to Government financing operations. The absence of the risk factor and the support of financial institutions make the Government bond market attractive while private capital movements are at a standstill.

The experience in this country has shown that when large amounts of Governmental borrowing take place, private and institutional investors do not absorb much of the new issues. The banking system owns a major portion, estimated at three-fifths to three-quarters of the new Federal issues floated since 1931. The common contention is that the purchase of bonds, either by individuals or banks, involves the "using up" of funds. This leads to the belief that a capital shortage, holding back recovery expansion, is created. It can be shown, however, that when individuals purchase Government bonds, deposits in the banking system are not reduced, since Government spending tends to create idle funds in a degree possibly equal to that in which governmental borrowing absorbs them. Furthermore deposits in the banking system as a whole can be decreased only through a repayment of loans to banks, through bank failures, through cash hoarding or through payments by depositors to the Government with the Government in turn withdrawing deposits from the commercial banks to the Federal Reserve banks. The result of a loan expenditure program is, therefore, an increase of Government bonds in bank portfolios and an increase in member bank balances at the Federal Reserve banks. The latter being created by virtue of the increased individual deposits at member banks. Any of the conditions leading to decreased deposits would counteract this tendency.

The chief objection to banks holding excessive amounts of governmental securities (as well as any other long-term investments) is that the liquidity of their portfolios has disappeared. Banks are ultimately forced to accept additional governmental issues because of various pressures and because of the need for maintaining the value of obligations they already own. This condition may lead banks to stress unduly the liquidity of their other assets and to prefer cash to commercial loans. This tends to contract the debt structure as well as the scope of industrial and commercial operations. This would nullify the effects of the expenditure program by its income and price deflation influences and would delay the desired expansion.

Another objection to excessive holdings of Government securities by banks is the risk of depreciation in the value of the obligations they own. In this country we have obviated the need for fearing this factor by a general substitution by the Government of its own credit for that of the banks. The measures achieving this include the new Federal Reserve legislation and the activities of the Federal Deposit Insurance Corporation and the Reconstruction Finance Corporation. The possible effect of a policy of governmental support for the banks is a postponement of any difficulties. If a collapse of governmental credit should occur, the severity of the crash will, however, be increased.

It is not true that ownership of Government securities by the banks necessarily involves a credit inflation in the sense that bank credit expands faster than production and encourages price increases. A credit inflation of this type might be desirable as a recovery measure, but it is not achieved by loading the banking system with Government paper.

A potential danger to the economy is involved in the building up of excessive bank reserves. In the present situation this reserve expansion has been achieved not only by Federal Reserve bank purchases of Government securities but by the monetary policy which is being pursued. Treasury disbursements out of cash, permitted by virtue of the gold increment and to a lesser degree of silver purchases, can add to the excess reserves. Gold imports are another factor leading to an expansion of reserves. While the monetary policy and gold factors are not related to governmental borrowing, their coexistence places an added obstacle in the way of justifying such borrowing. The danger mentioned is that excessive bank reserves may lead to a strong boom when normal business activity is resumed. It is possible to lessen the inflationary expansion due to these excess reserves by increasing the reserve requirements or by selling Government securities in the open market. Such action with respect to reserve requirements should be coincidental with the borrowing program. It is precisely this kind of a boom, facilitated by high reserve balances, which many fear and which they associate directly with bank ownership of Government obligations. In the popular mind this idea expresses itself in the fear that the direct or indirect use of Federal Reserve credit in the purchase of Government bonds is the equivalent of a direct exchange of paper between the Treasury and the Reserve System or "greenbackism."

It has already been noted that many of the difficulties encountered by our fiscal systems during the current depression were caused by factors in operation long before the economic causes started. Equally our banking system was not without faults in general and in many particular instances a highly unsatisfactory condition was present. Because of their unsound status many banks were in process of liquidation during the depression and could not successfully carry their share of governmental financing. Banks of a weak character were not aided by their purchases of long-term Government paper.

With respect to the expenditures made, numerous studies have described the mechanisms radiating the effects of Government spendings. Effective demand is said to be substantially increased. Assuming a work-relief program (though the exact routing of the outlay does not affect the ultimate conclusion) prices and wages will rise. It is not difficult to see how a major spending program, supported by a monetary policy such as we have had in this country, can cause a cessation of deflationary courses in private industry. The point is reached where prices rise, profits reappear, tax bases expand, and public finances improve. To some it is evident that the continued functioning of the system is dependent on further Government loan expenditure. Others see the Government spending providing for a higher consumption rate than otherwise and making it more feasible for industry to embark on a capital-expenditure program; the latter being essential for recovery. Equally there are cases where higher wage costs may retard capital expenditures. At present our spending program has not started the desired increased capital outlay by private industry. Undoubtedly factors such as the N. R. A. and the high costs of building materials, have been obstacles in a capital-expenditure expansion through their profit minimizing effects.

In all events no major changes in the financial system appears to result from the expenditure of the borrowed funds. Professor Robbins has indicated that the depression consumption and durable goods market relationships may return after a transition period.[4] This tends to support the conclusion that no additional disturbance of the banking system other than an increase in deposit and reserve magnitudes (primarily associated with the borrowing phase) results from the expenditure program.

The general conclusion appears to be that heavy governmental borrowing does not necessarily involve inflationary excesses. The common beliefs about capital shortages resulting from governmental borrowing do not appear to be substantiated. The financing implications of a borrowing program do not contain elements which insure a rapid recovery. A retardation of the deflation may be more rapid with Government spending than without it. At all events, the ulti-

4 L. Robbins—"The Great Depression" London, 1934."

mate success of a public works program and its financing measures is conjectural, and it is unwise to propose the adoption of a similar or related plan for future depressions until such time as the results may be viewed with a historical perspective.

The whole history of public works and their financing in this country offers no experience of any value in relation to major public works programs. Conclusions are valid only with respect to fiscal stabilization efforts to which normal public works must be related. It should be possible to coordinate Federal, State, and local construction in such a manner as to take advantage of the most economical financing methods. The activity of the State Advisory Boards indicate that major programs are being mapped out, though little consideration, if any, is being given to financing aspects. The experience with public works since the depression culminates in the P. W. A.; the economic effects of the financing methods, as has been stated above, are not yet discernible. It is reasonable to conclude from P. W. A. experience that within the framework of local finances, as they are today, public works must remain essentially a Federal problem. Local fiscal systems lack the mechanisms and the flexibility to deal with them effectively.

With respect to foreign public works programs, little conclusive evidence is available. Russia, with the biggest program, offers no experience which is applicable to our type of economy. Of the other nations, Sweden has during this depression embarked upon a public-works program to accompany its monetary experiments. Using borrowed funds, both the National Government and the municipalities have been carrying on construction programs comprising chiefly self-liquidating and revenue-producing projects. The absolute and relative amounts spent are in all ways comparable with a major program. The entire scheme, furthermore, has been absorbed into the regular financial structure. The program is said to be based on a recent memorandum prepared for the Swedish Government by Professor Myrdal which concludes with the recommendation that public-works programs should be expanded during depressions. The nature of their works projects, their industrial structure, and their fiscal system make the Swedish program inapplicable to our own condition. It is also important to note that the Swedish plan is based on the theory that an encouragement of savings is necessary, especially during booms. The Swedish have an increase of productive capacity as a primary desideratum. The problem of extensive public ownership in Sweden further obscures the app icability of the Swedish recommendation to our institutions. In all events, empirical experience and conclusions are lacking.

England's policy with public-works programs, neither during the post-war period, nor during the depression, offers any relevant conclusions. Public-construction efforts centering in the road fund and in housing have not been of any great magnitude. The road fund was withdrawn from the budget in 1929 by Churchill and the moderate expansion of the early years of the depression already has stopped. Housing projects financed by means of State aid to localities have been common. The absence of the need for public works as an unemployment and relief measure can be explained by the existence of provisions for welfare activities through other channels. In general, it may be stated that any credit expansion for governmental public works which did take place was discontinued before large-scale borrowing resulted. In 1931 all public-works expenditures were curtailed. The British budget now balances without any qualifications. English monetary theorists nevertheless continue to advocate inflationary Government loan expenditures as a recovery measure.

In France the depression policy until very recently has been decidedly deflationary and offers no opportunity for a study of public-works expansion. Following the monetary stabilization, a short period of approximately balanced budgets has been superseded by years in which considerable deficit financing for current services has been necessary. Because of colossal armament and fortifications work the ordinary expenditures may be said to comprehend considerable public works. This construction has not been related to recovery efforts. The extraordinary public-works budget ("Compte Special du Perfectionnement de l'Outillage National") which began with funds of its own and which was not intended for financing by loans, has not been the source of any great activity. French opinion as a whole, influenced by post-war difficulties, is antagonistic to excessive governmental credit expansion. The recently adopted plan for works programs in regions where there is severe unemployment calls for governmental borrowing and the raiding of several Government funds. There is no opportunity at this time to learn of the effect of this program on either the unemployment problem or on the financial system.

In Germany and Italy experience is available to show precisely the basic deflationary tendencies involved in a cessation of private capital activities induced by excessive Government expansion. In both countries difficulties with the currency standard have grown out of the expenditure program. During early years when foreign capital poured into these nations, there appeared to be no threats to the gold base. During recent periods exchange disturbances, due to the fact that the public works programs involve substantial increases in imports of materials, have arisen. Though the influences are not measureable, there is evidence that public works programs on the continent, which have not been coordinated on an international basis, have resulted in a disequalibrium of prices and have added to currency difficulties.

In the Reich the severe post-war inflation, the subsequent foreign-financed expansion of communal public works and the economic events prior to the overthrow of the Republic, indicate numerous points. The projects launched during the early years of the recent depression, involved heavy reliance on taxation. This proved unsuccessful and since the fall of 1932 borrowing has been relied upon. A scheme whereby the Reichsbank financed most of the projects was instituted. Exceptionally high rates of interest had been necessary to enable the governments to borrow in the open markets. The National Socialist Government has made a public-works expansion policy a feature of its general economic program. The ultimate outcome of the financial incidence is not known though there are indications that an unfavorable reaction is involved. It must, furthermore, be admitted that structural changes taking place in Germany may detract from the applicability of their experience.

In Italy monumental public works have been a feature of the general economic policy rather than of specific recovery efforts. In addition to two semipublic corporations using small government capital contributions and subsequently expanding on the basis of government guaranties, the major "Mussolini Plan" (Piano per la

Bonifica Integrale) has been launched.   Another rural public works fund has added to the total of approximately 25 billion lire which was spent on public works from 1922 to 1932.   The government is continuously expanding its program.   Agricultural development schemes have played a large role in the public-works projects.   The borrowing of this program, combined with the recurring general budgetary deficits, has placed a severe burden on the financial system, especially since the external credit, which helped finance the earlier projects, has disappeared.   There is a capital shortage and a general deflationary program has been embarked upon by the Fascist regime.   There is nothing in the Italian experience to encourage the belief that public works, financed by borrowing, have a salutary effect on the economy in general or the financial system in particular.

Foreign experience, if conclusive at all, does not indicate any substantial recovery benefits from public-works programs financed through credit expansion.   Difficulties arising out of the financing methods are apparent.   There is evidence pointing to the conclusion that the governmental borrowing programs exercise nullifying effects on the recovery efforts.   In foreign countries deficit financing has led to monetary inflation threats or has necessitated renewed deflationary activities.   In particular, adherence to an international gold standard appears to restrict the amount of loan expenditure which can be made.

Part IV

The dangers involved in financing a major public-works program point to the added necessity of insuring a maximum of fiscal stabilization.   The unemployment relief problem will undoubtedly make some program, to be financed by borrowing, inevitable so that it is important to study, recommend, and take action on increasing the stability of the fiscal system.   We may expect in this country a new social and economic philosophy, culminating in a planned economy having economic stabilization as one of its primary goals.   This may succeed in decreasing the amplitude of business fluctuations.   To the extent that deficit financing needs will be reduced, the scope for public-works expansion which will not involve credit operations, having perhaps an objectionable reaction on the economy, will be greater.   The objectives for future policy should be in terms of fiscal and general economic stabilization not necessarily linked with public-works programs.

It is extremely difficult to measure, as well as to give any significance to the present condition of the fiscal systems.   Norms, which concern themselves with the maintenance of sound fiscal operations and the avoidance of credit and currency expansion are hardly the proper criteria with which to measure the Federal finances.   The policy of the administration in segregating the emergency credit-financed spending program has resulted in the retention of a considerable portion of the fiscal operations on a normal plane.   The necessity as well as the desirability of such a policy may be evident,[5] but it is doubtful whether it will be possible to separate the two spheres of public policy with regard to future developments and reactions. Public opinion has recently been inclined to measure the entire

[5] The present writer has treated this problem more fully in The Emergency Budget of the United States American Economic Review, vol. XXIV, no. 1, March 1934.

Federal finances in terms of deficit financing, regardless of the underlying different policies.

In State and local finances, the crisis is still severe because the
burden or relief efforts has not as yet been completely absorbed by the
Federal program. Unless State and local credit improves, every
added expenditure will fall back on an already burdened and defective
tax structure. Particularly, the property tax dilemma is acute.
Tax delinquency threatens a major collapse which may not be averted
long enough for the ameliorating effects of the Federal loan expenditure program to take effect. Other taxes are yielding added revenues,
particularly the income taxes with provisions added during the
depression. The sales tax assures the States a direct link to any
retail sales improvement. The general purchasing power expansion
induced by the Government spending policy directly affects this.
Expenditures are, in most States and localities, still considerably
curtailed and fiscal balance does in no way imply a properly functioning financial system. It must be evident that with some seven million
(not counting dependents) people directly receiving Federal support
and the Federal outlay supplying a large portion of the national
income, the State and local finances are not in a position to function
independent of Federal support. The success of the Federal program
in permanently (as far as this depression is concerned) arresting the
deflation will insure a possibility as well as a probability that State
and local finances will soon operate on a normal basis. It is, however,
impossible to consider State and local finances at present without
reference to the nature of the influences which are expanding the tax
bases. The expansion of tax bases independent of Federal spending
effects is, with the exception of the new liquor levies, not sufficient
to warrant a conclusion that the improvement in the local finances is
indicative of recovery.

The structural changes and trends in the fiscal systems as a result
of the factors operative during the past few years which will influence
future fiscal stabilization needs and efforts, may be summarized, as
follows:

1. The new broadened sphere of expenditures, particularly in the
Federal Budget, will necessitate much larger scope for Government
finances. Apart from recovery measures which may show stationary
tendencies, new social policies (unemployment insurance, old-age
insurance, child welfare, etc.) and a trend toward public ownership
(particularly public utilities) will necessitate diverting a new high
level of the national income for financing these programs. The greater
the interest of the Government in the national economy, the more
important the problem of fiscal stabilization. Ultimately, fiscal
stabilization itself may influence economic stabilization. A result
of the trend in governmental functions indicates a particular need for
fiscal stabilization because of the specific social nature of the activities
and expenditures implied.

2. A definite trend toward new taxes and the overthrow of some old
taxes is evident. In State and local finances, particularly, a decline
of the property tax, is notable. Budgetary systems, tax legislation,
and the entire fiscal systems are so interrelated with the property tax
and its theories, that a continuation of the decline of the real estate
levy will imply a revolution in State and local finances. The growing
use of consumption bases, in both local and Federal tax systems,
though more strongly in the former, threatens to involve the dis-

placement of tax philosophies which have been guiding for many years. The income tax as a major fiscal instrument has received a temporary setback and is momentarily in disfavor because of the inadequate yields. The existence of several important States including California, Illinois, Michigan, and New Jersey, without income taxes, shows a potential field for expansion. Other trends in taxation indicate a possible revival of benefit notions (prices, fees, etc.).

3. With regard to borrowing, Federal policy is self-explanatory. For the States and localities, the need for new measures and limitations has become evident. Borrowing for deficit financing and for relief threw over many old notions regarding the scope of borrowing. The difficulties encountered as well as the fact that the older capacities have been used up, point to the conclusion that a new approach to State borrowing is probable. A striking example is afforded by the State of Washington where borrowing for financing relief expenditures was possible only through the invoking of the "insurrection" clause of the Constitution. Wholesale municipal defaults and the break-down of local credit indicate that the property-tax base for borrowing may change.

4. Budgetary procedures and the administrative aspects of finances will certainly benefit from the efforts to eliminate the glaring defects which have recently been brought into prominence. Particularly State and local finances suffered because of the prevalence of methods which made a constructive fiscal policy impossible. Unfortunately the American practice of putting into the Constitution specific and detailed financial legislation and budgetary procedures, instead of general principles has added to the rigidity and cycle sensitivity of the local finances. The lack of elasticity, flexibility, clarity, unity, and above all, the presence of dedicated revenues and specific use funds, made the effects of the depression on the finances of the political subdivisions much worse than they should have been. Improvements in the direction of greater executive authority over expenditures, revision of estimating procedures, and more wide-spread publicity have been promising. Similarly, the difficulty of working with biennial budgets was clearly demonstrated. Almost every State legislature held a regular or extraordinary session in 1933. This indicated the pressing need for frequent revisions of finances during emergencies. A trend for improvement in these mechanisms may be absent but the groundwork has been laid and the need for further action demonstrated.

5. Finally, the further clarification and coordination of Federal, State, and local relationships in finance achieved during the depression definitely indicates that steps toward a solution of this problem have been taken. The desirability for some integration has been clearly shown and much actual work looking toward this end has been completed. State and local relationships have been furthered with respect to functions and especially with State-collected, locally shared taxes. No real economic policy can be pursued by a community that subjects itself to the vagaries of one tax. Localities which depended almost exclusively on property-tax yields found it imperative to increase the number of levies and to diversify the risks from the failure of yields to live up to estimates. Expanded Federal and local relationships have been a new feature introduced by the depression. Not only has direct Federal aid developed, but the nature of the aid involves supervision and further contact between Federal offices and local finances. A durable contact has definitely been established. Federal and State relationships have been extended with respect to

Federal outlay, but tax and borrowing policy coordination (the latter practically impossible under our present legal system) have not made any actual progress. The break-down of many State systems and the difficulties encountered in the national finances have called attention to the need for developing a new scheme for administering our federated finances. There are indications that positive action along this line will be taken by the Federal Government and the States in the near future.

In general, the trends indicate a major reform movement in State finances, much of it as a result of depression experience, but not all of the trends are favorable to ideal fiscal stabilization requirements. There is evidence to support the contention that the States and localities are still further removed than they were before the depression from the concept of fiscal system best adapted to stabilization needs.

Summary

The glaring need for taking active steps, in the interest of the general economy, toward maintaining fiscal stabilization along lines consistent with cycle smoothing efforts, cannot be questioned. It precedes a major planned public-works program in importance and is a basic prerequisite for any other use of the fiscal system for recovery or antideflationary purposes.

The Planning Board is offered a field of activity along these lines which fits into the scope of its work. Particularly, under our institutional framework, it is essential that a central coordinating agency, using persuasive rather than coercive powers, should undertake the furthering of fiscal stabilization programs.

It has been a feature of planned economies elsewhere that fiscal reform lags far behind other economic changes. The pressure for revenue under which most fiscal systems operate all the time make reforms in the interest of any other but immediate revenue needs extremely difficult to achieve. It is only through the activity of agencies not directly concerned with administering the finances that efforts of the type here contemplated are possible. Specifically, the Planning Board should undertake the furthering of the integration of Federal and State finances. The pressure exerted by a body such as the Planning Board will materially aid those working for coordination from other angles. It is possible to formulate plans at present for working along these lines.

It is with respect to fiscal stabilization rather than to public-works programs, that foreign experience and theories are extremely valuable. Equally, the States and localities can contribute suggestions and devices which have proven successful and which are worthy of widespread attention. It would be advisable to encourage further study of fiscal experience in relation to fluctuating economic backgrounds.

In striving for fiscal stabilization, the Planning Board will find itself working for the general furthering of sound and orderly finances. Depression financing is essentially emergency financing. In emergencies fiscal plans and even legislation are usually only norms for fiscal morality. These are never rigidly adhered to. Specific planning for methods to meet emergencies cannot be achieved. Recommendations for fiscal stabilization, therefore, will deal primarily with sound economic and equitable tax systems, flexible and efficient budgetary mechanisms, and enlightened leadership in Government functions, activities, and expenditures.

O

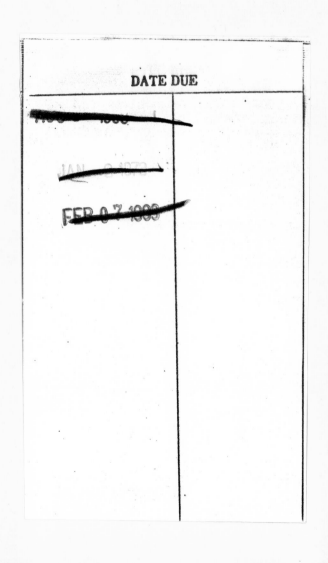